WHY WO̶̶̶̶ ̶W̶I̶L̶L̶
SAVE THE PLANET

Big cities don't have to mean a dystopian future. They can be turned around to be powerhouses of well-being and environmental sustainability – if we empower women.

This book is a unique collaboration between C40 and Friends of the Earth showcasing pioneering city mayors, key voices in the environmental and feminist movements, and academics. The essays collectively demonstrate both the need for women's empowerment for climate action and the powerful change it can bring. A rallying call – for the planet, for women, for everyone.

About Friends of the Earth

Friends of the Earth is the largest grassroots environmental network in the world. Friends of the Earth International unites more than 2 million supporters and 5,000 local groups across more than seventy-five countries.

For more than forty-five years, Friends of the Earth England, Wales and Northern Ireland has recognised that the well-being of people and planet go hand in hand – and this is what inspires its campaigns. Together with the support of hundreds of thousands of people, Friends of the Earth's work has led to the passing of laws and policies such as the landmark 2008 Climate Change Act and the 2003 Household Recycling Act. At a community level, Friends of the Earth has inspired hundreds of newly planted bee-friendly nature spaces and the development of community-owned energy schemes and safe cycling routes. Our role is to enable and support people to transform our environment into one that is flourishing, healthy, sustainable and fair.

We believe that the next generation should enjoy an environment that's getting better: a safer climate, flourishing nature, and healthy air, water and food.

You are looking at the second edition of this book – updated with new content and in a unique collaboration with the hugely influential C40. It showcases pioneering female city mayors, key voices in the environmental and feminist movements and academics. It demonstrates unequivocally that women's empowerment is essential to addressing climate change and other environmental issues. It also demonstrates that women bear a disproportionate impact from environmental degradation.

Use the book to learn more about the issues and to be inspired by what women are already doing, despite our unequal world. More importantly, use it to spread the word – women's empowerment and gender equality is as important to saving the world as the widespread use of solar panels or electric bikes/cars and other green technologies.

www.foe.co.uk/page/big-ideas-women

About C40 Cities

C40 connects more than ninety of the world's greatest cities, representing more than 650+ million people and one-quarter of the global economy. Created and led by cities, C40 is focused on tackling climate change and driving urban action that reduces greenhouse gas emissions and climate risks, while increasing the health, well-being and economic opportunities of urban citizens.

Powerful women have been key to tackling climate change and were responsible for delivering the Paris Agreement adopted at CoP21 (2015), which is why C40 is delighted to collaborate with Friends of the Earth for this second edition of *Why Women Will Save the Planet*.

C40's Women4Climate initiative supports and celebrates women leaders who are driving forward climate action. The initiative also aims to empower and build the capacities of future female leaders in cities.

'Helping new generations of women to rise in the fight against climate change will make our cities stronger, more resilient and more equal,' wrote eleven women mayors as the initiative was launched. And clearly momentum is building. In 2014 there were just four women mayors of C40 cities. As of now there are 17 women mayors of C40 cities.

In addition Women4Climate offers a global mentorship programme where promising young women receive support, advice and guidance from C40 mayors and committed leaders from the business sector, international organizations and civil society. The programme will represent a turning point in the lives of the women involved, providing them with tools they need to develop themselves and their sustainable activities and businesses.

The chair of C40 is Mayor of Paris Anne Hidalgo, and three-term Mayor of New York City Michael R. Bloomberg serves as President of the Board.

www.c40.org

WHY WOMEN WILL SAVE THE PLANET

SECOND EDITION

FRIENDS OF THE EARTH AND C40 CITIES

ZED

Why Women Will Save the Planet was first published in 2015 by
Zed Books Ltd, The Foundry, 17 Oval Way, London SE11 5RR, UK.

This edition published by Zed Books in 2018.

www.zedbooks.net

Typeset in ITC Galliard by seagulls.net
Cover design by Alice Marwick
Edited by Nicola Baird

A catalogue record for this book is available from the British Library

ISBN 978-1-78699-314-4 pb
ISBN 978-1-78699-316-8 pdf
ISBN 978-1-78699-317-5 epub
ISBN 978-1-78699-318-2 mobi

Printed and bound by CPI Group (UK) Ltd, Croydon, CR0 4YY

CONTENTS

ACKNOWLEDGEMENTS

First and foremost, Friends of the Earth and C40 are so grateful to all the contributors who have generously shared their expertise, energy and time to make this second edition possible. For those authors whose work is not in both editions of *Why Women Will Save the Planet*, please be assured that this bears no reflection on the importance of what they do, or the quality of their first edition chapter. As is hopefully made clear in the Introduction, it is simply because this new edition has a deliberately more urban focus.

It has been a huge help to have the book championed by mayors and staff in C40 as well as the staff, volunteers and activists at Friends of the Earth. A special thank you needs to go to Mike Childs at Friends of the Earth and Emily Morris at C40 for their support and expertise during the process of creating the second edition of this book. C40 would also like to thank Mark Watts, Anna Beech, Silvia Marcon, Josh Harris, Sophie Bedecarre Ernst and Emmanuelle Pinault.

From the Friends of the Earth perspective, a big thank you to Elaine Gilligan and Anna Watson plus all those at Friends of the Earth locally, nationally and internationally who used the first edition to spread the word and bring together women's groups and environmental groups to work in greater partnership. Hopefully you'll enjoy doing this again.

Jenny Hawley also deserves a very special mention. Not only did she lead on the first edition, which made the task of creating the second edition far smoother, she also helped create this partnership with C40.

Finally, we would like to thank the fantastic team at Zed Books.

Nicola Baird, Editor

FOREWORD
ANNE HIDALGO

Mayor of Paris and Chair of C40 Cities

Climate change does not affect all people equally. Certain countries – especially small island nations – are already feeling the disastrous effects of sea level rise and increasingly powerful and destructive storms. And certain populations are especially vulnerable – including the young, the elderly and, perhaps surprisingly, women. The severity of climate impacts is inextricably linked to economics, public health, inequality and gender.

Around the world, climate change-induced disasters affect women disproportionately, throwing into sharp relief the existing societal inequalities between men and women. Several studies have shown that, in too many countries, women are more likely to be at home when climate-induced disasters – such as heatwaves, violent storms or hurricanes – strike. They typically have less access to critical emergency response information. And as caretakers for the young or the elderly, they are often less likely to be able to evacuate. The devastating impacts of these events can be measured in both lives lost and economic opportunities destroyed.

But as we look to address the greatest challenge humankind has ever faced, we do so with one of the greatest possible resources: womankind.

Empowering women is key to creating cities and communities that are clean, safe and economically vibrant. This is true not only because women make up 50 per cent of the global population, but also because women are powerful advocates for solutions to long-term problems like climate change.

Women possess the ability to surpass great obstacles to make our world a better place. As women, we know we must work ten times as hard to attain the same opportunities as men. As women, we know that we will face discrimination and dismissiveness in any arena we enter. But we also know that responsibility for the future rests on our shoulders and we are prepared to rise to that challenge.

Decisive, dynamic women are already leading the charge. We must look no further than the great women who were not only the architects but also the contractors and builders of the Paris Agreement on climate change – one of the greatest diplomatic achievements of all time. Laurence Tubiana, Christiana Figueres (see her chapter on p. 5) and others made what many considered the impossible – a global agreement between nearly all countries of the world to address climate change – possible.

Empowering the next generation of women leaders is a concrete step towards securing a bright, sustainable future for all. Through this book, we are seeking to share the wisdom of a pioneering generation of women leaders with the leaders to come.

As the first woman chair of C40 Cities, I decided to launch the Women4Climate initiative, which offers support, mentorship, guidance and advice to ambitious young women fighting climate change. Together with other women mayors in C40, a global network of more than ninety of the world's largest and most influential cities, we are transforming how we think about our cities. For hundreds of years, systems designed by men have catered to men's needs, often making those systems inaccessible or even dangerous for women. Now, with women at the helm, we can be sure that solutions will accommodate both men and women.

In Paris, for instance, we are reclaiming the streets of the city by pedestrianising some of the most iconic segments of the city and by aiming to ban diesel by 2020. By reducing air pollution and expanding pedestrian and cycling opportunities, we are making the city a safer and healthier place for families and citizens.

There is no downside to investing in women and girls. Prioritising education for the 62 million girls globally who currently lack access to it will make them leaders in their own communities, preparing them to face the effects of climate change, increase resilience in their communities, and help their families and communities recover from the aftermath.

We know that women will shape the future. In order to build the most liveable, equal and economically empowered cities, we need women to lead. Unfortunately, women remain underrepresented in positions of power. That must change.

To all the thoughtful and dynamic women who have lent their voices and wisdom to this book – Patricia Espinosa, Zandile Gumede, Alexandra Palt, Karin Nansen and Vandana Shiva, among many others – thank you. Our sisterhood is strong, and I am delighted that readers – especially young women – will have the opportunity to learn from some of the world's most impressive women.

We must show courage, creativity and solidarity as we endow more young women with the skills and opportunities they need to lead the fight against climate change. We must remove obstacles for the next generation of women leaders. We must give them the tools they need to carry forward the work we have started. We must inspire a new generation of men and women to help tackle climate change. Our future depends on it.

Let's get to work.

Join the conversation at #women4climate.

INTRODUCTION
NICOLA BAIRD

This new edition of *Why Women Will Save the Planet* is much more than a partnership between the world's largest environmental organisation, Friends of the Earth, and C40 – a network of more than ninety of the world's cities representing 650+ million people – in a global alliance to tackle climate change. It's a direct result of the impact of the first edition, which came out in 2015, and a growing and broader recognition of the critical role of women's empowerment and leadership in achieving environmental sustainability. This time around *Why Women Will Save the Planet* turns its attention to cities

Why cities?

In 2009 the number of people living in urban areas (3.42 billion) overtook the number of rural dwellers (3.41 billion) for the first time.[1] Now, urban locations are where most people live, and increasingly will be living in the future. By 2050 two-thirds of the global population will live in cities. Historically, cities have big track records as centres of commerce, culture and innovation, and the birthplace of some of humankind's greatest ideas.

By teaming up on this book, the powerful C40 network of cities and Friends of the Earth hope that *Why Women Will Save the Planet* will put centre stage the need to think about environmental sustainability, women's empowerment and gender equality together.

So what's inside this book? You'll find a collection of articles and interviews by women that demonstrate the evidence, cover the history, offer methodology, showcase practical endeavours, and delve into inspirations. Read it sequentially, or dip into the chapters that most interest you.

Ten messages you'll find in this book

1. **Making the numbers count.** Women and girls make up more than half the world's population, but are often disproportionately impacted by climate change and other environmental harms.
2. **Gender equality and environmental sustainability are interdependent.** It is not possible or desirable to achieve one without the other.
3. **Solutions have to work for everyone.** We may take it for granted that cities 'are what they are', but discover overwhelming arguments in the chapters by UK academic Susan Buckingham and Berlin-based consultant (and physicist) Gotelind Alber for city planners to use more gender awareness.
4. **Women's leadership and participation are critical to solving this global crisis.** Not only because we need to use 100 per cent of the talent available, but also because all perspectives are needed in order to deploy solutions effectively.
5. **Women are providing leadership on climate change right now.** Women leaders such as Christiana Figueres, Anne Hidalgo, Ségolène Royal and others[2] were instrumental in the lead-up to the Paris Agreement (CoP 21) and are key to achieving its goals. Increasingly, many of the cities leading on climate change – Paris, Washington, Sydney, Cape Town – are run by women.
6. **Gender diversity and women's representation need to increase at every level**. Women are under-represented in national delegations to the United Nations Framework Convention on Climate Change (UNFCCC) and climate decision-making globally. In politics, business, the media, community groups, etc., ensuring increased gender diversity leads to more climate-sensitive policy and practice.
7. **Joined-up thinking.** Those working to tackle climate change and environmental degradation must consciously integrate

gender equality into their work, in order to be effective and achieve equitable societal outcomes. Equally, feminists, if they aren't doing so already, need to embrace environmental sustainability as part of their work.

8. **Paying attention to vulnerable and marginalised voices.** Climate change will bring more flooding and sea-level rise. Around 90 per cent of the 150,000 people killed in the 1991 Bangladesh cyclone were women.[3] These women were marginalised in their communities – many women died as they waited for their relatives to return home and accompany them to a safe place. Since the 1991 cyclone, many women in Bangladesh are now involved in various disaster preparedness committees at the local level, initiated by the government, the Red Cross and NGOs.

9. **Adapting to climate risks and extreme weather events is essential for a climate-safe and equitable future.** Droughts hurt everyone, wherever they live, although in the city water and food supplies may be more available than in rural areas. But hotter weather has a bigger impact on city dwellers. Urban heat islands are caused by tall buildings, roads, pavements, and closely sited, dark buildings absorbing more heat from the sun. This means that cities can be considerably hotter than the countryside, depending on location. For example, in 2003, around 15,000 people in France – many elderly and 65 per cent of them women – died from heat exhaustion, dehydration and heat stroke during a six-week heatwave.[4] On just one August night the combination of high temperatures and air pollution led to as many as 3,000 Parisians dying early.

10. **Inspiring the next generation of women to lead the fight against climate change with hope.** This book shares ideas and women leaders' hard-won experience, and gives confidence to women to take action. In today's political context, the impact of women leaders working together to defend jointly human rights and our planet inspires optimism and innovation. You can see more about this at www.c40.org/women4climate

Stand up for change

To echo the words in the introduction to this book's first edition, know that achieving gender equality, social justice and environmental sustainability is not possible without people like you agitating for change, whether in your workplace, in politics or more broadly in society. We all have a part to play, whatever that may be. If you are already involved, then you deserve applause. Achieving the changes suggested in this book would be transformational or, in the words of Friends of the Earth, a Big Idea. So if you want to do one thing after reading this book, get involved and stand up for change.

1

CHRISTIANA FIGUERES

Architect of the Paris Climate Change Agreement, Conference of the Parties (CoP) 21

The power of stubborn optimism

This Q&A with Christiana Figueres, the architect of the Paris Climate Change Agreement, took place while Christiana was in her home city of San José, Costa Rica. She was talking with a London-based journalist, on the UK's hottest June day for forty years (34.5°C).

Can you explain how you developed your thinking about how to negotiate the un-negotiable – the Paris Agreement in 2015? Is your approach a business leadership technique or special to you?

I actually wish that the reality were that there was a methodology that was clear in my head, but that's actually not true. There were two big ingredients for me: my values and principles, *and* my intuition. The values and principles form the basis of the work and then how I moved and constructed the basics was very much intuitive.

People often hide strongly held values when they go to the office. Should they?

I've chosen to be very open and I wear my values, principles and convictions on my sleeve. I think it is more transparent and people know where I'm coming from, and then they can then make their own choices – do they want to join? They know how I'm setting the scene. I operate out of a very deep love and respect for every other human being, independently of where that person is born, irrespective of their gender or age.

When I got to the United Nations (UN) secretariat in Bonn in 2010, the first thing I did was not figure out what the admin requirements for the UN were, even though I'd never run a UN agency before. It was rather asking: how are the people doing? What is the morale of the staff? I knew their morale was pretty bad after Copenhagen 2009, so I dedicated the first year to understanding the 500 people who worked at the UN Framework Convention on Climate Change (UNFCCC) secretariat.

The first thing was doing all sorts of projects for the people working there, to increase the quality of their life, not their performance. I said: 'Please tell me what stops you from coming to work with a smile on your face?' The Smile Project identified all sorts of things they would like to see changed, and then we developed a project around that. But that deep love and respect for human beings comes first within the secretariat, and then outside the secretariat it's the same values, the same principle and the same conviction of truly, deeply respecting the fantastic diversity that we have among human beings ... their cultural traditions, their beliefs, their needs, their interests and really truly respecting those differences. And it has to be without an expectation that the people would have to change the way they think or act, or the way they interact with each other.

That's one value. The other one, which was very helpful, was deep listening.

Deep listening I actually learned on the road – and I learned it because I had a very serious personal trauma, which happened halfway through my period in the secretariat, and I was personally deeply desperate. I turned to Buddhism for solace and for understanding. In my study of Buddhism I learned the art of deep listening from Thích Nhất Hạnh – founder of Plum Village. The art of deep listening is very consistent with the first value (because it stems from respect for the other person), but it puts you actively into a non-judgemental position and in the mode of asking questions, and listening clearly and deeply to the people with whom you are interacting. It was very helpful for me personally, but it was also helpful professionally. That deep respect is more passive, but listening is the active part as you interact with people. You don't tell them what to do; you ask them how they feel and what they think.

Stubborn optimism is something else I developed on the road. It came when I realised that, while the global framework for dealing with climate change was not sufficient, it was definitely necessary. There was so much evidence, so many things happening against that, and I knew I had to be really very tied to my optimism. My optimism was necessary because there was no other way to do this, but I also needed to be stubborn in the sense of realising that there were so many barriers – not to minimise them, but to be clear on the end goal and know that somehow we would get over the barriers, and work with the barriers or work around the barriers, or through the barriers, whatever way it was, but we had to get to our end goal.

So my stubborn optimism is a provocative way of saying 'relentless optimism'.

What difference in dynamics have you seen – or would you want to see – when dealing with a meeting that has a more equal proportion of men and women?
It's very simplistic and irresponsible to make a broad statement like that – the generalisations don't really apply. Having made that disclaimer, I think there is a female energy (which many men also have) to have an open attitude, and higher capacity to deal with complexity and differences of opinion. But, of course, 'most women' and 'most men' are never one formula.

But I tend to observe that most women are more open to differences of opinion and are used to working through those differences to end up with a collaborative result, rather than an imposed result. Women tend to use collaboration and collective wisdom – what I call collective leadership – to deal with issues.

Can you explain more about collective leadership?
Collective leadership is one of my favourite concepts. I realised very quickly that I didn't have the answers to everything; I didn't have any answer to anything! But I knew, collectively, we could all develop the answers.

Instead of keeping people out, or institutions out, I was very deliberate in opening up the tent to as many stakeholders, voices and opinions as possible. It is very clear to me that wisdom is always wiser when it is collectively produced. Two minds always think better than one; ten minds always are better than two; and 1,000 are better than ten. It does make things much more complex and the process slower, but in the end I think the result is stronger.

You've lived and travelled widely. Is there a city that allows opportunities for work and well-being irrespective of gender or pay grade?
I don't think that's a yes or no question. It's about a range of possibilities women have – a little bit more, and a little bit less – a relative positioning. Let me put it another way: one could place different cities around the world along a very broad gamut of the opportunities, or equal opportunities, that women have. I'd say my home city of San José, Costa Rica offers many opportunities for women, certainly now, though perhaps not so thirty to forty years ago. When I am home I observe the fantastic crop of brilliant young professional women who are shoulder to shoulder with each other, and with fantastic men, and are moving quite smoothly, and comfortably, into positions of leadership. While there are, of course, many cities and countries where we are much further behind in this, it is very exciting to see that it is beginning to take place in some developing countries.

I now live in London. London is a good city for most women (and it's never completely true, by the way, for all people). In most developed countries, cities recognise the value of working with 100 per cent (male and female) of social potential. Using only 50 per cent of the social potential will not get us much further than where we are now. Engaging 100 per cent of our potential is clearly a stronger driving force for good.

What is difficult about making a sweeping statement is that it is never the reality of every single woman. I would not want the impression that every single woman in Costa Rica feels she has equal opportunities. The fact is that if you take a range, or average,

I would say women have a pretty good average in San José. Within that you'll always find women who have no problem getting to where they want, and with equal pay, but you will also find women who are actually very oppressed.

As a society we are moving in the right direction, but we all spread ourselves along a very broad gamut. And there is more complexity. It could be that a woman who is personally very oppressed happens to have professional success; and it could be the other way round. Personal and professional success do not always go hand in hand, although they do very often.

You've called for radical shifts in flows of finance from fossil fuel industries to ensure that the world can meet its obligations to reduce emissions and meet climate change targets. Since 2015, how positive do you feel about this happening?
It's definitely happening. Fortunately we are increasing pace and scale, though not as quickly as I would wish. It's definitely increased in the green bond market, where we have gone from US$10 or US$11 billion just a few years ago, to US$40 billion, then to US$80 billion, and this year (2017) it is estimated at US$123 billion. And that is just one financial instrument – not the only one. We see some movements in the whole divest/invest movement also shifting over from carbon-intensive to less carbon-intensive technologies. We're seeing it. Though, as I say, not as quickly as we would want.

Most of us feel we are powerless to help big world problems. When you had the power to make changes in the run-up to the 2015 Paris Climate Change Agreement you made use of stubborn optimism. How can women practise this stubborn optimism to help create the big changes that are needed?
We're all motivated by something in life. We are all passionate about something. In my case I'm consistently, and constantly, motivated by my daughters – two fantastic young women (now aged twenty-seven and twenty-nine years old). I'm very proud of my daughters, but to me they also represent future generations who are going to be living the effects of climate change. The two

of them keep me moving forward and working as ardently as I do. That's my personal choice.

In general, I've always thought we should work at issues for which we have a passion. Somebody who gets up and goes to work just because 'that's their job', I just don't think that person can bring 150 per cent of potential to their job. When my daughters are choosing between jobs, or areas of work, I always ask: which are you more aligned with? If you work with your passion then you mobilise so many more components of who you are as a human being. You don't just mobilise your intellect in a profession, you mobilise the fullness of yourself as a human being. Somebody who is only working with their head is minimising the impact that they could have. Working with your head, your heart and your soul all aligned together has a much deeper impact on whatever you do. My choice was climate change, but anybody else should choose wherever they can have impact.

What made climate change your passion?
When I was a little girl I travelled with my parents – both of whom have always been in politics – to every single corner of Costa Rica, and one amazing thing I saw was a little golden toad that was endemic to a national park in Costa Rica. I just thought it was fantastic. By the time my daughters were more or less the same age I discovered the toad had disappeared, gone extinct. [The golden toad was last spotted in 1989 in the Costa Rican cloud forest of Monteverde. Its disappearance was the first extinction to be blamed on global warming caused by human activity.]

I was really taken by the fact there was extinction of a species in my lifetime. I thought: 'This is not what parents are supposed to do, to turn over a diminished planet to their children. They're supposed to turn over an improved planet.' And that's when I started to consider what on earth is going on here.

In your opinion, why will women save the planet?
I don't think women are going to save the planet on their own. Women and men need to join forces and maximise their collec-

tive and joint potential in order to improve the world. I think the complementarity of the approaches that we'd bring between the two genders is exactly what we need. We can't move forward in a meaningful way with one approach. You need a balance. We need both masculine and feminine characteristics.

And for men you need the same things – they need to balance out their masculine characteristics with feminine characteristics to have greater impact. This need for a balance is as true for one person as it's true for a family; both characteristics are needed for an organisation, a country, and certainly for the planet to be able to balance. The problem is we've had a predominance of male characteristics for thousands of years. If women are given equal opportunities to contribute to the global condition we will be able to create a safer, more just and more prosperous world. Universal well-being created by universal participation.

2

PATRICIA ESPINOSA

Executive Secretary, United Nations Framework Convention on Climate Change

Empowering women to power up the Paris Climate Change Agreement

We live in challenging but also exciting times. Our era is a moment of both grave threat and great opportunity. The threat comes from many sources, and climate change more often than not makes these challenges worse.

The loss of lives and livelihoods from the impacts of climate change and other threats is unacceptable. The human and economic costs of failing to act are too high.

Acting on climate change also presents a great opportunity. It is a path to lasting peace and widespread prosperity. Climate action can lift people out of poverty and ensure their needs are met, even as the population grows to close to 10 billion by 2050.

In this moment, the multilateral system is being tested. National governments alone cannot deliver lasting prosperity without a transformation of social and economic development that seeks to minimise risk and seize the opportunity we have.

Transforming our societies and our economies is an agenda that requires the participation of all.

It is clear that responding to climate change requires a rapid transition from 'business as usual' to a low-emission, resilient world economy.

It is also clear that this transition must happen in a way that is inclusive, fair and just. Countries have articulated this vision through the Paris Climate Change Agreement, the 2030 Agenda for Sustainable Development and the Sendai Framework for Disaster Risk Reduction.

A common thread running through these agendas is recognition that gender equality and the empowerment of women and girls are key to successful implementation.

Including and empowering women and girls to develop and implement climate solutions is the right thing to do. It is also the smart thing to do.

Smart collaboration

There is compelling evidence that links the inclusion of women in climate policy and solutions with better results, enhanced economic growth and more sustainable outcomes. However, we cannot take for granted that gender equality and the empowerment of women and girls in the context of addressing climate change and sustainable development will happen automatically.

Across the world, barriers that are too often cultural, structural and institutional must be overcome to ensure that women have the voice, agency and authority to fully and effectively contribute to – and benefit from – climate solutions.

Leadership from governments, companies, intergovernmental organisations and civil society is required to raise awareness, drive action and ensure that climate policy is truly gender-responsive.

It will also require an unprecedented level of collaboration and cooperation between these actors.

The Paris Agreement and the 2030 Agenda provide a framework for tracking progress both by national governments and by those who must be engaged for successful transformation, such as cities, regions, businesses and investors, among others.

Comprehensively capturing this collective effort will be critical to take stock of progress and make necessary, timely adjustments to each nation's contribution to the Paris Agreement or climate action plan.

Women can and must be empowered to contribute to the success of our global goals.

Initiatives such as C40's Women4Climate can make an important contribution to this effort, as their research on the links between gender, cities and climate change starts to generate results. These comprehensive data sets strengthen and improve climate policy because they ensure that the needs, perspectives and preferences of the entire population are represented.

Women make up 50 per cent of the population and cannot be excluded from development decisions.

Another ground-breaking initiative is the OECD Development Assistance Committee's first-of-its-kind study that tracked how women benefit from climate finance, in the form of bilateral official development assistance to climate change.

The study found that the overlap between climate development assistance and support for gender equality accounted for just over 30 per cent of bilateral aid in 2014 – a total of US$8 billion. By elevating equality as a top objective, those who provide support ensure that this support flows to those who need it most. This is the foundation for truly transformational change and lasting resilience.

Another key finding is that more needs to be done to improve women's opportunities to participate in the green economy. It is true. We must do more.

I urge every county to review their climate plans and better integrate gender considerations to ensure more effective and sustainable climate solutions. It is excellent that sixty-four countries have already started this effort by including gender-responsive approaches to action taken under the Paris Agreement. However, more must be done.

Countries stand to benefit greatly from finding the synergies between climate action and action towards women's empowerment. This is one of the most important lessons we have learned from cities and regions partnering on the ground with many diverse civil society, private sector and local women's organisations.

There is growing worldwide recognition of the urgent need to increase the number of women in decision-making and leadership roles to address climate change and sustainability. But persistent barriers remain across all sectors of the economy – in private enterprise, public and political institutions and entrepreneurship.

Give women a voice

One key agricultural sector barrier is gender bias in land ownership and access. For example, in Tanzania a woman's right to legally access land is not sufficient because men make many of the decisions about land ownership, making it harder for women to expand or diversify their farming activities. This can slow or prevent responses to climate impacts.

This entrenched dynamic is far too prevalent and this story plays out far too often, in far too many places. It is a dynamic we can and must change. For example, the leadership focus in the C40 Women4Climate initiative facilitates dialogue with current leaders and the mentorship of young women, who must be part of our next generation of leaders.

I am very pleased to be a global mentor under the initiative and I am working to enable more young women to step up to the challenge of climate change in their own communities.

In June 2017 I was fortunate to be offered the opportunity to join the International Gender Champions network and help empower more women leaders. I am doing everything I can to create more space that gives women a voice.

As one of my commitments, I signed the panel parity pledge, meaning that I will request organisers of any event at which I am speaking to aim for gender balance among speakers in panel discussions. I plan to hold all organisations to account.

I want to ensure that when we talk about a topic as significant as climate change, women who are working in this field are provided with an equal opportunity to share their knowledge and perspectives. This both enriches discussions and raises the visibility of strong female leaders and experts.

The UN Climate Change secretariat's own Momentum for Change initiative is also raising the visibility of women acting on climate change. The Women for Results pillar has brought to light a wealth of creative, innovative local initiatives led by women.

In recognition of the importance of leadership in driving change towards more gender-responsive climate action, the

Women for Results pillar includes for the first time in 2017 two separate focus areas: one on women's empowerment and one on women's leadership.

Open to change

We will continue to shine a light on efforts such as Dar Si Hmad, the 2016 Women for Results lighthouse activity in Morocco, the host of the 2016 UN Climate Change conference. This women-led group designed and installed the world's largest operational fog-water harvesting system. They use 600 square metres of special nets to harvest fresh water from fog, which provides water for more than 400 people in five vulnerable communities on the edge of the arid Sahara Desert.

A valuable and scarce resource, water plays a central role in women's lives, often requiring more than three hours per day to travel to distant, depleted wells. This innovative solution to persistent water stress is inspired by ancient water practices, but with a modern twist that will deliver lasting results.

Once infrastructure was installed to collect and distribute fog water, female villagers were equipped with mobile phones and trained to report on the fog-water system, maintaining their ancestral role as managers of water resources.

As Jamila Bargach, Director of Dar Si Hmad, explained to me, it is not just about the environment and building climate resilience: 'Women have gained back half a day that they have put into economic activities like argan oil production. This has been good for them, for their households and for their communities.'

This is just one example among many that illustrate the multiple benefits that can be achieved when women lead the design and implementation of climate solutions.

At the Conference of the Parties (CoP) 23 held in Bonn in November 2017, the Parties to the United Nations Framework Convention on Climate Change (UNFCCC) will review technical information to understand the challenges to full and equal participation of women in UN Climate Change meetings. This review of options for increasing the number of women participants should offer ways to break down barriers that hinder women at the highest level of global governance.

So we see progress at the community level and at the international level.

Women are gaining ground in rural agricultural communities and in the largest, fastest-growing cities. But by all accounts it is not enough.

We must share what has been learned through studies, technical papers and on-the-ground projects. We must look at projects showcased by Momentum for Change, by C40, and by so many others who are working to empower women, so we can successfully lift up women in every community in every country.

Those who are in power now need to create the space at the table and deliver the opportunity to be heard. Leaders must listen to all voices, especially the historically under-represented, and listen with sincerity and serious thought. Be open to change.

Climate action offers the opportunity to transform social and economic development for the better. We must take this opportunity to elevate women and girls as equals in a stable and sustainable society marked by lasting peace and prosperity. That is how women will save the planet.

3

SUSAN BUCKINGHAM

Independent gender researcher and consultant
and feminist geographer, Cambridge, UK

The hissing of summer lawns: cities, gender and climate change

Cities both exacerbate climate change and can pioneer ways in which climate change can be managed and mitigated. At their best, even the largest and most unruly of cities can be creative, beguiling and intoxicating. They can give women and men the freedom to be their authentic selves, and provide us all with opportunities to live together constructively regardless of our religion, culture, ethnicity, sexuality, age, parental responsibilities and other differences. Cities provide the context and arena for social, environmental and political change – from mass protests to community eco-projects and imaginative art – which encourages us to think about the ways in which we can live better together and with nature that is not human.

At their worst, however, cities can be alienating and divisive. Extreme and even 'merely comfortable' wealth allows those who enjoy financial security to exist in a bubble, which mostly insulates them from the underside of cities – including those who are homeless, have substance addictions, are street sex workers or form gangs.

Cities are constructs, influenced by social, economic and cultural structures: from bombastic signifiers of capital such as the skyscrapers that house investment banks; private shopping malls from which the poor are discouraged and sometimes forcibly evicted; gated communities of and for the rich. As such, cities carry the imprint of gender inequality – buildings and urban planning often create barriers to accessibility and feeling safe, generating a sense of hostility, or they simply dismiss the importance of women. For example, how many statues celebrating the lives of women can you think of, compared with the hundreds of statues of male military and political figures which are positioned in cities worldwide? The simple explanation for this is that cities are largely built by men for men, and can thereby alienate women and prevent them from taking a full and active part in urban life.

However imaginative architects, planners, urban designers and developers may be, it is impossible for them to fully understand the lives and concerns of people who they are not.

And so those unimagined people continue to be marginalised as cities sprawl outwards and upwards. Even the garden cities and new towns, designed to free households from the dark, damp, over-crowded and unsanitary conditions of British cities in the twentieth century, failed to attend to the concerns of women. And cities that reinforce gender inequality tend also to exacerbate climate change.

Who designs cities?

Despite initiatives for girls to study STEM (science, technology, engineering and maths) subjects worldwide, the majority of developers, planners, architects, surveyors, urban designers and civil engineers are men. So are those municipal and national politicians who make decisions to commission buildings and to build, demolish and rebuild urban areas and infrastructures. Arguably, many urban developments are vanity projects designed to enhance the image of the companies funding them, the politicians who sanction them, and the 'star' architects who design them. Major road projects are often envisaged and built as entities in themselves, rather than as serving the neighbourhoods through which they run. North Kensington in London was bifurcated by the expanded and elevated motorway section built in the 1960s. Although it was fought against energetically by the local community, the Westway road was pushed through, solidifying a barrier between the prosperous south of the borough of Kensington and Chelsea and the north, now typified by high-rise council accommodation and notorious for the Grenfell Tower fire in 2017. The road links central London with the affluent suburbs and dormitory towns of neighbouring western counties, enabling drivers to travel swiftly, and oblivious to the destruction of the community beneath them, polluting the rough sleepers under the structure, and to the lives of those living in the Lancaster West Estate, of which Grenfell Tower was a part, built following the construction of the Westway in the 1970s.

Earlier, the architectural journalist and author of *The Death and Life of Great American Cities*, Jane Jacobs, was more successful in drawing attention to the municipal, political and financial interests and processes that supported the building of highways through huge swathes of large US cities.[1] These roads were flanked with high-rise housing and office blocks, and reflections of them can now be found in most cities the world over. Her critiques and local activism in the 1950s galvanised successful protest against the destruction of the nineteenth-century Greenwich Village and Washington Square in New York City. Her celebration of the human scale was criticised by the celebrated US urbanist Lewis Mumford as promoting 'Mother Jacobs' Home Remedies', and her observations of daily neighbourhood activities denigrated as 'little flirtations that season a housewife's day'.[2] This criticism assumes that activities which involve the unpaid caring for children, neighbours and older relatives and provisioning for the household are less valid than those of paid and commuting employees. Such an assumption remains in discussions about the school run, for which car journeys (mainly made by women) are seen as more dispensable than commuting journeys (mainly made by men).

And yet it is the latter – the commuters – who are the beneficiaries of rapid transport links built as part of urban development and renewal. For example, main roads, such as the Westway, are primarily radial, designed to aid the commuter to paid work, even though 'he' is likely to have to make only one return journey a day, compared with 'her' multiple trip-chaining for the main household caring and servicing activities. Despite this disparity, women are more likely than men to rely on public transport, involving them in complex, time-consuming journeys as they escort children to nurseries and schools and other dependent relatives to doctors' surgeries and hospitals, and as they go shopping for their own and neighbours' households, while also fitting in full- or part-time paid work. They are also usually paid less than men.

Urban historian and Professor of Architecture Dolores Hayden has critiqued the outer suburbs of North American cities as being planned to fossilise a culturally specific and aspirational household of a male 'householder' earning money and a female 'housewife' whose work in the home and with their children is unpaid.[3] Dormitory suburbs in which each household unit is isolated from the next have both social and environmental costs: they require multiple car journeys over unnecessarily long distances, while each house and garden is independently kitted out with appliances, which stimulates environmentally destructive consumption and further isolation – an affluent lifestyle Joni Mitchell poetically observes in her 1975 song *The Hissing of Summer Lawns*.

Another impact of separating (extensive) housing from (intensive) centres of paid work, and high-income housing from low-income housing, is the added burden on those who service the offices and homes of the rich. Research in both Istanbul[4] and Santiago de Chile[5] has analysed the journeys taken mainly by poor women between their homes in peripheral areas, and their cleaning, childcare and other domestic work in central offices or rich people's homes. Journeys of up to three hours each way, made longer by searches for cheaper methods of transport, add to these workers' already stretched lives, while such commutes also contribute to climate change. A city of shorter distances – one that Berlin aspires to – would reduce carbon emissions and make such women's lives easier.

In addition, planning decisions and policies on health and education, particularly from the late 1990s in the UK, have consolidated high schools, hospitals and universities as well as shopping and business parks in locations not always well served by public transport. This generates additional road traffic and greenhouse gas emissions, as well as adding to the care work of many women and some men. In arguing for a mobility of care, Ines Sanchez de Madariaga presents European data from the Harmonised European Time Use Survey which shows that women spend more than double the amount of time than men in caring and household work and that without a transport system which recognises how important it is to minimise travel both the quality of women's lives and the quality of the environment are compromised. Sanchez de Madariaga's solution to this is a city of short distances with an emphasis on the local, thereby minimising environmental damage and expanding opportunities for neighbourhood interactions.[6]

Online shopping may be seen as one solution for those with time constraints, but it is one in which women's needs and environmental impacts need to be carefully thought through. While there is not yet much research on the environmental impacts of online shopping, one US-based research project found an increase in the burden of travel time, delay, average speed and greenhouse gas emissions on the urban transportation network.[7] An Australian women's group, 1 Million Women, which aims to build a 'movement of strong, inspirational women and girls acting on climate change', also draws attention to the substantial increase in demand for cardboard as a result of online shopping.[8]

Many planning and design decisions have also created cities that are perceived as unsafe, and political decisions compound this. Lighting, for example, is a contested issue in which the need to reduce energy consumption compromises safety; this was recently challenged by women's groups in Cambridge, UK, when the roads authority sought to make economic savings by reducing night-time lighting. Unsupervised streets and public areas feel unsafe and are created when mixed uses are replaced by a single activity. Jane Jacobs writes elegiacally about the daily urban ballet which starts with the early opening of shops and departure of commuters on trains, and continues with children escorted to school by their mothers, who themselves shop and socialise in the park and in the street.[9] The day closes with restaurants and bars active until late in the evening. With such a mixture of activity there are always eyes on the street. When such diverse activity is replaced with monocultures of flats, or offices, or shops, then not only are the numbers of journeys, pollution and levels of isolation increased, but people – and especially women – feel less safe.

So who builds these cities? Surveyors, planners, civil engineers, architects and other built environment-related professions are predominantly male and, arguably, masculinist.[10] The Royal Town Planning Institute reported that 35 per cent of its members were women in 2015 (though not of all of these would have been practising planners),[11] while *The Architects' Journal* reported in 2016 that 25 per cent of professionally registered architects in the UK were women.[12] A 2014 sector-wide study of the architectural profession in Europe reported that 39 per cent of architects were women, but that men earned a third more than women.[13] In the USA in 2014, 30 per cent of associate members of the professional association of architects were women, but only 25 per cent of those working as architects.[14] 'Star' architects are overwhelmingly men: one in sixty-nine Gold Medal winners in the USA is a woman; only one woman has won the prestigious Pritzker Architecture Prize (and two women jointly with men); and only one woman has independently won the RIBA Gold Medal – and that was awarded posthumously. Gender pay gaps, and unhelpful working conditions that do not support caring responsibilities, are reported in the sixth 'Women in Architecture' global survey by the *Architectural Review* (2017).[15] Sexism, discrimination and bullying in the workplace are identified by more than half of women respondents as contributing factors to women 'losing their faith' in the profession, suggesting that there is unlikely to be much change in who designs buildings and cities in the short to medium term.

What can we do?

Is this an inevitable trajectory for the twenty-first-century city? Cities made less safe and harder to negotiate by increasing the segregation of activity and social class also lead to higher greenhouse gas emissions. Massive development projects will produce heavy carbon footprints. Can a focus on gender equality contribute to cities that are less environmentally damaging and fairer for women? And if cities are better places for women to live in, won't they be better for men as well?

There are many examples of urban projects that have already tried to combine gender and environmental justice. Women's housing projects have been developed in northern European countries such as Sweden and the Netherlands, where older women living alone, or younger mothers of dependent children, can live more cooperatively, sharing kitchens, childcare facilities or tool sheds, reducing isolation and increasing energy efficiency by pooling some material resources. The Frauen-Werk-Stadt (FWS) in Vienna was built as a result of a female-only competition as one way to break the stranglehold of master planning competitions to which no women architects had been invited. This was enabled by The Women's Office, which was established in Vienna in 1992 and still works to foster gender- and environmentally sensitive design. A second FWS project was developed in the 2000s, which focused on living in old age. Such a focus has a particular resonance for women, who outnumber men in older age – but it benefits older men too. The guiding principles of both schemes are flexibility of space (rooms which can be used for different purposes), intergenerational living, visual contact with play areas inside and outside the flats, communal facilities and storage rooms, social spaces, and spaces that are and feel safe.[16]

This initiative inspired Berlin in 2001, when it legislated to require a consideration of gender relations and how these interact with other social, demographic and cultural features in city planning and building.[17] Such planning strengthens community and sense of place by increasing the mixed use of buildings, accessibility, mobility and a focus on the compact city. Gender-sensitive housing includes attention to social and intergenerational mix, provides robust and flexible housing to minimise the number of moves a household needs to make, and conserves resources, including through energy efficiency. Such measures can make a contribution to reducing greenhouse gases and the city's carbon footprint.

Berlin has a rich tradition of alternative housing options with environmental and social benefits: for example, one co-housing website reports 1,000 eco-housing units, in which households combine private spaces with communal facilities to different degrees with social and environmental benefits.[18] Lidewij Tummers has researched co-housing across Europe to understand the symbiosis between gender equality and low carbon impact. Recognising the power of the built environment to reinforce particular behaviours and lifestyles, she concludes that the social disruption needed to achieve gender equality 'may be the key to resolving the challenges that climate change presents in a just manner'.[19] Of course, as ecofeminists have long argued, this requires a rethinking of gender relations to ensure that gender equality is achieved by changing the dominance of industrial masculinity that sets current male norms of behaviour, including their relationship with non-human nature.[20]

Small-scale projects, designed collaboratively with the communities they are intended for, are likely to serve both women and the environment well when they take into account the complex lives and multiple tasks of people involved in the design process. Examples of this include Col.lectiu Punt 6 in Barcelona,[21] which was set up in response to national legislation to include a gender perspective in the design of urban spaces and facilities, and Urbanistas, a women-led network that works with professional planning organisations in the UK and Australia to encourage 'women to draw on both personal values and professional know-how to lead and deliver projects […] to [achieve] equality and social justice'.[22]

Conclusion

Both the informal and formal strategies presented here illustrate how women can be involved as urban professionals and community participants to address current gender inequalities and improve the lives of different women, and men, in cities. These strategies also have a lighter impact on the environment than prevailing planning, development and design. Given the vulnerability of urban areas to climate change, and the contribution that current urban formations

4

ZANDILE GUMEDE
Mayor of Durban, South Africa

What's happening in Durban: from 'tree-preneurs' to trendsetters

Women are nurturers by nature. They have been taking the lead in climate change action to ensure environmental sustainability and protecting the needs of future generations for years, without even realising it.

In Durban, South Africa, approximately 67 per cent of the eThekwini municipal area is rural in nature with thousands of people living below the bread line, despite the advances in economic growth and service delivery since the birth of South Africa's democracy. The risks associated with climate change in Durban include increased pressure on water resources, energy security, health services, food security, loss of biodiversity and sea level rise, which will impact on tourism. These impacts could result in loss of life and livelihoods and damage to infrastructure.

Much of the African continent too is rural. Climate change therefore has a direct impact on rural women, who remain most vulnerable because it is women who are responsible for keeping the home fires burning. Rural women still forage for firewood, fetch water from the rivers, attend to their meagre food garden and see to the needs of their families. They are the group most reliant on natural resources for their livelihoods and yet have the least capacity to respond to natural disasters such as droughts and floods. And climate change impact poses a threat to the natural resources that they are largely dependent on.

Due to poverty, most South Africans live a minimalistic life. For centuries women have been responsible for ensuring that there is no wastage; everything is repurposed and reused. Dishes are washed with only as much water as is needed. Whatever water is left is used in the vegetable garden. Kitchen scraps are used as compost in the garden. Tin cans and bottles make excellent storage containers and newspaper is used as cheap yet effective disposable tablecloths and shelf liners. Plaited plastic and grass make excellent mats. This scenario is not unique to Durban or even to South Africa, but rather to the African continent.

This protective and minimalistic lifestyle is still entrenched in many women today, especially those of the older generation, who disapprove of lavish and excessive modern-day living. We certainly need to take a leaf out of their books and look back at how economical they can be.

The response to climate change depends on lifestyle choices and young women need to be trendsetters for a green lifestyle, especially in light of the many environmental challenges faced by the world today.

Inspiring all women

In South Africa, the month of August is dedicated to celebrating the women who led thousands of women from all races to fight against the apartheid government on 9 August 1956. As women in South Africa, we remain inspired by these women and we believe that we should continue fighting in all facets, which includes the area of climate change. Women from all walks of life can play a pivotal role in climate change mitigation and adaptation – whether homemakers or the youth or the career-driven professional women. Their knowledge and experience in sustainable practice is a resource to be tapped into for the greater good of the community. We have found that their meaningful participation enables a greater response and cooperation.

We should be inspired by the likes of Professor Wangari Maathai (1940–2011), the founder of the Green Belt Movement and recipient of the 2004 Nobel Peace Prize. Professor Maathai introduced the idea of community-based tree planting that developed into a broad-based grassroots organisation, the Green Belt Movement, whose main focus is poverty reduction and environmental conservation through tree planting.

Professor Maathai was internationally acknowledged for her struggle for democracy, human rights and environmental conservation. Her record is well known for numerous activities and initiatives, which included playing a visible role in Nairobi and being appointed as a United Nations Messenger of Peace in 2009 and a member of the Millennium Development Goals Advocacy Group in 2010. She received a string of awards and honorary doctorate degrees for the unselfish work she did.

I am inspired by her wise words: 'We cannot tire or give up. We owe it to the present and future generations to rise up and walk.'

Here in Durban we are proud and privileged to have one of our own to help us, Dr Debra Roberts. Dr Roberts previously headed the Environmental Planning and Climate Protection Department that leads the city's climate change adaptation agenda. She now leads the city's Sustainable and Resilient City initiative, while acting as a co-chair of Working Group II for the Sixth Assessment Report by the Intergovernmental Panel on Climate Change (IPCC). She is the first South African and local government official to fulfil this role. Her passion for biodiversity and climate change adaptation in developing cities has made her a world-renowned and a highly respected figure in the field.

While these two women are examples of women who have influenced global agendas and policy, women are central to Durban's various ecosystem-based adaptation reforestation projects, such as the 600 hectare Buffelsdraai, 250 hectare Inanda Mountain and 200 hectare Paradise Valley community reforestation projects, as well as the 78,000 hectare Durban Metropolitan Open Space System (D'MOSS).

More than 400 households, which are led by women, have benefited from these programmes. They perform various functions from collecting indigenous seeds to planting them and nurturing the seedlings for sale back to the city for reforestation projects. Local communities are also employed in planting the forests and eradicating alien invasive plants. We have coined the term 'tree-pre-neurs' for these hard-working women.

Waste management is also a huge challenge in a fast-developing city such as Durban, especially for residents of informal settlements. Through the initiation of a community-based waste management project, however, things are improving for the informal settlement community as a group of women have initiated a recycling programme to curb waste problems. The establishment of green economy initiatives by our 'waste-preneurs' is one of the fundamental goals for climate adaptation in the city. Such initiatives bring multiple benefits, including job creation and poverty alleviation, and so should be supported and replicated throughout the city to support climate change adaptation.

Their employment has impacted greatly on the women's lives as they are now in a much better position to provide for their families. Besides this, these women have been empowered with information and also act as advocates for the protection of the environment in their communities. The value of this grass roots-level interaction and education is immeasurable. It allows communities to take ownership of their environment, protect it, and value the services it offers.

Using a gender-sensitive plan

In conclusion, eThekwini municipality is very strict on gender equity matters, and aims to eliminate discrimination in the workplace. We want to see more people from previously disadvantaged communities being employed, especially women, youth and those with disabilities.

Already females make up at least 48 per cent of the team that specialises in environmental and climate change issues in the city.

There is a shortage of suitably qualified employees from designated groups of Africans and women, particularly in certain skill areas such as science and engineering. A gender-sensitive plan for the period 2014–18 has been developed and is being implemented to meet employment equity targets.

eThekwini municipality has partnered with a local university to develop climate change response tools and develop local capacity. This scheme, which has 60 per cent female students, has already produced two PhDs and fourteen master's graduates. Education is the very best way for women to become empowered. Cities can leverage on programmes such as Women4Climate scholarship to uplift young smart ladies into powerful women to lead the climate change agenda.

Mentorship is critical in developing confidence and fine-tuning the skills of young women. This will ensure that each future generation has strong influential women to carry on the legacy that was started by the few.

There is space for all women to lead action against climate change – whether they are planting trees or are involved in river protection or recycling of waste, involved in policy and decision-making, a suburban mum running her household, or an environmental activist. Wherever we see women's empowerment, it always extends to the greater good of the community.

5

DIANE ELSON

University of Essex

Women's empowerment and environmental sustainability in the context of international UN agreements

Introduction

Why should environmental activists be interested in women's empowerment? Not because women are intrinsically closer to nature than men, and better equipped to save the planet. But because neither environmental sustainability nor women's empowerment can be achieved without challenging patterns of economic growth and configurations of economic power that do not take into account non-market resources, not only climate and oceans, but also the unpaid care work that is vital to human well-being, and which is disproportionately women's work. There are important synergies between environmental sustainability and women's empowerment that need to be explored, and the social movements focused on each goal can be strengthened through collaborative efforts. These arguments are explored here in relation to UN agreements pertaining to the environment, and the struggle over what 'green economy' will signify in practice.

International UN agreements on the environment and women's empowerment

Beginning with the UN Conference on Environment and Development in Rio in 1992, a series of international agreements have linked the participation of women in activities related to the agreements as important for fulfilment of the aims of the agreements. Thus, Principle 20 of the official Rio Declaration on Environment and Development states that the full participation of women is essential to achieving sustainable development.[1] The trio of global environmental conventions that followed this conference – the United Nations Framework Convention on Climate Change (UNFCCC), the Convention on Biodiversity (CBD) and the United Nations Convention to Combat Desertification (UNCCD) – all make reference to the importance of enhancement of women's participation in relevant public bodies.[2]

A concern with women's empowerment is repeated in the outcome document of the Rio+20 United Nations Conference on Sustainable Development, *The Future We Want*:

> We recognize that gender equality and women's empowerment are important for sustainable development and our common future. We reaffirm our commitments to ensure women's equal rights, access and opportunities for participation and leadership in the economy, society and political decision-making. We underscore that women have a vital role to play in achieving sustainable development. We recognize the leadership role of women, and we resolve to promote gender equality and women's empowerment and to ensure their full and effective participation in sustainable development policies, programmes and decision-making at all levels.[3]

However, despite the lip-service paid to women's participation in decision-making, it appears that there has been little of substance, with efforts ranging from 'exclusion to nominal inclusion'.[4] The discussion on gender and climate change focused primarily on local-level vulnerabilities and adaptation; with only limited attention to gender issues in discussions involving large-scale technology, market-based initiatives and climate finance.[5] A pioneering effort to construct an environment and gender index included indicators for presence of women in Conference of Parties (CoP) delegations and policy-making positions, and inclusion of gender issues in UNFCC reports, UNCCD reports and CBD reports. It found that the global average for women was 36 per cent of those participating in intergovernmental negotiations on climate change, biodiversity and desertification.[6] The Conference of Parties in 2012 adopted a resolution to promote gender balance in bodies of and delegations to UNFCC and to include gender and climate change as a standing item on the CoP agenda. However, these negotiations are only one space among many, and there is little data on women's ability to exercise decision-making power in environmentally sensitive production and consumption processes, especially those dominated by multinational corporations.

There is indeed evidence that women's participation in environmental management can make a difference: for example, their effective involvement in community forest management bodies has yielded positive outcomes for both forest sustainability and gender equality.[7] However, a recent UN Women report argues that there has too often been a presumption that women could be harnessed as 'sustainability saviours' based on the assumption that women are especially close to nature and have time to spare:

> Women–environment connections – especially in reproductive and subsistence activities such as collecting fuel wood, hauling water and cultivating food – were often presented as if natural and universal rather than as the product of particular social and cultural norms and expectations. Ensuing projects and policies often mobilized and instrumentalized women's labour, skills and knowledge, adding to their unpaid work without addressing whether they had the rights, voice and power to control project benefits.[8]

Moreover, it is vital to recognise that some measures to address environmental sustainability may have adverse impacts on some women. For instance, biofuel production could run counter to the ability of women smallholders to provide food for their families. Higher consumer prices for energy may encourage consumers to 'econo-mise' in their use of energy and not to waste it, but in the context of poverty and inequality may confront low-income women with the terrible dilemma of providing 'heating or eating' for their families.

What matters is not the simple presence or absence of women in climate change delegations or on committees to manage envi-ronmental resources. What matters is how women's empowerment and sustainable development are framed, how the determinants of gender inequality and harmful climate change and environmental degradation are understood, and what kinds of measures are intro-duced to reduce them both. Are the means of implementation profit-driven? Or are they rooted in collective social investment and regulation, recognising the importance of resources and activities that are not commercialised?

Meanings of empowerment and sustainability

Both of these terms can be understood in narrow ways, disconnected from rights and justice. For instance, women's empowerment can be understood as more women being present in the public sphere, participating in the market economy or being elected to parlia-ments and other public bodies. But this ignores the question of the quality of this participation. Do women enjoy the rights at work that are set out in human rights treaties and ILO Conventions? Are women earning a living wage? Are their jobs secure? Are they able to combine employment with caring for other people without being penalised by low wages, poor promotion prospects, lack of security, unhealthy working environments? Are the women in parliaments, and other public bodies, mere tokens, subject to sexist practices, with most women unable to exercise real decision-making power? A much broader understanding is offered by the UN Committee on the Elimination of Discrimination Against Women, which suggests that women are empowered 'by an enabling environment to achieve equality of results' in terms of enjoyment of all human rights,[9] some-thing that applies to the private sphere of the home and community, as well as to the public spheres of the market and the state. This requires transformation of existing societies and economies and not merely integration of women into the public sphere, as Articles 3 and 5 of the Convention on the Elimination of All Forms of Discrimination Against Women indicate. This has been spelled out by the UN Committee on the Elimination of Discrimination Against Women, which has said that governments must adopt measures to bring about 'a real transformation of opportunities, institutions and systems so that they are no longer grounded in historically determined male paradigms of power and life patterns'.[10]

The disproportionate responsibility that women bear for carrying out unpaid work is an important constraint on their capacity to realise their rights, as has been emphasised in a recent report by the UN Special Rapporteur on Extreme Poverty and Human Rights.[11] Thus, a key transformation is the recognition, reduction and redistribution of the unpaid work of caring for families and communities, so that unpaid work that is drudgery (such as collecting fuel and water) is reduced, and other unpaid work, such as caring for children, is redistributed, some of it to men in households and communities, and some of it to paid workers in public and private sectors. Both women and men need time to care for their families and communities, and time free from such care – something that is often discussed in Europe in terms of 'work–life balance'.

Environmental sustainability can be understood in terms of not breaching the planetary boundaries that have been identified as keeping the planet within a safe operating space for humanity.[12] But this ignores the question of inequalities between people, the distribution of the costs and benefits of actions to avoid breaching critical thresholds, and the foundational importance of respect for human rights.[13] It is important to keep in mind intergenerational issues so that we can 'meet the needs of the present without compromising the ability of future generations to meet their own needs'.[14] But in doing so, we must not ignore the fact that many people are dying today because of unmet needs – for instance, the maternal mortality of low-income women in developing countries has remained stubbornly high despite the Millennium Development Goals and many avoidable deaths are occurring. Thus we need to be not only Friends of the Earth but also Friends of the Poor, and those subject to discrimination. These considerations are perhaps addressed by the post-Rio+20 discourse about the three dimensions of sustainability: social, economic and environmental. But this can be a cover for a wish to simply maintain unequal patterns of profit-driven economic growth, hoping to avoid social disruption, economic crises and environmental disasters through piecemeal adaptation and mitigation measures, rather than transforming our economies and societies.

Both 'empowerment' and 'sustainability' as used in most UN documents are ambiguous concepts, whose meaning is revealed only in the context of specific practices. If the practices of profit-driven economic growth dominate, this will severely restrict the kinds of 'empowerment' and 'sustainability' that are possible to those that are profit-conforming, and may in fact prevent the transformations that are necessary for women to be fully empowered, and use of natural resources to be fully sustainable.

There is evidence that strongly suggests that the underlying causes and consequences of unsustainability and gender inequality are deeply intertwined and rooted in profit-driven economic processes.[15] These involve market liberalisation, productive and financial activity geared to short-term profits; unrestrained material consumption; unparalleled levels of militarism; privatisation of public goods and services and reduction of the capacities of governments to regulate and redistribute. As well as environmental degradation and harmful climate change, these processes have caused in many places crises of care, which entails the breakdown in the abilities of individuals, families, communities and societies to sustain and care for themselves and future generations, undermining people's rights and dignity.[16]

Green economy: gender equitable and environmentally sustainable?

The idea of promoting a green economy has become popular in UN agencies as a way to address environmental sustainability and create 'green' jobs.[17] There are several variants of 'green economy', though most embrace the goal of economic growth; the difference being mainly in terms of the relative roles of public and private investment. Dominant variants of green economy assume continued, even enhanced, profit-driven economic growth, through green business investments and innovations that increase energy and resource efficiency, and prevent the loss of ecosystem services. They call for financial valuation of 'natural capital', payments for ecosystem services, and schemes for trading carbon and biodiversity credits and offsets, arguing that the problem is that markets fail to price natural assets and ecosystem services, resulting in overuse of 'natural capital'. Governments must define private property rights in ecological assets and create markets to trade them.[18] However, UNEP has a broader vision, seeing a green economy as one that ends extreme poverty, improves human well-being and enhances social equity while reducing carbon dependency and ecosystem degradation, and furthering sustainable and inclusive growth.[19]

The case for 'green' public investments was much discussed and promoted as part of the (short-lived) counter-cyclical macro-economic policies adopted in the wake of the 2008 global recession in both developed and developing countries, often framed as a 'global green new deal' (GGND) in which government spending would be directed towards technology and employment generation in ways that enhance environmental protection and raise efficiency, for instance by retro-fitting energy-inefficient buildings or infrastructure.[20] UNEP's version of GGND emphasised the principle of common but differentiated responsibilities of developed countries, emerging economies, countries with economies in transition, and least developed countries. A 'fair and just GGND, therefore, should consider including developed countries' additional support to other countries, especially least developed countries, in the areas of finance, trade, technology and capacity building in the interest of effectiveness as well as fairness'.[21]

Gender equality has been a marginal concern in most of the green economy proposals. Given the extent of gender segregation in employment, there is a risk that efforts to 'green' industry will not only bypass women, but actually marginalise them. Sectors targeted for green employment expansion, such as energy, construction and basic industry, are very male-dominated. Among 'green' jobs that already exist, women tend to have low representation and/or occupy the lower value-added rungs. For instance, in the OECD, where women hold more than half of university degrees, only 30 per cent of degrees in science and technology (key areas for green jobs) go to women.[22] In developing economies, women are highly concentrated at the low value-added end of existing green jobs, for instance as informal workers in waste collection and recycling. However, there have been efforts to organise waste pickers worldwide, and women are more likely than men to participate in waste picker organisations, perhaps because they tend to be concentrated in lower-earning waste picking activities, and are typically paid lower rates than men for equivalent work.[23] Organised waste pickers are better able to circumvent middlemen and negotiate fair prices for their materials from buyers. There are also attempts to better incorporate waste pickers into waste management and recycling activities, countering the push towards incineration and landfill technologies, and instead promoting zero waste strategies that maximise recycling and provide decent employment for the poor.[24]

UN Women[25] has called for targeting specific skill development and education for women, and efforts to break down gender stereotypes, while at the same time pointing to several examples of new 'green' jobs that have included women. For example, in the 'Working for Water' project in South Africa, where peope were trained to remove invasive alien plants to enhance water security, successful efforts were made to specifically recruit women, youth and people with disabilities to take part. In Bangladesh, as part of a larger project to extend electricity to rural areas by installing solar home systems, women were trained to install and repair solar panels and electrical outlets, serving as 'rural electricians'. In the United States, the Women Apprenticeship in Non-traditional Occupations (WANTO) programme gives grants to community-based organisations that provide openings for women into non-traditional occupations, such as pre-apprenticeship programmes, with recent rounds emphasising green jobs.

But there are other important dimensions of a green economy besides the gender-equitable creation of green jobs. A key issue is what kinds of ways of life are supported by the goods and services produced.[26] Do they support a competitive, 'privatised' way of life, built around individual consumption, in a consumerist culture in which possessing more material goods than your neighbours is always better? No matter how energy efficient the shopping mall, no matter how many jobs, both for women and men, have been created in its construction, if this becomes the emblem of the good life, and entry into it an aspiration for all those now excluded, it is hard to see how this can be socially and environmentally sustainable, and genuinely empowering for women.

An alternative would be production that is environmentally sustainable and supports a cooperative way of life, central to which is the production of public goods that are used by all – public health, education, transport, water and sanitation, energy, streets, parks etc. Some services might be free at the point of delivery, such as health services. For others, such as water, multi-part tariffs, which charge the better off more per unit than the poor, could be used. This alternative would incorporate a substantial amount of collaborative production by non-profit institutions such as cooperatives and community enterprises; and services run by the local or national state would be organised in partnership with the users of services. For-profit production would be regulated to serve the public good, rather than the shareholders.

Conclusions

A system that supports a cooperative way of life is better equipped to take into account goods and services that are not priced and paid for in money, such as the non-market realms of nature and family care. The ability to take into account resources that are not marketed and not produced for a profit, whether unpaid work caring for family and friends, or the atmosphere and oceans; not taking them for granted as 'bottomless pits', able to absorb any demands made on them; recognising both their importance and the distinctive value of not subjecting them to a commercial calculus – all this is central to the attainment of both women's empowerment and environmental sustainability. Many environmental campaigners know a lot about how to take into account environmental resources without subjecting them to the calculus of monetary profit and loss. Many campaigners for women's empowerment know a lot about how to take into account unpaid care without subjecting it to a calculus of monetary profit and loss. The two sets of campaigns can be mutually strengthened, both in the context of UN agreements, and at national and local levels, if they work together.

6

ALEXANDRA PALT

**Chief Corporate Responsibility Officer,
L'Oréal, Paris**

Walking the talk: empowering tomorrow's women leaders

Here, Alexandra Palt discusses the ways in which corporate social responsibility can improve society.

Corporate social responsibility is meant to improve society. Your role at a major global company puts you in a key position to do this, so how does L'Oréal contribute to a healthier and more sustainable society?

At L'Oréal, we see sustainability as a licence to operate. It is what our consumers expect, and will expect more and more in the future – and it is integral to our mission of bringing beauty to all. Put simply, sustainability is who we want to be – a responsible business that creates a positive impact on society and the environment.

As the largest beauty company in the world, we have a responsibility and an opportunity to help address the major challenges faced by humanity today, including climate change, resource scarcity, poverty and social inequality. This will contribute directly to our long-term success. Through our global vision for 2020, 'Sharing Beauty with All', we are transforming every aspect of our value chain – all the way from raw materials sourcing to consumer interaction with our products.

We have the full support of our CEO, Jean-Paul Agon, and we are empowering our employees worldwide, across every brand, to contribute to this profound movement of change. This new paradigm has changed the way we design, produce, distribute and communicate about our products.

Firstly, we want 100 per cent of our new or renovated products to have an improved environmental or social footprint by 2020. This means that whenever our teams invent or renew a product, they enhance its formula by improving biodegradability or using responsibly sourced raw materials, while optimising the packaging. A product's environmental and social impact is now just as important as other factors in the design and creation process. It is a huge global effort, and we have already reached 82 per cent of our target. For example, various L'Oréal brands have developed products with high levels of natural ingredients and biodegradability, such as Kérastase with its range Aura Botanica, and Matrix Biolage RAW.

We are taking action to cut the carbon, water and waste impacts of our production by 60 per cent. In 2016, we had already reduced our manufacturing CO_2 emissions by 67 per cent (compared with 2005), four years ahead of target. I am proud that L'Oréal is one of two companies globally to have received three 'A' rankings for its climate change, forest management and sustainable water efforts from CDP, an independent, not-for-profit entity that evaluates companies' environmental performance.

We want all our brands to help raise consumer awareness of living sustainably by 2020. By making sustainability desirable, we are encouraging people to make healthier, more sustainable lifestyle choices. Walking the talk is very important here. We are being clear with our consumers about how we are improving the footprints of our products. Half of our brands had conducted campaigns by 2016. Our target is 100 per cent by 2020.

Sharing our growth with all our stakeholders – our employees, suppliers and the communities in which we operate – is central to fulfilling our vision. We focus on collaborating for positive change, empowering people to give of their best, and promoting social inclusion. By 2016, we had helped 67,500 people from underprivileged backgrounds find access to employment through one of our social inclusion programmes.

As a woman, do you feel you approach social responsibility and sustainability through a different lens than a man would? If so, how?

I have always been passionate about fighting injustice and standing up for human rights. That is why I studied law and began my career defending human rights. Throughout my career, I have witnessed the diverse challenges and significant obstacles women face. The way I approach social responsibility and sustainability is directly influenced by what I have seen and experienced – from women pushing for equal rights in the workplace to women in developing communities overcoming cultural barriers to take ownership of improving their livelihoods.

I have total confidence in the abilities and potential of women, and I believe that if women had more power in their communities, in business and in politics, the march towards sustainable development would be far higher up the global agenda. It is clear to me that women are motivated more by the greater good and less by power.

As a young graduate, I was lucky to have a wonderful mentor – Barbara Lochbihler of Amnesty International (now an MEP) – who inspired me to transform my ambitions to lead positive change into reality. Throughout my career, I have pushed forward, drawing energy and inspiration from both success and adversity. That is why I believe so strongly in the importance of empowering tomorrow's women leaders to stand up for what they believe in and be tenacious, despite any resistance.

From a personal point of view, I have approached sustainability very differently since I became a mother. I am less concerned by the idea that humans might face difficulties in overcoming the great changes to come, and far more concerned by the thought of the human suffering that will inevitably accompany these changes. Climate refugees, armed conflicts for resources but also the disappearance of nature, as we know it today, frighten me for the generations to come. So yes, I think being a woman changes my viewpoint on sustainability because empathy and long-term thinking are at the centre of my life.

What does L'Oréal do to address climate change specifically? How do these programmes also empower women?
While climate change is a major challenge, and we are already seeing its effects on the most vulnerable populations, our commitment to tackle climate change is stronger than ever. We are active in reducing the carbon impacts of our plants and distribution centres, optimising our energy consumption, expanding our use of renewable energy and opting for more sustainable transport. We have exceeded our 2020 carbon emissions target four years early, cutting our emissions by 67 per cent in absolute terms between 2005 and 2016, while growing production by 29 per cent. In doing so, we have proved that it is possible to decouple our growth from our environmental impact.

By 2020, we plan to have become a 'carbon-balanced' company – we will generate enough carbon savings in our raw materials supply chains to balance our remaining manufacturing carbon emissions. Women are playing a critical role in this, since they sit at the heart of our sourcing communities. Across the world, our sustainable, 'solidarity sourcing' projects are helping women to overcome the risks posed by climate change and improve their livelihoods, while strengthening our ability to continue sourcing some of our most iconic ingredients.

Let me give you an example. In south-west Burkina Faso, we source shea butter, one of our top ten raw materials, from 35,000 women producers. They live in communities that depend on firewood for energy. For thousands of years, they have harvested and prepared shea butter. However, the women face distinct barriers, including poverty and a lack of access to knowledge, finance and markets. They often see the majority of their profits go to middlemen. Additionally, the intensive processing of shea nuts deforests 100,000 hectares of forest every year, which has a devastating impact on the environment and local communities.

So, at L'Oréal, we saw an opportunity to support these women, protect the environment, and improve our own efficiency and profitability. In partnership with our supplier Olvéa and Burkinabe social enterprise Nafa Naana, we launched an effort to provide producers with a fair income, offering training and support to improve production methods and reduce carbon emissions and deforestation. To boil the water used to scald the shea nuts, we are also introducing cleaner cook stoves, which save the women time and money and reduce their exposure to smoke.

This is an important example of how we take action to empower women. This is not charity. This is about preparing women – and our company – to meet the world's environmental and social challenges.

You took part in the first Women4Climate conference, organised by C40 Cities in New York City in March 2017, and L'Oréal became the first company to partner with C40 on the larger Women4Climate initiative. Why did you and L'Oréal get involved, and are there other similar women empowerment initiatives that L'Oréal takes part in?

I am very proud that L'Oréal is a founding partner of the C40 Cities Women4Climate initiative. This was a strategic decision. It is an important way for us to build momentum on two of our major ambitions: empowering women and protecting the world's climate. When you consider that C40 Cities connects more than ninety of the world's biggest cities and more than 650 million citizens, there are huge potential social, economic and environmental gains to be made. Our partnership stands to drive climate action, boost economies and improve people's health and well-being.

As a global beauty company whose business touches millions of people around the world, the majority of them women, we want to enable women to apply their full creativity and resourcefulness to addressing climate and environmental challenges. By partnering with the inspirational C40 mayors, we want to empower the next generation of women leaders in the fight against climate change.

This latest commitment builds on L'Oréal's existing, long-standing efforts to empower women, promote gender equality and recognise the achievements of remarkable women – both within our company and beyond. We have consistently sought to empower women within our company, promoting diversity and inclusion initiatives, and fostering a strong understanding of the strategic importance of gender equality at work. We are very clear about the business case for diversity – it increases the well-being and performance of our employees, fuels creativity and innovation, and helps accelerate our growth. That is why women account for 46 per cent of the L'Oréal board, and why 58 per cent of our brands are led by women. Women also play an important role in our sourcing communities.

And our corporate foundation, the Foundation L'Oréal, has awarded prizes to brilliant women scientists for twenty years. For Women in Science recognises excellence and remarkable contributions to science, honouring five laureates each year. We support women researchers and rising talents through their careers – to date we have granted 275 doctoral and postdoctoral fellowships in 115 countries.

If women are to save the planet, what needs to change to make sure they can forge ahead? How can companies such as L'Oréal work with mayors and other government representatives, as well as citizens, to make much needed changes in their communities? Firstly, mindsets across the world need to shift. Everyone – men, women, boys and girls – must become aware of the equal roles that men and women can and should play in our society. This starts with teaching our children about the importance of equality. Girls must grow up knowing that they can do anything that boys can do.

Beyond that, it is important that women everywhere are able to achieve economic independence. We want to see a future where women play an equal role in the home, take ownership of improving their livelihoods and earn a fair income to support their families. This means pushing for equal opportunities and pay in the workplace.

We will continue to support women at the forefront of climate and environmental research, and pave the way for more women to stand up and speak out on addressing fundamental human rights and environmental issues. I already see many inspiring examples across the world every day. But we need to take this to the next level – to empower the next generations of women to rise up and lead the charge.

Through the Women4Climate initiative, we will help to mentor at least 400 young women by 2019 who are developing solutions to limiting the impacts of climate change in multiple C40 Cities, from Paris to Mexico to Cape Town. We will mobilise women leaders from our own teams to support future leaders and strengthen their leadership capabilities. L'Oréal will also support research exploring how climate change impacts women, and fund projects that address gender-specific consequences of climate change.

Finally, we will continue our efforts to help women in our sourcing communities transform the way they produce and sell raw materials, and improve their livelihoods. And we will continue to empower our consumers – both women and men – to make sustainable choices.

While meaningful change takes time, I am confident that it will happen. What's more, I believe that women will be at the forefront of accelerating humanity's epic sustainability journey.

7

LOLA YOUNG

House of Lords, London

How holistic thinking benefits people and the planet

Lola, Baroness Young of Hornsey, is a social justice campaigner, working mainly in the cultural and creative sectors, as well as through parliament. As chair of the Man Booker Prize 2016–17, her verdict on the panel's long list was that the thirteen books had 'a spirit in common: though their subject matter might be turbulent, their power and range were life-affirming – a tonic for our times'. You might call Lola, who is a cultural critic, Arsenal fan and fashion aficionado, a tonic for our times too, thanks to her work on transparency in supply chains (Section 54 in the Modern Slavery Act 2015). In this Q&A she discusses the ways in which social and environmental justice overlap.

What made you join up your thinking about climate change and social justice?

When I started to work with the Centre for Sustainable Fashion I began to realise more about what was going on in the fashion industry in terms of its role in environmental degradation and abusive labour conditions. I'd only read about these issues before or seen television programmes on the subject. When we set up the All-Party Parliamentary Group (APPG) on Ethics and Sustainability in Fashion, in 2011, I was educated in all kinds of ways about fashion's role – from the fact that 90 per cent of corporate uniforms have a short life and end in landfill to the meaning of the term 'transparency in the supply chain', which was then unfamiliar to me. I guess that was the moment when I really began to link social justice and environmental issues.

Can you provide an update on the Modern Slavery Act and supply chains?

Well, it's the law now. The part of the Modern Slavery Act of 2015 with which I am most concerned is Section 54, 'Transparency in Supply Chains'. The underlying premise is that companies with a turnover above a certain amount (£36 million) have to produce a statement to say what it is they're doing to try to root out coercive and abusive forms of labour from their supply chains. There's a lot more work to be done to make this piece of legislation more effective. A big weakness is that there's no official body to monitor the implementation of this part of the Act.

What motivates you?

In terms of the role of our craving for fashion in ruining people's lives, a key turning point for me and many others was the Rana Plaza disaster in 2013 in Bangladesh, where more than 1,100, mainly women, were killed as a direct result of very poor labour and health and safety practices. Everybody is complicit in this process in one way or another: we want cheap clothes; companies want to make a profit; the factories want to win contracts and have to try to keep up with the fast fashion production turnover, no matter what. So no matter that there are cracks in a building indicating that there's something seriously amiss; no matter that some people may be locked in so that there's no escape in the event of fire; no matter that there are children working under these conditions producing this stuff – as long as everybody gets what they think they want, it's OK. But it's not.

To me, it's perfectly legitimate – indeed necessary – to be able to point to a specific tragedy and say, 'OK, if we can introduce a piece of legislation that might curb some of those practices that led to that disaster, then that's what we should be doing.'

There was a cross-party desire to have the original Modern Slavery Bill, but for Section 54, 'Transparency in Supply Chains', there was a very strong lobby, including lots of businesses. For businesses that have a good reputation, it makes sense: your customers trust you and you want to maintain that trust. One of the ways of doing that is to say, 'Look, we're not perfect, but we're doing what we can to make sure these abusive practices aren't happening in our supply chain.'

There's a crossover here with the environment. People who are fleeing terrible impacts of climate change often become some of the most vulnerable refugees, who are then more likely – because they are vulnerable – to be trafficked and/or put into forced labour or bonded labour situations. Again, within that, women and girls are currently the most vulnerable – and children, boys and girls.

We don't have really robust data on how many climate refugees there are yet because it depends on who or what you're reading and how you define a refugee. But if you're in a rural situation where, because of drought year on year, your family says, 'OK, here's my teenage girl or boy and here's a man who says he can get them a job in Italy working in the fashion industry or as a Premier League footballer. And if I pay him what little money I've got, he'll see to it that they send money back' … And then off those teenagers go, and maybe that's the last you hear of them, is that a climate change refugee?

This displacement and exploitation of the poor is particularly common in the Indian sub-continent and also in parts of sub Saharan Africa, and there are variations of it within Europe as well. Hardly any of these practices are confined to any one continent, and some people are surprised about the extent to which these practices go on here in the UK.

The other link to the environment is that both fashion and major sporting events have a considerable impact. Huge amounts of textiles go into landfill, and plastics from clothing are washed into the sea – and then there are the dyes used and the toxic chemicals used in dry-cleaning. Additionally, and this returns us to forced and abusive labour practices, there's the impact of these cocktails of toxins and carcinogens on the people who work with these substances, without effective health and safety protection.

In Uganda recently I was at a workshop on modern slavery organised by the Commonwealth Parliamentary Association with the Africa Region. There were representatives from a number of the key sub-Saharan African members of the Commonwealth. Time and time again, we hear stories of desperately poor people. The reasons why they are poor are very complex. I tend to think people are discouraged from thinking holistically. We don't join the dots. We don't think, 'Oh, because that's happening over there, that might be a direct consequence of something we've done here', or vice versa. I think we need to know more about the number of people who leave their homes because they've been displaced by environmental factors and then who, or how many of those, actually end up in forced labour and bonded labour.

How does football fit into this?

There's a huge amount of potential in garnering some of the energy and enthusiasm that exists around football, particularly in the context of the Premier League. All the top-tier clubs have to make statements because their turnover is above the threshold for companies to report their anti-slavery strategies in Section 54, which I mentioned before. I know that there are also environmental organisations working with a number of teams to decrease their carbon footprints.

Potentially good models for engaging football clubs and their fans with modern slavery and environmental issues are Let's Kick Racism Out of Football (renamed Kick It Out), the Rainbow Laces to celebrate LGBTI, and a lot of community-based socially aware activities around, for example, people with disabilities, young people and so on.

I think there is a growing momentum around this now. Women leaders have been crucial to the development of my understanding of these issues and many are at the forefront of the debates and practical strategies for combatting these negative consequences of our scant regard for people and the planet.

Businesses are, I think, edging very much closer to this idea of human rights and business being not just 'something you shove under the heading of corporate social responsibility', but something that is integral to the way you do business. You respect people's human rights; indeed, you promote people's human rights and you don't adopt practices which undermine those. It's heartening that a lot of young women seem to be looking to work in this area: I think they're seeing the links between a more equal society locally and a more equal global community. The problems that emerge when you don't have that should be abundantly clear to everyone by now.

Do you have any tips for ways to make this happen faster?
It's really important to be confident when you speak. So how do you build your confidence up to enable you to speak in a way that gets you listened to? First of all, you must know what you're talking about, and have the facts and evidence on which you've based your case or argument to hand.

I've worked with some brilliant young women and sometimes they talk really quietly or they do that interrogative thing and say, 'Maybe we should do this?' or 'Should we do this?'. I'm not saying you've got to try to speak like a stereotype of a man, because one of the most effective people I ever watched on committee was actually a great listener. He didn't speak unless he had something new to add and did so with authority because it was clear that he had taken on board what had been said and written, then synthesised and analysed it. Watch people who you think are really effective in meetings and work in a style that would suit you. And don't be afraid simply to observe and to ask for opportunities to attend high-level meetings or events, again to see how these things work.

Also recognise who your real friends are – which isn't to say that you can't have critical friends, because if you've got an honest and open and trusting relationship with somebody, that's great. It's those people who always say, 'No, you can't do that', 'No, you're really big-headed', 'No, you can't go there', 'Why should you be doing that?', 'How come they've asked you to do that?' They're not the type of friends you need if you want to be in a leadership role.

Finally, the idea of leadership has become quite narrowly defined: 'as a leader' has come to mean somebody who leads an organisation, or who is at the front of a campaign. What I prefer to think about is how you can be a leader in any kind of role that you're in. As long as you recognise that there's something that needs to be done, you think you can make a contribution towards doing what's needed, and you do it and gather other people in support of that, that's leadership. It might be that you organise a group of people to volunteer to teach English conversation to refugees or it might be as simple as following up a thought like 'I'm fed up with seeing all this litter on our streets; I'll organise a monthly litter pick-up', or 'Let's all decide that instead of walking head down straight past people, we will smile'. Small things that can improve the quality of people's lives – and that can be achieved through encouraging a kind of distributed leadership.

8

NATHALIE HOLVOET and LIESBETH INBERG

University of Antwerp

How gender-sensitive are National Adaptation Programmes of Action? Selected findings from a desk review of thirty-one sub-Saharan African countries[1]

Introduction

There is nowadays a growing acknowledgement of the fact that policies to address climate change are influenced not only by technological development but also by the local institutional factors and norms which generally shape human behaviour.[2] The sociocultural construct 'gender' is such a set of norms which influences how men and women are affected by and respond to climate change. In addition to factors such as income, class and caste, gender relations determine the degree of access to and control that individuals have over different types of resources, their division of labour within productive, reproductive and community activities, as well as their level of involvement in decision-making at household, community and (inter)national levels. This differential positioning in society affects individuals' vulnerability to climate change, their capacities to adapt to climate change as well as their needs and potential contributions with regard to adaptation and mitigation. The growing realisation that ignoring the mediating influence of gender relations may put into perspective the effectiveness of adaptation and mitigation policies has gradually brought gender issues onto the agenda of national and international fora.

The 2010 Cancún agreements adopted during the 16th Conference of the United Nations Framework Convention on Climate Change (UNFCC), as well as the more recent 2012 Doha Conference, are a case in point. While the original 1992 UNFCC was totally gender blind and even disregarded one of the principles of the Rio Declaration on Environment and Development,[3] the 2010 Cancún Agreements refer for the first time to the importance of gender,[4] and recognise that 'gender equality and the effective participation of women and indigenous people are important for effective action on all aspects of climate change'.[5] In line with this, the Declaration of the recent Doha Conference explicitly highlights that women continue to be under-represented and recognises that a more balanced representation of women from developed and developing countries in the UNFCCC process is important in order to create climate policies that respond to the different needs of men and women in national and local contexts.[6]

Prior to the Cancún agreements, the importance of integrating a gender dimension in adaption programmes was already acknowledged in the 2002 list of principles that guides the preparation of National Adaptation Programmes of Action (NAPAs). NAPAs are country-owned policy documents in which countries that are most vulnerable to climate change diagnose the (likely) effects of climate change and identify priority adaptation projects to address their most urgent needs.[7] One of several stipulations of the NAPA guidelines,[8] developed by the Least Developed Countries Expert Group, states that NAPA teams should include gender expertise and that processes should be participatory and involve both men and women at grassroots level as they have knowledge of existing adaptation practices, while at the same time being among the most affected by climate changes.[9]

Confronting discourse with praxis, however, demonstrates that the locally grounded knowledge of rural women and men has thus far largely been disregarded when designing national adaption policies[10] while, in addition, gender issues have hardly been taken on board when elaborating NAPAs.[11] A 2009 internal review of thirty-nine NAPAs conducted by the Gender Advisory Team of the

United Nations Office for the Coordination of Humanitarian Affairs (OCHA) points out that several of the NAPAs mention gender equality and women's empowerment as principles, though very few demonstrate a clear commitment to these principles by mainstreaming gender throughout the document. About half of the NAPAs identify gender-differentiated impacts from climate change without, however, translating this observation into project selection and/or design.[12]

Our study connects with this research agenda and complements the internal reviews with a more comprehensive gender analysis of the thirty-one sub-Saharan African NAPAs[13] that have been elaborated between 2004 and 2011. First, it examines and compares the integration of a gender dimension into the different phases of the NAPA cycle. Next, it assesses whether the different sectors that are most directly related to climate change, such as agriculture, energy, forestry, water and sanitation and health, score differently on gender sensitivity. In addition to this more quantitative assessment we also analyse in more detail the way in which women and gender issues are conceptualised in the NAPAs as well as the gender sensitivity of the underlying processes.

Our mapping of the gender sensitivity of sub-Saharan African NAPAs' contents and processes aims to feed into the work of the Gender Office of the International Union for Conservation of Nature (IUCN)[14] to render future NAPAs and National Adaptation Plans (NAPs)[15] more gender sensitive. In doing this, we aim to avoid another case of 'gender retrofitting', which is particularly relevant against a background of mounting budgets that are nowadays channelled through climate funds.

Before presenting and discussing the findings of the gender analysis below, we briefly discuss different discourses and approaches towards gender and climate change.

Gender and climate change: different discourses and approaches

The rationale for the integration of a gender dimension into climate change adaptation (and mitigation) policies and activities is generally argued on the basis of welfare, equality, poverty and efficiency grounds. Browsing in more detail through the relatively recent but rapidly expanding literature on gender and climate change highlights that the different discourses resonate well with the different approaches to women/gender and development which have subsequently been designed and implemented from the 1950s onwards.

The two most frequently heard claims to promote the integration of a gender dimension in adaptation (and mitigation) policies[16] relate to women's 'vulnerability' and 'virtuousness' with respect to climate change. First, women, and particularly poor rural women in the South, are considered to be particularly vulnerable to climate change because they have less access to and control over land, money, credit and information while also having a lower personal mobility than men, which are all factors that affect the ability to adapt to climate change. They tend to be disproportionately affected by water and fuel scarcity and land degradation because they are predominantly engaged in household reproductive activities such as gathering water, fuel and other biomass resources, food preparation and caretaking.[17] Secondly, because of their higher dependency on natural resources, women are simultaneously considered to be more environmentally conscious and their contributions are considered vital for a more effective and efficient management of common property natural resources.[18]

This conceptualisation of women as 'vulnerable victims' on the one hand and 'responsible heroines' on the other hand neatly fits the pre-WID (Women in Development) welfare and WID anti-poverty and efficiency approaches. While there are important differences between the pre-WID welfare and the WID anti-poverty and efficiency approaches, at the same time they are highly similar in that they largely focus on women in isolation, while neglecting the importance of underlying gender relations to explain the observed inequalities between men and women. The importance of the sociocultural construct 'gender' has mainly been emphasised in the Gender and Development (GAD) approach, which starts from the idea that interventions in all thematic areas and at all levels (global, macro, meso and micro) are influenced by the existing structural features in societies, which differentiate among different individuals. Conversely, the assumption is that all interventions also potentially influence gender (and other) relations. Disregarding this mutually influencing relationship may lead to policy failures and a worsening of the already existing male bias in terms of allocation of resources and decision-making power.[19] This also holds for interventions in the agriculture, energy, forestry, health, water and sanitation sectors, which are those most closely associated with climate change and in which evidence exists demonstrating that the neglect of gender leads to further environmental degradation, something which in itself may intensify already existing gender-based inequalities.[20]

From the vantage point of this mutually influencing relationship between 'gender' and 'development', there is a need to integrate a gender dimension throughout the different stages (diagnosis, planning, implementation, budgeting, monitoring and evaluation) of all types of interventions at any level, i.e. gender mainstreaming. In addition to a top-down approach there is also a need for more bottom-up interventions that aim to modify the underlying gendered structures of constraint, this being particularly important in areas that are strongly regulated by gender norms. While institutional changes are never easy to achieve,[21] literature and history have shown that they are more likely to be possible when individuals act as a group through collective action. Such instances of collective action that lead to marginal institutional changes may also arise in the context of interventions in typical 'climate change sectors'. Well-known examples are cases of water and sanitation or forest conservation projects that initially started as welfare or efficiency initiatives aimed at satisfying practical gender needs, but which gradually evolve into instances of collective action where groups of women increasingly gain decision-making power with respect to water, land and forest management both inside and outside the household.[22] This also hints at the fact that interventions originally designed from a welfare or anti-poverty perspective can also gradually evolve into interventions that aim at tackling the more deep-rooted gender norms, or serve as entry points for this type of intervention.[23] However, when using instrumentalist framing to get gender issues onto the agenda, one should also be on the lookout for 'myth creation' and 'essentialism'.[24]

Discussion of findings and way forward

Despite an increasing acknowledgement of the importance of integrating a gender dimension into interventions related to climate change and reference to gender in the NAPA guidelines, the findings of our own stocktaking exercise of all 2004 to 2011 sub-Saharan African NAPAs lend credence to evidence from earlier research[25] and point at a low degree of gender sensitivity in NAPA's content with ten of the thirty-one NAPAs being entirely gender blind. When a gender dimension is included, it is mostly in sections dealing with the identification of projects and fails to be translated into budgets, indicators and targets. This dilution is indicative of the phenomenon of policy evaporation, which is particularly prevalent in the area of gender mainstreaming. When comparing gender sensitivity over different sectors, we do not come across substantial differences in gender sensitivy. While the agricultural sector outperforms the others when it comes to the selection of interventions, this pattern does not hold true for other phases.

The fact that none of the NAPAs include an in-depth analysis of gender issues in their diagnosis section already hints at the absence of a Gender and Development (GAD) approach in the NAPAs under study. As a GAD approach originates in the idea that there is a mutually influencing relationship between climate change and gender relations, some gender analysis would be expected at the outset of the NAPA which would then feed into the selection of interventions. The absence of a GAD approach does not entirely come as a surprise and is in line with Terry,[26] who highlighted that a GAD approach is not yet common in work and discussions on climate change. In the NAPAs under study, there is in particular a strong tendency to depict women as victims, a conclusion which was also arrived at by Rodenberg[27] in her review of climate change discussions and processes. Women are often lumped together with children and the elderly under a heading of 'vulnerable' and several NAPAs specifically refer to female-headed households in this respect. Interestingly, the other myth of women being 'virtuous' and more environmentally conscious is much less present in the NAPAs under study. The only prominent case is the NAPA of Mauritania, which explicitly highlights that 'women are often the chief guardians of vital local and traditional knowledge'.[28] Although at this relatively early stage of gender & climate change work, NAPAs are drawing particularly upon welfare arguments when including gender & women issues, it is highly likely that a WID efficiency approach which stresses more heavily women's virtuousness will become more prevalent in the future. What both these myths of 'vulnerability' and 'virtuousness' have in common is the fact that the importance of the underlying gendered structures which influence men's and women's constraints, opportunities and incentives with respect to adaptation remains out of the picture. This ignorance of the interplay between gender and adaptation influences the type of NAPA interventions designed, their effectiveness and their impact, both on adaptation as well as on gender equality outcomes.

Information with respect to diagnostic and decision-making processes was available only for a limited sub-sample of NAPAs, which might affect the external validity of these findings. For the specific sub-sample under study, the process was more gender sensitive than the content and no correlation was found between the gender sensitivity of the content and the process. This might partly be due to the relatively limited track record of combined gender and climate change expertise, which is also evident from the absence of operational gender mainstreaming tools and approaches that are framed in 'climate change' terminology. Such framing of gender issues alongside the 'frames' of the area or ministries has proved important in triggering the implementation of gender mainstreaming by non gender experts.[29] As Cornwall et al.[30] put it, 'when development actors seize upon feminist ideas they want them in a form that is useful for their own frameworks, analyses and overall policy objectives'.[31]

Brokering of relationships among local and central-level gender actors who have different comparative advantages when it comes to influencing climate change processes, as well as bridging gaps among gender and climate change experts, are areas in which climate change funds might invest part of their resources. It is, in particular, such exchanges and networking among actors with different knowledge and experience bases which might trigger more gender-sensitive processes with a long-term pay-off in terms of the content of future NAPAs and NAPs. Another area for further investment, research and experimentation is gender budgeting, which refers to the analysis of the differential impact of government budgets on women and men, as well as to the systematic integration of a gender perspective throughout the budget cycle. Gender budgeting is particularly relevant and timely when set against the background of the considerable amount of resources that are currently being channelled through climate change funds.

Finally, insights from the current desk study might obviously benefit from complementary field research focusing on a small number of well-selected cases, such as the relatively more gender-sensitive NAPAs of Burkina Faso and Malawi. Such in-depth field research would be interesting as a reality check for the findings of the desk study, but might also enable a better understanding of the underlying factors that have contributed towards the higher level of gender mainstreaming.

9

ATTI WORKU

Founder and CEO of Seeds of Africa, a non-profit changing the face of education in Adama, Ethiopia

Why educating girls is essential for a sustainable future

The idea is simple – gender equality is key to a sustainable future. And educating our girls is key to gender equality. So educating our girls is an investment in a sustainable future for all of us. The first step towards this future is investing in educating our girls. Here's why.

Picture a little girl growing up in a village with no running water or electricity, she did not have an opportunity to go to school and she was married off at the age of fifteen. Today, because of the lack of education, encouragement and access, she's a subsistence farmer in the Horn of Africa, a region suffering from one of the worst drought-fuelled famines in decades, exasperated by the impacts of climate change. Now picture that same girl, growing up with parents who invested in her education and made sure she went to school, did not marry her off at fifteen, and encouraged her to do anything she could dream of. This girl is me. My grandfather was a subsistence farmer; he lived in a small village outside my home town of Adama, Ethiopia. My mother and father were both the first generation in their families to go to school and attend college. I often think about how different my life would have been if my father had not left his village to go to school or if my mother had been illiterate.

I believe educating girls is essential for a sustainable future because I have seen first-hand how critical an education is. If I had not received an education, my reality would have been similar to the realities of millions of women around the world, especially those who live in poor and marginalised communities that are more vulnerable to the impacts of climate change. UNICEF is clear that girls' education is both an intrinsic right and a critical lever to reaching other development objectives.[1] Providing girls with an education helps break the chronic cycle of poverty. That's because educated women are less likely to marry early and against their will, less likely to die in childbirth, more likely to have healthy babies and more likely to send their children to school. When all children have access to a quality education rooted in human rights and gender equality, it creates a ripple effect of opportunity that influences generations to come, making it key to creating a sustainable future.

How does climate change impact women?

According to the Intergovernmental Panel on Climate Change (IPCC), an increase of greenhouse gases in the atmosphere will boost temperatures over most land surfaces. Some of the outcomes of an increase in global temperatures include an even greater risk of natural disasters such as droughts and intensified storms. Factors such as gender, socio-economic status and access to resources determine the degree to which people are impacted by climate change.

There are several areas that illustrate gender-based vulnerability to the adverse effects of climate change, especially in poor and marginalised communities. Women are hardest hit because they depend on climate-sensitive livelihoods such as agriculture, as they are often tasked with securing water, food and fuel for their families. These resources become scarcer during climate change-related natural disasters, and this scarcity places girls and women at increased risk. The lack of resources diminishes their ability to adapt, making them more vulnerable and forcing them to continue to depend on unsustainable practices to support their families. Research published by the United Nations Statistics Division suggests that two-thirds of the world's 781 million illiterate adults are women,[2] which significantly impacts their earning potential, economic independence, and access to information and resources, all of which are essential to escaping or avoiding climate change-related danger.

Why women?

The impact of these disasters is disproportionately worse for women than for men. The reasons are varied, but women often escape last, because they try to make sure everyone is safe and may stay behind to take care of the elderly and children, which makes their death toll higher. To make matters worse, women often do not receive life-saving information about natural disasters. And even if they survive, they may lose their wealth and livelihood as their community tries to recover from a disaster because women still have less political and economic power than men in these regions. In short, women are less able to cope with the adverse effects of climate change.

As if all these disadvantages were not bad enough, women are not well represented in leadership positions that would allow them to influence mitigation and adaptation strategies. According to McKinsey's 2016 report *Women Matter Africa*, only 5 per cent of CEOs and less than 30 per cent of cabinet members and parliamentarians in Africa are women.[3] These numbers are embarrassingly low, and prove only one fact: the higher you look up the leadership ladder, the fewer women we find. Women now have about 37 per cent of undergraduate STEM (science, technology, engineering and maths) degrees in the United States, but their representation varies widely across those fields. Women receive more than 40 per cent of undergraduate degrees in maths, for example, but just 18 per cent of computer science degrees. The researchers analysed more than 1,200 papers about women's under-representation in STEM, and from those identified ten factors that have an impact on gender differences in students' interest and participation in STEM. Then they winnowed the list down to the three factors most likely to explain gendered patterns in the six STEM fields: a lack of pre-college experience, gender gaps in belief about one's abilities, and a masculine culture that discourages women from participating.

Fighting climate change through mitigation and adaptation strategies requires significant economic and political investment. Since women are hardest hit by the impacts of climate change, we need more women in leadership positions so they can participate in strategies and implementation that impacts their very survival. So how do we get more women into leadership roles? We have to start by educating our girls.

What do we need to build a sustainable future?

A sustainable future is one where we understand the interconnectedness of economic, social and environmental issues; where we acknowledge that rural areas, cities, countries and continents need to find a way to develop without depleting natural resources such as the land we farm, the water we drink and the air we breathe; where we are producing our food – whether farming, meat production or fish production – in a way that does not deplete our resources; where we continue to build communities that are resilient and less dependent on fossil fuels; where we significantly decrease our emissions of greenhouse gases and our carbon footprint.

The creation of a sustainable future requires significant technological advances for both mitigation and adaptation strategies and a change in how we live our lives. Since women influence more than 80 per cent of global consumption decisions, the more educated they are, the better consumption choices they will make, choices that are more friendly to our environment. Investing in a girl's education, therefore, is essential to influence environmentally sustainable livelihoods and future consumption choices such as food, water and energy sources. This makes women powerful agents in the transition towards a more sustainable future and in building more resilient communities.

An investment in girls' education requires a significant commitment from a variety of actors, such as individuals, businesses, governments and civil society.

Women's positive impact on sustainable development

In order to build a sustainable future we need women scientists, business leaders, women in government, women in leadership and women in financial decision-making. The advantages of having more women in leadership are clear. In business, companies with a gender diverse leadership perform much better than companies that do not have the same leadership diversity. As women influence more than 80 per cent of global consumption, having more women involved in decision-making helps companies relate to consumers better, leading to financial success.

In politics, there is growing evidence that when more women are involved, they improve the political process. This is because women:

» are more interested in working across party lines;
» champion issues of gender equality, from working to eliminate gender-based violence to fighting for equal pay;
» design policies that have an impact on their communities for generations, such as making school and the workplace more compatible for girls and women.

Those women then become mentors and role models for young women who are starting out their careers, or for girls who are in school. And if girls get educated, they grow up with the tools and resources needed to adapt their livelihoods to the changing realities of climate change. Their knowledge can be utilised in mitigation and adaptation strategies and can make them essential agents of change.

When women hold leadership positions, communities do better during natural disasters, from preparation for a disaster to reconstruction afterwards. They do this already with limited resources in making sure that they are prepared for hazards, making sure that their families and communities have enough food and water to survive during a natural disaster, and taking care of children and the elderly.

Women's greater participation often enhances the effectiveness of policies and the sustainability of solutions, as women care more about the long term and about families and communities. They do a much better job when it comes to risk management and reduction in preparing for natural disasters. Most importantly, women in leadership often focus on building resilient communities that move away from climate-sensitive livelihoods and invest in mitigation and adaptation strategies.

When girls are educated, they grow up to be women with better income, better access, and so on, and therefore they improve the quality of their family's life: for example, stopping using toxic energy sources in favour of clean energy, which both saves their family from carbon monoxide pollution and decreases their family's carbon footprint in the world. As decision-makers, they vote for clean energy initiatives that are important to them – and the world –from both an environmental and an economic angle.

What is the status of girls' education today?

We have not done enough to educate our girls, especially those girls living in marginalised communities who are not getting equal access to quality education.

According to a report by the United Nations Statistics Division, nearly two-thirds of the world's 781 million illiterate adults are women.[4] Girls make up more than half of the out-of-school children population in the world. Additionally, girls continue to be at a significant disadvantage globally. In sub-Saharan Africa, school enrolment rates drop off considerably as girls move up from primary education (75 per cent of girls[5]) to secondary (38 per cent of girls[6]) and tertiary (6 per cent of women[7]).

Poverty, social exclusion, distance from school facilities and poor-quality education create even greater disadvantages when coupled with gender disparities.

Conclusion

If we want to save our planet, we need to invest in early childhood education and make quality education available and accessible to girls at all levels, especially those who are marginalised and disadvantaged. We need to invest in girls' achievement and look into the quality of education, not just access. We need to encourage girls to get into the fields of STEM, finance and politics, which are traditionally dominated by men, because when women get involved in those fields they bring diversity in leadership, which is important in making better decisions for society. If we adopt these approaches, our women and girls will be the scientists who will continue to inform us about what we can do to mitigate (or exacerbate) climate change, the political leadership that will make decisions on energy policy and general policy that protects the environment, and the people who will run businesses that are energy efficient and leave a very small carbon footprint. They will create jobs from sustainable businesses.

But in order to achieve this vision, we need to provide adequate legal protection for girls from harmful cultural practices that become barriers to going to school or to having a career, such as early marriage.

Finally, our investment in education needs to be matched with progress in the employment market that makes jobs and economic opportunities available for women.

Recommendations for action

1. Integrate gender perspectives throughout climate change programming in order to effectively address both women's and men's needs and priorities.
2. Ensure the full and meaningful participation of women and achieve gender-equitable outcomes.
3. Integrate gender considerations and women's issues into the planning and implementation cycle of climate change policies and projects.

4. Ensure that mitigation and adaptation efforts also address sources of gender-based vulnerability, gender inequality and poverty.

5. Ensure that policy and programming recognise that, because of their central role in environmental, social and economic development, women's empowerment and gender equality are beneficial for family and community well-being and livelihoods and are key factors in promoting the resilience of economies and communities.

6. For efficient, effective and inclusive financing, gender must play an essential role, informing all policies and programming. Gender-sensitive structures, guidelines, projects and tools need to be developed for all climate change financing mechanisms supporting adaptation and mitigation actions, at all levels.

7. Finally, to help address the historical, political and socioeconomic constraints faced by many women, as well as larger sustainable development objectives, gender-based criteria should be developed for fund allocation, including project identification, design and performance objectives.

10

SHUKRI HAJI ISMAIL BANDARE and FATIMA JIBRELL

NGO leaders

Women, conflict and the environment in Somali society

Somali women have been at the forefront of environmental activism since the early 1990s. Two of these inspirational leaders are Shukri Ismail Bandare and Fatima Jibrell. They have both founded non-governmental organisations (NGOs) to help local communities protect their environment and use natural resources more sustainably. The vital role of women and gender equality in environmental protection has been at the core of their work. In the face of civil war, a fragile arid/semi-arid environment, poverty and a traditional patriarchal society, the achievements of these women and their colleagues are immense. In interviews in late 2014 and early 2015 for Friends of the Earth, they contributed their experiences and ideas on gender equality and environmental sustainability.

Shukri Haji Ismail Bandare has served as the minister for environment of Somaliland[1] since 2013. Previous to her political appointment, she was an active campaigner on environmental issues and founded a local NGO, Candlelight for Health, Education and Environment. The charity continues to deliver training, education and healthcare programmes with communities across Somaliland. Shukri served six years on the first Election Commission in Somaliland as the only woman and participated in three successful elections when Somaliland was moving from a clan-based system to a multiparty system. She explains her motivations for her work:

'The charity was born in 1995; we saw there was a real need. The Somaliland people were in the midst of war – having suffered the onslaught of the [Siad] Barre forces they were now experiencing a period of great instability involving inter-clan wars. There were no schools for children of internally displaced people (IDPs) and they were growing up with so much fear and hostilities, we didn't want another generation lost to the war.

'We set up a school. With education, we soon realised there was a dire need for a health awareness campaign and so we decided to run campaigns including the dangers involved with FGM [female genital mutilation]. The conditions of the camp made us see how important sanitation was – and the environment as a whole – and so began our work on environmental hazards. I had a lot of help from people and the charity was by no means a one-woman show. The charity is one the biggest NGOs in Somaliland and its focus continues to be on the environment.'

Fatima Jibrell is the founder of the international NGO Adeso: African Development Solutions (previously known as Horn Relief), whose mission is to work with communities to create environments in which Africans can thrive. In 2014 Fatima received the Champions of Earth award from the UN Environment Programme for her outstanding contribution to conservation. She talks about her experiences as a child in Somalia and returning as an adult:

'I was born to a pastoral nomadic family in Somalia in 1947 and until I was seven years old I lived in an area that was savannah-like, with lions, leopards, all kinds of wildlife. I first visited Somalia again about thirty years ago – the land that I had remembered as a lush green savannah was total desert, with only huge sandstorms blowing. So I became interested in seeing if it could be brought back to life. After the civil war it seemed the best time to help people. There was an influx of people from big cities like Mogadishu coming to my area. I wanted to see if I could support them in any way to understand the environment, so they don't trash it further – that was my main reason to come back.'

Trees for people and the environment

One of the main causes of Somali environmental degradation has been deforestation and desertification – in particular from people cutting down trees to make charcoal for cooking fuel.

Shukri Haji Ismail Bandare explains: 'The environment is the most essential necessity in our lives as we depend one hundred per cent on it. Without a good, healthy environment it is impossible to exist as a people. The effects of [deforestation] on a land such as ours, which can be described as arid or semi-arid land, are acute. The scarcity of forests and woodlands means any loss of trees has significant environmental deficits.

'The trees we have in mountainous areas are our equivalent of forests and they are fast being eroded. In a large part this is due to the lack of education and awareness people have about the effects of cutting trees; also some people do not have alternative livelihoods other than cutting trees to make charcoal. The people remain reluctant to use alternative means of energy due to many factors and this continues to fuel the use of coal.'

'We are content to cut down a tree but not plant one in its place. The need for trees remains the same yet that need is being unmet with our current attitudes.'

The Somali rural population is traditionally pastoral and nomadic, moving with their livestock to find grazing pastures. These communities depend upon a healthy natural environment for their survival in the hot, dry climate with irregular rainfall.

Fatima Jibrell recalls the traditional respect for trees: 'There were all kinds of laws that almost all Somalis, even those who have not been pastoralists, know about. At that time nobody dared to cut a tree more than one or two branches – they will trim and take one branch and go to another tree and take one branch, and so on, to make a fence for their temporary homestead to protect their live-stock for the night from lions and hyenas that could easily prey on their livestock. People, usually women, made ropes and other mate-rials to construct their house and this was mounted upon camels when they moved. That house was all made of trees, but they would take part of the tree bark and not actually skin the whole tree – which they do now because they don't care about the tree.

'I remember the training that my mother was given as a child, I remember her telling me: *if you want to take off the skin of the tree to make a rope, you take just a little bit off so that you can make what you want without killing the tree.* I knew from that time that we needed the trees because I was eating fruit from them, we were using them to lie down [in the shade] when the sun was out, so it was well understood! My mother expected me to be a pastoralist like her and taught me to use the environment.'

Conflict and the environment

One of Fatima's most notable accomplishments is securing a prohibition on the export of charcoal from north-east Somalia (since 1998 an autonomous region of Somalia known as Puntland), which was driving deforestation. She united people and groups, and tirelessly advocated for an end to the charcoal trade that used the region's acacia trees to make charcoal destined for the Middle East. Through her advocacy and coordination, the Puntland government prohibited the export of charcoal through Bosaso port in 2002. Fatima also recognised the need to find an alternative fuel for household cooking; so she co-founded Sun Fire Cooking to promote the use of the butterfly-design parabolic solar cooker.

Illegal charcoal exports from Somalia continue today and have been recognised by the UN Security Council as a significant source of revenue for the terrorist group Al-Shabaab. The work of Fatima and others has put this issue on the international agenda and highlighted its humanitarian, security, environmental and economic consequences.

'For example,' says Fatima, 'the urban youth are being lured into the rural areas through payments to make charcoal, yet the international community are not prioritising the environment or youth rehabilitation in their efforts.'

There are deep-rooted links between the environment and conflict in Somalia and Somaliland, as people are so reliant on their environment for their livelihoods, cultural identity and security. Shukri Haji Ismail Bandare stresses this point: 'Environmental issues play a key role in conflict in Somaliland, I would go as far as to say such issues play a daily role in conflict situations across Somaliland. Confrontations frequently occur over disputes over grazing lands, watering holes and land that has been sealed off by individuals for private use. All these problems demonstrate the key role land features in the lives of Somalis, their existence remains tied to the land as with their nomadic forefathers.'

Challenges of environmental governance

Shukri Haji Ismail Bandare reflects on her experience as a minister: 'Our Ministry of the Environment is an emerging ministry; a lot of our efforts have been on training and building our staff capacity to facilitate an adequate working environment. Though the ministry was first created in 1997, it has not received the same level of attention or focus as the ministries for education or health, and so it has been somewhat neglected. The challenges we face within our ministry are overwhelming; we are constantly under pressure due to budgets and because we know that time is of the essence where environmental emergencies are concerned. We are facing too many environmental emergencies including prolonged droughts, flash floods across dry river beds and the increasing number of industrial factories, which require preventative measures to ensure industrial waste is properly disposed of. We face all the challenges associated with a post-conflict society but I keep telling myself: "Rome was not built in a day". Since we are all trying.'

Fatima Jibrell points out the challenges and opportunities for better environmental governance: 'Before the war and the collapse of the Somali state, there was a whole department of environment that would protect the trees. Tourists were not allowed to park everywhere. We were not allowed to consume as much as we wanted. Today it is still a challenge! Sixty per cent of jobs in Somalia come from a pastoral environment. There is no opportunity to help Somalis, particularly young people from pastoral families, to get involved in environmental or marine conservation. We have the longest coastline in Africa – that could provide a job for everyone.'

Women and the environment

'Women's livelihoods are entwined with the environment,' explains Shukri Haji Ismail Bandare. 'As a traditionally pastoral-nomadic society, it is the women who herd the livestock, they are the first to witness changes in our environment. Even in the urban setting of Hargeisa there are women (many of whom are the family's breadwinners) selling goat's milk and camel's milk from their live-stock. We are a people dependent on the environment, especially water as there is no life without water. If we do not act against environmental degradation, women will be the first casualties of any environmental disasters that result from limited actions from ourselves and the international community at large.

'Women are intimately concerned with the changes in weather pattern and rainfall, they have to personally calculate how long to walk to get water, how far to take their herd for watering and pasture. Those of us in government are also aware of the challenges facing such women. We constantly keep ourselves updated on the areas where drought is present in order to send whatever reinforce-ments we can.

'I think equality is not necessarily the same in everyone's eyes. As a woman I am aware of my physical limitations to that of a man and similarly I am sure a man could not match my resilience as a woman. Equality has taken on this forceful, confrontational connotation and I would like to move away from that and instead promote a complementarity between the sexes. As for the planet I don't believe we can save the planet without first creating a fair and harmonious society for humanity.'

Fatima Jibrell sees the struggle for gender equality as central to environmental protection: 'There's a very strong connection between the marginalisation of women and youth and the environ-mental degradation in Somalia. The degradation is making poverty even worse for so many people; politics and gender inequalities are at the heart of it.

'It's not possible to achieve environmental sustainability without gender equality, because women work in the environment, they put food on the table, bring water. Women who are doing all this and looking after children have no chance to do anything else, to get involved in politics. They are carrying the whole society on their back.'

Gender in society and politics

Women in Somali society are traditionally seen as potential peace-builders and peace emissaries, able to facilitate communication between warring groups. Women have been at the forefront of local and national peace-building across the Somali regions since the civil war. However, time and again women have been excluded from peace talks, or permitted only as observers on the sidelines rather than as equal participants with men. Unlike women, young men have no traditional role to play in conflict resolution, but like women, young men are marginalised and kept on the sidelines during peace talks.

In principle, the constitutions of the Somaliland and Puntland governments and the Federal Government of Somalia all provide for equality between men and women in relation to political participation. But in fact, all three governments are almost exclusively male forums and promises of quotas for women are variously rejected and flouted.[2] This is despite international conventions, such as the United Nations Security Council Resolution 1325 (UNSCR 1325), which calls for women's participation in peace negotiations and in post-conflict reconstruction.

From 2012 to 2014, Adeso ran a project to promote gender equality, women's empowerment and political participation in Somalia to foster the development of an inclusive, transparent and accountable society. This project, Promoting Women's Political Participation in Somalia, provided training to more than three hundred female civil society representatives and councillors in political representation, advocacy, understanding of gender equality, and the role of women in peace-building. It also offered both technical support and capacity-building to the Ministry of Women Development and Family Affairs (MOWDAFA).

The project also facilitated the construction of Community Women Centres in the four target districts of Badhan, Bocame, Carmo and Xarfo. These centres continue to be a resource for local women in Puntland, giving them a place to consult, report and share their views and experiences. The targeted women in civil society, local councillors, teachers and community leaders in the four districts learned skills to challenge and change social attitudes and cultural factors that constrain their lives, and advocate on behalf of their communities.

Fatima believes that this is the future: 'Unless men talk to women and youth, government will not improve and women will not move forward. I hope the United States and other countries that are supporting the [Federal] Government of Somalia will talk to women because each nation comes and talks to male politicians. We need every nation that comes to Somalia to talk to women separately and equally – that's how you start equality.'

Shukri Bandare shows how political and social empowerment are intricately linked: 'There was a time fifteen to sixteen years ago when the question of gender was not on the agenda; many in our society were looking at us [women in politics] as though we had committed an unspeakable taboo. But I believe we have come a long way since then. We live in a rigidly patriarchal society riddled with contradictions. On the one hand we are witnessing more girls in schools, all the way to universities, but in the end that girl is still supposed to conform to the role of stay-at-home mum. Many parents will entertain the idea of their daughters having an office job but entering politics, especially at an official decision-making level, you can be sure to face every hurdle they can throw your way.

'There have been attempts to set up a female quota in the House of Representatives but unfortunately that bill did not pass. Nonetheless, there are prominent women's associations including Nagaad Network, which is an umbrella group of many grassroots women's organisations in Somaliland. As a founding member of this network, my ministry continues to foster a close relationship with the network in the promotion of greater women's empowerment in society and politics.

'We must find a platform that encourages discussion and an open dialogue on the environmental issues we face and that is what I want to be part of, the start of that conversation.'

11

KARIN NANSEN

**Chair of Friends of the Earth International,
Uruguay**

The close ties between social and environmental justice

Karin Nansen is an environmental justice campaigner and co-founder of REDES, based in Uruguay. As Friends of the Earth International chair she is constantly on the move at policy meetings. This Q&A took place on the London tube – Karin had been in meetings in Togo, then Amsterdam. She was on her way to Derbyshire for a Friends of the Earth England, Wales and Northern Ireland AGM, and then was going to a UN meeting in Europe.

What's your city like?
I live in Montevideo in Uruguay, South America. Montevideo is a nice city, but as in other parts of the world, the capital city of the country is an expression of the socio-economic inequalities that characterise society nowadays. Increasing territorial fragmentation, associated with wealth concentration, class divisions and market dynamics threaten to dominate by reorganising the city – not according to sustainability principles, people's needs and to nurture the social fabric, but via the decisions of the private sector's profit priorities.

The positive side is that for more than twenty years there have been progressive governments in Montevideo. They have been trying to introduce some limitations to the market forces and the logic of capital accumulation, with public policies aiming to reclaim public spaces for the people, foster collective and cultural activities and guarantee fundamental rights. But we are in need of a good public transport system, and cycle tracks, to offer a real alternative to the increasing numbers of cars on the roads.

What is women's role in saving the planet?
At Friends of the Earth International and in our regional structures and national member organisations, we want a systemic change that focuses on analysing and challenging the power and privilege that are an inherent part of a capitalist system that is also patriarchal, classist and racist. This system, run by global elites, endangers life on the planet as we know it, through the exploitation of the environment and our labour force.

At Friends of the Earth International we want women to be recognised as political agents for change, and not because women are 'closer to Mother Earth' or because we are naturally caring or environmentally conscious.

Historically, and as a result of the socially constructed sexual division of labour between men and women, women are responsible for so much care work. That's not to deny the importance of care work, but responsibility should be shared between men, women and the state. I really believe in the need to transform this sexual division of labour, which leaves women with all the weight of care work but does not recognise care work as important for the economy.

This sexual division of labour also cuts across class. Women with more money are often able to hire other, poor, women to do the care work for them: cooking, cleaning, childcare, and nursing the sick, vulnerable and elders. This is not the society we are working towards. We want more equity and for the responsibility of care work to be shared between men, women and the state.

You've been involved for years with rural women's struggles. Can you explain the thinking behind Via Campesina?
The Via Campesina struggle is for the right of peasants to produce healthy food, a struggle for the right to land, seeds and water, with women playing a central role. The historical struggles of Via

Campesina led to the principle of food sovereignty – the right to food, the right to produce food in culturally appropriate ways in the countryside and the city, and the right to have enough healthy and diverse food to eat.

This is a different concept to that of food security. Friends of the Earth International has joined Via Campesina in promoting and incorporating the food sovereignty principle into our campaigning and policy work with local communities, at the national level and internationally. Food must not be treated as a commodity and the food system must be under people's control, not the control of transnational corporations. The fundamental questions of what we produce, how we produce it, who we produce it for and how we distribute it must be answered through democratic and ecological food systems based on justice in all its dimensions. And it must recognise the vital role of women in production and decision-making.

How can the successes of Via Campesina be replicated in cities?
Via Campesina enables women to be key actors. In agriculture they are cultivating food in family gardens, producing food for local markets, saving seeds and preserving the knowledge. In the same way, women are important at the city level, trying hard to make neighbourhoods sustainable and to protect livelihoods.

There's a need to build closer links between the countryside, farmers, peasants and people in the cities. These can be developed through a different relationship between consumers and producers, based principally on reciprocity, fairness and justice. For example, consumers can get a fair and just price for the food they buy. But it's also important for farmers to get a fair and just price for the food they produce, and that means reducing the distance between producers and consumers. That's vital in the city.

The experience of Via Campesina can be replicated in the cities and towns. At Friends of the Earth International we believe in the need to build a new food system to guarantee people's rights – such as the right to land, water and seeds – and to address the multiple crises we face, including the food crisis, the climate crisis and biodiversity erosion. So this radical change of the food system involves both the rural areas and the cities.

Via Campesina has accomplished a lot in terms of defending peasants' agroecological production, building new relationships with consumers in the cities, and trying to make sure that healthy production is not only for the elite, but has the objective that poorer groups have the right to eat healthily too. This needs public policies that ensure farmers get a fair price, and all types of people in the cities have access to this healthy, fresh food.

We have many examples of success – new types of markets in which consumers buy food baskets or boxes, pick food from the farm or organise communal kitchens. We want to see states favour, and buy, food produced on smallholdings, and/or ecologically, for schools and hospitals. Buying directly from farmers has worked in Brazil. Now in Uruguay it's starting to work too, thanks to a new policy of public procurement from farmers using ecological methods. This solves two problems by ensuring that schoolchildren no longer eat poor-quality food (instead, students receive a healthy meal made from local and seasonal food bought directly from the farmers), and it guarantees a market for peasants and small-scale farmers.

The changes we propose to rebuild the food system will also reduce emissions. They will also enable local areas to become more resilient if farmers gain more autonomy and diversify more in ways that are appropriate to the ecology and culture of each territory and city.

Building alliances between rural and urban women has a transformative power. It can strengthen political agendas in both spheres.

As Friends of the Earth International's chair, what have you seen in cities around the world that has inspired you?
In the city, we are seeing the reduction of public spaces. We see the privatisation and corporate control of our public services, with rising prices for health, education, transport and other services that should be a human right. But there are good things and inspiring alternatives being developed in cities too. Recently in Togo I saw

women tending many different crops, including cassava and maize, on the side of the road. It's so inspiring to see women – and also men – who don't have a plot of land to grow food on figure out ways to produce food in urban areas.

I've also been inspired by seeing women defending their community's right to water; or cooking together in community kitchens, perhaps started up in times of crisis or when neighbourhoods are very poor, so that their children have food to eat. It's impressive seeing how often women constantly try to breach the separation between the domestic and the public that is imposed within society.

Throughout Amsterdam I've seen many community gardens, looked after by people of all ages, and I've heard that the city council offers spaces where the neighbourhood can produce its own food. In a big city you're more or less anonymous, and through this kind of collective experience and type of work, your well-being is improved and you really get to be involved in the social fabric of the communities. That is also so important for the environment. There are so many examples of social justice and environmental justice going together.

What can women and environment justice activists learn from each other?

We cannot achieve the system change we want – for a socially and ecologically just society –without radical changes in society based on our fight against patriarchy and oppressions and injustices based on race/ethnicity, sexuality, age, disability, etc. Women are most impacted by environmental problems, but women often also have the knowledge about how to change things and women are already building their alternatives. So we are not only victims – we are also the agents of change, and we need support for this role of ours.

Women have so much to contribute, so we're exchanging ideas with each other and learning what are the main structural issues of each struggle. We then join these struggles together with movements such as Via Campesina and the World March of Women, because you cannot win your struggle without winning the other struggles. That's why Friends of the Earth International is part of the same movements and networks, in terms of climate justice and food sovereignty: together we are strengthening our work and our organisations.

One of the things that brings this relationship closer is the fight against the 'commodification of everything' in our lives. Women and the feminist movement have been fighting against the commodification of our bodies, against the commodification of public services, etc., and at Friends of the Earth International we are fighting against commodification and the privatisation of nature. It's a common fight that brings us together.

How could cities be improved?
One of the problems in many countries is that the public transport system is not good, with many people spending long hours getting to and from work. Those who have money are encouraged to buy cars, but so often traffic jams bring cities to a standstill.

Environmental injustice is very clear in cities. Poor people often live in neighbourhoods that are more polluted, while the richer people live in the areas that are much more environmentally healthy, and with more green space.

That's why Friends of the Earth Brazil is working with people without housing, campaigning for public policies that allow people to have the right to a house and also to fight against this trend for the privatisation of land and streets in cities.

Cities should be organised in a way that allows for sustainable livelihoods and for the meeting of people's rights. That implies people self-organising, but also the right to develop collectively public policies, to change our transport systems and the way the land is used and to secure the right to land within the city, the right to a house within the city, the right to water, the right to free time and culture. It's really about how we reorganise cities to secure people's rights and sustainable livelihoods.

With so much accumulated experience of care work, and concern and care for the lives of other people, women have extensive knowledge and understanding about the domestic sphere. And we have also always worked – especially working-class women and Afro-descendent women – for the survival of our families and communities, and so we have extensive knowledge of the public sphere too. It's not only important to take care of your house; it's important to take care of your neighbourhoods and your city – there is so much to learn from women's experience and our way of looking at things. We need to value this knowledge. Which is why we should not develop any public policy without women's active participation.

City planning must take into account women's perspectives and needs, especially our use of public transport, the education system, etc. With democratic and participative spaces and processes, we can learn together and build together. We can make mistakes together and learn by doing.

12

GOTELIND ALBER

GenderCC: Women for Climate Justice, Berlin

Engendering urban climate policy

What is gender-responsive climate policy? In the United Nations Framework Convention on Climate Change (UNFCCC) process, this question has remained unanswered. Despite a growing number of provisions calling for gender-responsive adaptation and mitigation, there is a broad variety of interpretations, rather than an official definition of the term 'gender-responsive'. Some think of gender balance, others of capacity-building for women, or even clean cook stoves.

GenderCC believes that cities are an ideal place to learn what gender-responsive climate policy is, and to put it into practice. GenderCC, a global network of women's organisations, gender experts and activists based in Berlin, Germany, has been set up in the context of the UNFCCC negotiations with the aim of integrating gender into climate policy. GenderCC has been the first organisation to examine the gender and urban climate policy nexus[1] and to seek feasible approaches and solutions. Cities are under pressure to effectively respond to climate change in order to reduce greenhouse gas emissions and enhance resilience. At the same time, inequalities and injustices are particularly apparent in urban areas; these tend to be aggravated by climate change impacts, and sometimes even by the effects of climate policy. Cities can, and should, therefore play a pioneering role in developing gender-responsive climate change responses, applying experimental approaches and interventions and building on available urban experience, such as gender-sensitive urban development or gender-responsive budgeting.

During GenderCC's work with partners around the world – for example, with women's groups in Mumbai, India, Makassar, Indonesia, and Johannesburg, South Africa[2] – an approach was developed for a gender and climate assessment of urban institutions and procedures, as well as of mitigation and adaptation policies. Gender impact assessments have been developed and applied in various contexts to examine the design and implementation of policy interventions in detail. Yet, it is also essential to look at the city's entire climate action programme.

To analyse a portfolio of policies and measures from a gender perspective is a novel approach. To date, portfolio analysis in climate policy has been applied mainly to the cost–benefit considerations of technology options: namely for greenhouse gas abatement cost curves. In contrast to this, we looked at policies and their benefits beyond climate change responses.[3] We drew up a comprehensive catalogue of adaptation and mitigation policies and measures in the various sectors – housing, settlements and urban planning; transport supply and demand; energy supply and demand; water supply and demand; waste management; disaster risk reduction and so forth. For each policy, we identified environmental and socio-economic benefits, such as cleaner air, cost savings, job creation, and the potential benefits for gender equality – such as facilitating care work, the just distribution of newly created jobs, and alleviating energy poverty, all of which affect women the most. The assessment, which drew from research findings, our own experience and plausibility considerations, was based on gender criteria derived from the underlying reasons for gender inequality:

1. **Representation and participation in decision-making.** In policy areas relevant to climate change such as energy and transport, the share of women is still small, resulting in a bias in planning and implementation. Moreover, there are questions about what extent women have an equal say in decision-making at household and community levels.
2. **The need for and access to resources, such as food, housing, time, space, education and training, services,**

infrastructure and technologies. Policy should contribute to better access for all to these services, and should take gender-specific needs, consumption patterns and possibilities for action into account.

3. **The care economy plays a crucial role.** Even in countries with a high degree of gender equality, women still spend considerably more time on housework and family care. Urban policies should acknowledge care work, and provide infrastructures and services that both facilitate these everyday activities and contribute to a fairer distribution of care work.

4. **The conventional 'productive' economy and the gender bias in income.** Questions need to be asked to see if policies put an additional financial burden on people with lower income, with more women among them, and to find out who public investments and subsidies will benefit.

5. **Body, health and safety**, including sex-specific vulnerabilities, safety issues in public spaces, and access to health services.

6. **Rights and access to justice.** For example, in some countries, women are denied land rights, and the question is whether policies can remedy this problem and assist people to be aware of and exercise their rights.

7. **Structural gender issues.** These must be considered when tackling prevailing male norms. In most societies, women, and what they do, are considered inferior to men and what men usually do. In order to contribute to gender equality, policies should challenge these norms and privileges.

Applying this approach, we have identified priority strategic approaches and policies and are now using the prioritised portfolio as a benchmark in the appraisal of real-world adaptation and mitigation action programmes, in order to identify gaps and weaknesses from a gender perspective. In the following, we briefly explain the priority fields of action we have identified, which are valid for both industrialised and developing countries.

Urban planning and urban design

This creates layouts and structures that may last for many years, thereby massively influencing carbon footprints and the resilience of present and future populations. The layout and structures of many urban areas are heavily biased towards a masculine-connoted model of 'productive' work, accessible by motorised private transport, while activities attributed to women such as family care and securing livelihoods, including climate-friendly transport modes, are neglected and marginalised. Therefore, avoiding urban sprawl and working towards dense cities and mixed-use development, which reduces transport distances and emissions, can also have positive effects on gender relations, as it facilitates everyday activities, access to services and jobs, and care work and its combination with paid work. Creating such urban layouts and structures is an extremely important, though longer-term, strategy. In practice, it means exploring new ways to develop cities, abandoning the zoning approach and redistributing existing space in favour of non-motorised transport and purposes that benefit everyday life for all, such as markets and public services, playgrounds and parks. Vienna is a good example of how gender considerations can be included in urban planning, and the city has published a guidebook on gender mainstreaming.[4]

In middle- and low-income countries, upgrading informal settlements in collaboration with the people who live there has a very high priority, as slum dwellers are the most vulnerable to climate change impacts, and women make up the majority of slum dwellers in many cities. Activities need to include climate-proofing of settlements and the provision of basic infrastructure for water and sanitation. UN-Habitat has published a guide on gender in housing and slum upgrading.[5]

Resilience, health and livelihoods

Building resilience is particularly important to address the proven higher vulnerability of women to climate hazards. It includes reliable livelihoods for citizens, food security, housing, access to basic infrastructure for energy, water and sanitation, unconstrained mobility, information and skills, and cohesion in the community. Yet, it is often difficult to make a clear distinction between actions to build resilience and development in general, thus impeding access to climate finance for these efforts.

Kampala, for example, has developed a gender-sensitive approach to addressing vulnerability, using neighbourhood exploratory walks and gender-inclusive focus groups.

Mobility and transport

The gender dimensions of mobility are particularly striking. Gender differentials include trip purpose and distance, and transport modes. Women tend to work closer to home, or at home, and make more frequent trips for family care, such as shopping and escorting children and the elderly, resulting in more complex trip patterns. Women have less access to motorised means of transport, and consequently they walk more, and over longer distances, and are more dependent on public transportation services than men, who often choose private motorised transport and may also prefer larger, more fuel-consuming vehicles. Moreover, a lack of safety in public areas and in transportation massively constrains women's mobility and contributes to social exclusion. These observations are valid for most low-, middle- and high-income countries. Access to clean, affordable, accessible and safe transport services for all is therefore paramount.

The city of Bogotá, Colombia, is famous for its innovative transport policy. To a certain degree, it also took gender issues into account, with actions and campaigns to improve the safety of women, and efforts to achieve an equal distribution of newly created jobs.

Disasters and emergencies

Women who are in charge of family care and often lacking formal employment are among the worst affected by disasters. Moreover, sexual harassment and gender-based violence are often more severe during and after disasters. Therefore, disaster risk reduction and emergency provisions must meet women's needs, including gender-sensitive communication and training on disaster risk reduction. For example, early warning systems must ensure that women are reached, and emergency shelters must accommodate women and children.

Energy demand

In many low-income countries, women lack modern energy services and have to rely on traditional biomass and hard manual labour for family care. However, energy poverty is a phenomenon that occurs in high-income countries as well, due to the gender pay gap mainly affecting women, in particular the elderly or single mothers. Urban energy policy should therefore address both poverty and affluence by developing strategies to provide access to clean energy on the one hand, and, on the other, by reducing energy demand from those with high levels of consumption. For energy upgrading programmes, including offering advice and incentives for more efficient devices, gender-sensitive approaches and communication are crucial in order to reach women, who are often users and decision-makers at the household level.

Additional fields of action

From a gender perspective, cities in middle- and low-income countries need some further priority fields of action. One is **water management**, water supply and sanitation, as family care and personal hygiene needs require a reliable water supply. Another is **waste management**, with waste contributing substantially to greenhouse gas emissions in middle- and low-income countries. Often, poor women are involved in waste management and recycling and would lose their income if waste management were to be professionalised without taking them into consideration. Furthermore, waste management in private households often falls on women, and the separate collection of waste and other measures might burden them with additional work. Finally, **urban agriculture** is a further field of action that many poor women consider to be a priority area. Cities should provide them with access to space for urban gardening and agriculture in order to improve food security.

Next steps

One of our recommendations is a multidimensional approach for cities integrating climate change, environment and social and gender issues. This requires a commitment to work towards becoming a low-carbon, climate-resilient, equitable, gender-just, inclusive and caring city. As a first step, the gender balance in planning and decision-making should be improved. Participatory processes should be enhanced to give people, in particular women, a voice that can be heard. For baseline emissions inventories and vulnerability assessments, relevant data should be collected – for example on poverty, mobility and energy consumption – through surveys, focus groups or collaboration with community groups. To do this, gender-sensitive methods such as community-based vulnerability assessments should be applied. During policy formulation, the priorities listed above should not be missing. Certain groups may require specific policies, such as slum dwellers and female-headed households. During the design of measures, social and gender assessments should be carried out, in order to improve the design if necessary. During implementation, citizens and community-based organisations should be involved. Finally, evaluation should examine gender-differentiated impacts and use established methods such as gender-responsive budgeting.

There are many compelling reasons why urban climate policy should follow a gender-responsive approach.

Both women and men have a right to be meaningfully involved in climate policy planning and decision-making, whether at city or neighbourhood level. The equal participation of women and men enhances the legitimacy of urban climate policy and builds a sense of ownership. It makes sense to tap into the opportunities to work towards more healthy, liveable, sustainable, equitable and inclusive cities.

Climate policy is not only about technology; it is also about people. People and communities are subject to the impacts of climate change, and their consumption and mobility are the underlying causes of greenhouse gas emissions. Hence, climate policy will only be effective if people, their gender roles and tasks in society are taken into account. This makes urban climate policies and measures more acceptable, viable and efficient.

Urban climate policy should respond to the needs and capacities of all citizens and address poverty and marginalisation as well as affluence. Otherwise, a vast array of human resources, innovative potential and traditional and practical knowledge remains untapped, as well as a large potential for greenhouse gas reductions.

Moreover, international agreements, such as the Paris Agreement (2016) and the New Urban Agenda (2006), call for a gender-responsive approach. The Green Climate Fund has been built on an architecture that integrates gender provisions. Therefore, cities are well advised to develop gender-responsive actions if they seek to access climate finance.

The good news is that this situation is beginning to evolve, even in industrialised countries where the gender and climate nexus is often neglected. For example, the city of Potsdam, Germany, has involved gender experts in drawing up its ambitious mitigation programme, which aims to lead to a carbon-neutral city by 2050.

13

LYLA MEHTA and MELISSA LEACH

Institute of Development Studies,
University of Sussex

Why do gender equality and sustainability go hand in hand?[1]

Gender inequality and patterns of unsustainability

Dominant patterns of development have not delivered. In a world that is ever more globalised and interconnected, poverty and inequality are increasing, not decreasing. Ecological shocks such as floods, droughts, polluted land and oceans, destroyed landscapes and livelihoods are creating deep threats to the well-being and survival of future generations. These ecological changes are particularly affecting a third of the world's population directly dependent on natural resources for their livelihoods and well-being.[2] Furthermore, every day thousands of children die from waterborne diseases, more than a billion people go hungry, more than a thousand die in pregnancy and childbirth, and many lack the secure, decent jobs they need to provide dignified lives for themselves and their families. The poorest 20 per cent of the world's population control only just over 2 per cent of global income.[3] The recent multiple crises of climate, food, finance and resource scarcities also indicate that neoliberal market-driven processes have largely failed. There needs to be a refocus on the problems arising out of unfettered growth and unsustainable patterns of production and consumption on the part of the rich and the middle classes around the world, as well as the negative impacts of extractive and polluting industries and manufacturing.[4] These deeply interlocked economic, social and environmental problems point to a crisis of unsustainability. They also indicate that unsustainability and its counter, sustainability, need to be recast and reanimated as political terms that can help us recognise and tackle the drivers that have led to the current predicament, and spur vigorous debate and action towards more prosperous and just futures for all.

Since the 1992 United Nations Conference on Environment and Development (UNCED) there has been widespread acknowledgement that sustainable development is not possible without gender equality. Despite several differences in the various conceptual debates around gender and the environment (e.g. ecofeminist, Women, Environment and Development (WED), Gender, Environment and Development (GED) and feminist political ecology, FPE), there is now a wide consensus that the environment and sustainable development are not gender neutral. They are shaped by and shape gender relations which in turn determine environmental outcomes. Feminists and gender analysts have also called for a radical rethinking of capitalist modes of production and consumption as well as the social justice and equity concerning resource use. In sum, without gender justice there can be no environmental justice or sustainability.[5] Thus, it is surprising that despite much of the progress made in the 1990s on firmly placing gender on the map of sustainable development issues, current high-level debates on the green economy, planetary boundaries and the Anthropocene have been surprisingly gender blind and not adequately radically transformative.[6] This chapter highlights some of the fault lines in current global thinking, in particular from a gender and social justice perspective, before highlighting alternative pathways to sustainability that promote both social and gender justice.

Whose Anthropocene and who sets the boundaries?

Highly influential currently is the rise of scientific concepts and arguments centred on notions of the *Anthropocene and 'planetary boundaries'*. These concepts are grounded in an emerging set of earth system sciences suggesting that we have entered a new geological epoch, the Anthropocene, in which human activities have become the dominant driver of many earth system processes, including climate, bio-geochemical cycles, ecosystems and biodiversity. The extent of human influence, driven by intensifying material production and consumption, has grown rapidly since the Industrial Revolution and has accelerated dramatically since the 1950s (see the following section). A series of nine planetary boundaries has been identified, referring to the biophysical processes in the Earth's systems on which human life depends.[7] Together, these serve to keep the planet within Holocene-like conditions and thus define a safe operating space for humanity. Potentially catastrophic thresholds are in prospect, it is argued, which will compromise development both globally and locally. It is thus urgent that development pathways reconnect with the biosphere's capacity to sustain them.[8]

While the science is still developing, the concept of planetary boundaries has been rapidly taken up within policy debates, including those around Rio+20. Yet many actors, including developing country governments, have contested the concept, interpreting it as anti-growth and anti-development. Some suggest that planetary boundaries bring a return to 'limits to growth' thinking and a privileging of global environmental over local concerns, justifying top-down interventions that protect the environment at the expense of people and their livelihoods. It is also worth asking: who defines which boundaries and for whom? Boundaries at local and regional scales will be different from global ones; women and men and rich and poor people will define boundaries differently. That steering development within planetary boundaries should not compromise inclusive development that respects human rights has been proposed by Raworth,[9] whose 'doughnut' concept takes the circle of planetary boundaries and adds an inner circle, representing a 'social foundation'. In between these is a 'safe and just operating space' for humanity, within which development must take place. Yet even this fails to address the possible divergences and trade-offs between some people's notions of a good life and visions for the future, and scientifically defined environmental limits. Meanwhile, the new, neo-Malthusian narratives of impending scarcity and catastrophe implied by some interpretations of planetary boundaries arguments risk justifying a return to draconian policies and unjust responses that limit people's rights and freedoms. To date, and with the exception of Raworth,[10] who introduces 'gender equality' as one dimension of the 'social foundation' of humanity's safe and just operating space, discussion and advocacy arising from the planetary boundaries concept has been gender blind.

Green economies: business as usual?

The idea of '*green economies*' is capturing the attention of governments, businesses and NGOs alike. According to UNEP, which launched its Green Economy Initiative in 2008, a green economy is 'one that results in improved human well-being and social equity, while significantly reducing environmental risks and ecological scarcities. In its simplest expression, a green economy can be thought of as one which is low carbon, resource efficient and socially inclusive'.[11] Although this would appear to demand an integration of environment, economy and social development no different from other conceptualisations of sustainable development, in policy and practice green economy thinking has come to drive a particular range of approaches. These include a focus on business and private sector action, albeit motivated and regulated by the public sector, in investments, technologies and innovations that enhance energy and resource efficiency, and prevent the loss of ecosystem services. There are opportunities to deliver profit, employment and environmental sustainability at the same time in forms of 'green growth', it is claimed, provided investments are correctly targeted. Indeed, it is argued that the emerging green tech economy – in areas such as renewable energy – will be worth $4.2 trillion annually by the year 2020.[12]

While these approaches assume that continued economic growth can be reshaped in green directions, others argue that environmental constraints will require much-reduced rates of growth – or even no growth – as well as different types of growth. Thus

Jackson[13] argues for a shift in economic thinking and strategy to emphasise the pursuit not of growth, but of prosperity and well-being. Investments in services and care, as well as in 'green' action in the areas of sustainable food production and marketing and clean energy, are seen as key. These arguments link with growing debate around alternative economies and solidarity economies,[14] drawing on evidence from mostly local-scale modes of organising, and social movement activism, around the world. Green economy thinking also calls for a focus on maintaining and enhancing natural capital, supported by valuation and accounting measures that build on, but extend, the environmental economics work of the 1990s,[15] and on market-based approaches to environmental protection. The latter include an array of schemes to value and trade aspects of ecosystems now (re)defined as commodities to include schemes for trading carbon credits and offsetting emissions, such as those associated with clean energy, forests and agriculture under the CDM, UN-REDD and voluntary schemes. While livelihood benefits to local people are often claimed, it is highly variable whether these are realised in practice. Critics point to mounting evidence of such financialisation and commoditisation of ecosystems being linked with forms of land and resource dispossession, or land, water and green grabs.[16] Little wonder, then, that many women's organisations from around the world have resolutely rejected this concept.

While green investments and technologies are important areas, questions of justice and social values are often missing in the debate. Thus narrow forms of financial value – on ecosystems and resources – overlook social and cultural values, including those that have emerged from the long coexistence of people and ecosystems. And attention to the differentiated social – and gender – implications of 'decoupled' and green economies – and even prosperity-focused care economies – is often lacking. Not addressed is whose priorities count, and who may gain or lose from the resulting policies and interventions. Also, even though there is some mention of MDG3 on gender equality, the Green Economy Report makes no mention of the differentiated impacts of the green economy on men and men and what exactly the transition to the new economic model will mean for different groups of women and men.[17]

Critics see the green economy concept as one that continues with the business-as-usual gobal economic model which is the root cause of global environmental destruction, social exploitation and inequality.[18] It has also been criticised for being a market-based approach that justifies the commodification and enclosure of resources, and carbon schemes such as REDD that undermine local livelihoods, justify land grabs and also displace local people, especially women subsistence farmers who comprise most of the food producers in developing countries.[19] In all the recent approaches outlined above, we find an overly technocentric and economistic focus; in different ways, each opens the way for either a techno-regulatory, top-down style of development, or a neoliberal market-led one. At the same time, new and problematic narratives of environmental catastrophe and crisis are afoot. Underplayed are questions of power, and of social values, distribution and justice – including gender – both in how problems of sustainability emerge and how they, and responses to them, are experienced.

By contrast a gender-equitable sustainable development framework would combine care economy and green economy approaches to address the exploitation of women's largely unpaid care work and also question the use of natural resources and the environment as an inexhaustible source of productive inputs. There has also been new work from feminist economists and analysts reinvigorating earlier critiques of the separation between production and social reproduction and the power relations that uphold these.[20] There are also calls to replace efficiency with sufficiency,[21] with sharing, redistribution and 'commoning' as the guiding principles. By a so-called 'caring economy' feminists are calling for a redistribution of labour and value creation that goes beyond the market, efficiency and remuneration[22] and for a new conception of what constitutes 'the good'. All these different strands are calling for a new transformatory politics that will lead to different pathways across different scales, like those being advocated by 'green economy' and planetary boundary specialists.

Pathways to gender equality and sustainability

If one thing is clear from this account of recent thinking, policy and practice, it is that sustainability and sustainable development are political. Dimensions regarding what to prioritise, and what actions are undertaken (or not), are all subject to diverse interests and perspectives, and are thus contested. Sometimes contestation is across spatial scales, as when global and local priorities conflict; sometimes across timescales, as when governments struggle to reconcile long-term environmental agendas with short-term domestic interests and political cycles; and sometimes between social groups with diverse positions and values. Even if not explicit at the outset, such contestations have often proved to undermine even the best-conceived sustainable development policies and programmes. This means that sustainable development policy and practice cannot simply proceed as a technical and managerial exercise, but must embrace a more normative, politicised approach.

There are also gender-related problems around different approaches to sustainable development and gender that need to be avoided. In the name of environmental protection, local women and men have sometimes been dispossessed from their lands, forests and water resources; problematic linkages between women and nature have led to the essentialisation of the roles of women as so-called 'carers' of nature, and they have been made responsible for environmental chores that have drawn on their voluntary labour. Such past mistakes and pitfalls must definitely be avoided in future.

Linking gender equality and sustainable development is therefore vital for several reasons. First, this is a moral and ethical imperative: building more equitable gender relations that support the human rights, dignity and capabilities of women, intersected by differences of class, race, sexuality, age, ability and circumstances, is a central requirement of an ethical world order. Secondly, to avoid women becoming victims, the all-too-common pattern whereby women suffer most from environmental, climatic and economic shocks and stresses, undermining their vital roles in sustaining their families and communities, must be redressed. But thirdly, and most significantly, it is vital to build on women's agency. Attention to gender offers routes to improving resource productivity and efficiency, to enhancing ecosystem conservation and sustainable use, and to building more sustainable, low-carbon food, energy, water and health systems. Not just victims, women have been and can be central actors in pathways to sustainability and green transformation. Yet crucially, this must not mean adding 'environment' to women's caring roles, or instrumentalising women as the new 'sustainability saviours'. It means recognition of and respect for their knowledge, rights, capabilities and bodily integrity, and ensuring that roles are matched with rights and control over resources and decision-making power. Here we respond to a growing consensus that gender equality and sustainable development can thus reinforce each other, in powerful ways.[23] Also, attending to gender differences and relations provides a vital lens on and way to address the social and political, as well as economic and environmental, challenges and opportunities that must be core to pursuing sustainable development, and highlights ways that women can be powerful agents of green transformation. Finally, gender-focused and feminist analysts and movements have long provided strong and radical alternatives to patterns of unsustainability that promote gender inequalities, as well as other forms of injustice. They call for a reimagining of sustainability in which gender equality is a key element, and provide powerful tools to enable such alternative imaginaries and transformations.

The concept of pathways helps to capture this. Pathways are the alternative directions in which social, technological, economic and environmental systems might co-evolve.[24] Pathways are shaped by values, by selective kinds of knowledge, and by power. They can encompass particular policies, projects and interventions. It is clear that dominant pathways of change – the motorways, to extend the analogy, of global development – are moving in directions that are thoroughly unsustainable and not enhancing gender or social justice. Challenging such current unsustainable pathways, and identifying and building alternative pathways to sustainability that embrace gender equality, is the challenge of our age.

The pathways approach helps in conceptualising how institutions, power and knowledge can interact to create and sustain pathways that are either unsustainable or – alternatively – offer routes to sustainable development. Thus a local example might be the interactions of water and food, gender divisions of labour and responsibility, and different water management systems (including irrigation) that provide water for productive users. Nationally, we might be concerned with the interactions of state policies and markets involved in food systems. And a global example might be the interactions of dynamic climate processes with international regulation, carbon market schemes and finance aimed at curbing greenhouse gas emissions and impacts. Yet most sustainability challenges involve interactions across scales. Thus we might be concerned with the impacts of global climate processes on local land ecologies and uses, or with the ways that household, state and market institutions interact to shape the dynamics of food and water access. For gender equality to flourish, pathways therefore need to generate multiple capabilities and freedoms that go beyond basic material needs and rights. They also need to include opportunity and process freedoms that allow people to convert resources to multiple capabilities.[25] The hope is that these then feed back to sustain ongoing processes of pathway generation and maintenance that further reinforce sustainable development and gender justice. But this will often not be a linear process; there will be unexpected events, opportunities and setbacks, to which people, institutions and ecologies will need to adapt and respond. Also, pathways, by virtue of their dynamic nature, have unintended social, technological and environmental consequences which also affect outcomes in terms of gender (in)equality. Thus, it is important to build inclusive learning and deliberation processes and ways to monitor exclusion, trade-offs and emerging opportunities.

Fortunately, this is a time of opportunities. Alternative concepts such as 'Buen Vivir' and 'Sufficiency Economy' are being proposed in different parts of the global South. There are many alternative pathways to sustainability and gender equality but these are currently unrecognised. They exist in urban and rural spaces where

14

NAOKO ISHII

CEO and Chairperson, Global Environment Facility, Washington DC

The benefits of using a gender lens

We are at a defining moment for the future of the planet and for human well-being. Our planet is reaching the limits of what it can provide to humanity in a sustainable manner. The global commons that support life on Earth – the land, seas and atmosphere we share, and the ecosystems they host – are under severe threat from human activities.

The good news is that we still have a window of opportunity to change the course we are on, but it will not last long. The decisions we make over the next fifteen years will determine what kind of world we will have for the rest of the century.

To get on the right path to a better, safer future, all stakeholders need to work together on common and systemic solutions and to address the drivers of environmental degradation. We need to change the systems that support how we live, how we eat, how we move and how we produce and consume. Women's role in this transformation is critical.

If we want to ensure that women play a catalytic role in safeguarding our global commons, we first need to improve our understanding of women's roles, perspectives and needs.

It is increasingly evident that women's involvement and leadership in environmental solutions help deliver successful and long-lasting results. Nonetheless, despite some efforts to promote women's empowerment, more must be done.

One thing that Global Environment Facility (GEF) has learned over the years is not to assume that environmental projects are gender neutral. When the GEF started to require gender analysis as part of the project planning, we realised that many projects perceived to be gender *neutral* were, in fact, gender *blind*. These projects failed to take into account their differentiated impact on women and men.

Today we know better at GEF. If we do not proactively identify and address gender issues, environmental projects could potentially perpetuate disparities and widen the gap between women and men. We also know that women and men are impacted by changes in the environment to different degrees and have different needs and opportunities to benefit from as well as to contribute to the GEF investments and initiatives.

Take the case of the provision of clean energy, where the distinct roles of women and men have often been overlooked in project design. Our experience at GEF has shown that energy projects can deliver transformative results when they support the productive use of locally available renewable energy sources and provide training and resources to women entrepreneurs. These projects not only guarantee a reliable source of clean energy services but also increase women's income and leadership.

Adding gender analysis improves project design

A better project design starts with a gender analysis. By asking the right questions and engaging with potential beneficiaries beforehand, we tailor project activities to improve women's participation in a more effective way. For example, using a gender lens to address questions on safety in public transportation, usage of energy, management of ecosystem services, agricultural practices, climate vulnerabilities, water dependence and community participation will provide better insights in understanding the perspectives and needs of both women and men.

In order to get a better understanding of the connections between gender analysis and project design, let us look at some of the projects funded by GEF in recent years:

» A project in the state of **Uttarakhand in India** addressed the crucial link between ecosystem services and livelihoods of women in fragile watersheds. As the primary users of forests and other natural resources, such as fresh water, women played a significant role during the project implementation. Their inclusion in the decision-making processes was achieved through various tools and mechanisms, such as an initiative called 'women motivating women' to raise awareness and enhance social mobilisation. Also, the project encouraged the participation of women in various committees and institutions and developed an emphasis on women-led income-generating activities.

» In **The Gambia**, where only 35 per cent of the total population has access to electricity and women are traditionally isolated from entrepreneurial activities, GEF funded a project to promote renewable energy-based mini-grids in rural areas. In this project, women received assistance for developing renewable energy projects under the renewable energy fund of The Gambia. The project supported skills training and income generation activities for women, including practical training courses for women to become renewable energy technicians. The fund specifically made sure that half of the funding would be earmarked for projects led by women, with additional support to women to develop proposals.

» In **Burkina Faso**, one project worked with the traditional beer-brewing sector to install energy-efficient cookstoves to promote clean technologies and also ensure safe and decent work for women. The intervention developed clusters of women beer brewers to generate collective gains and facilitate their integration into the local value chain. The project increased women's financial inclusion and improved their leadership in the community. Moreover, by providing the cookstoves and reducing the amount of firewood consumed by 40 to 50 per cent, the project lessened the vulnerability and risk of physical and sexual violence faced by women and girls when collecting fuel.

No more gender-blind projects

At GEF, we are now starting to see the impact of integrating gender analysis early on in the project design. At the same time, we realise that we might have missed opportunities in the past – not only did we not maximise women's contribution to safeguard our global commons, but, like the rest of the international community, we are failing to reverse the sharp downward trend in the global environment.

We have made progress, but our work is not done. There have been many good initiatives, but initiatives are too often fragmented and isolated, and have come up short in shifting the needle in the right direction, let alone in bringing about transformational change.

We have made the leap from gender-blind to gender-aware projects but we still have to work on translating this awareness into action. We need to promote women's entrepreneurship and leadership; enable opportunities to access the financial system; connect them to the current digital revolution; guarantee equal rights to land ownership; and enhance their participation in the expanding renewable energy sector.

To move forward this agenda, GEF – along with other international financial institutions – is working to make sure that our future projects are always gender-sensitive. This effort involves actions on many fronts, such as promoting an equal voice in planning and decision-making among key actors and strengthening the skills that will allow women to engage in and benefit from climate, energy, food and urban solutions.

Every intervention that offers an opportunity to make a difference for the global environment also offers an opportunity for women to play a more active role in the solutions we design. Widening our understanding of the complementary roles between women and men at the project level will lead to better results at the global scale. Today, the risks for the planet are simply too high and we cannot afford to miss any opportunity to drive transformative change. Without greater women's leadership and empowerment, we cannot safeguard our global commons.

15

CAROLINE LUCAS
UK Green Party MP

Is there a specific role for women in helping to achieve environmental sustainability through politics?

> We are not meek and we are not weak. We are angry – on our own behalf, for our sisters and children who suffer, and for the entire planet – and we are determined to protect life on Earth.
>
> Petra Kelly, German Green MP (1947–1992)

It was a potent image.

Just a woman in jeans, arms laden with sunflowers, a beaming smile.

But to me, it encapsulated a great deal. The woman's name was Petra Kelly, a founder of the German Green Party. The image captured her entry into parliament on her first day as a Green MP.

It represented to me a new kind of politics, politics as something personal – as everything we do from the moment we awake, as all the choices we make, as people-centred.

Certainly Petra was the greatest inspiration of my political life, and a person you might say summed up the Green movement. She embodied feminism, peace, activism, and inspiration – an amazing politician. She had a formidable intellect, spoke passionately of the Green Party as the 'anti-Party Party' – a party that went beyond the usual party politics, embracing grassroots democracy and non-violent direct action.

And here she was, a woman, a Green – an elected MP.

It gave me tremendous hope. It made me feel bolder – and Westminster somehow closer.

I've taken great inspiration from the pioneers like Petra, who, when faced with fierce opposition, even ridicule, persevered and pushed for change regardless. When finally I found myself within Westminster's halls – a Green MP in the heart of the British Parliament – their wisdom impressed itself upon me more than ever.

It's often been said that it's not easy being a woman in politics. I think perhaps it's harder still when your work centres on a passion for people and planet. But I firmly believe that women do have a specific role in helping to achieve environmental sustainability. And I believe we can do so through politics.

But Parliament's priorities are thoroughly back-to-front. We have £500 billion to bail out the banks in the financial crisis, £100 billion for a new nuclear deterrent system. But when it comes to protecting our most precious assets, to preventing catastrophic climate change – to talking sustainability, renewables, emissions reduction targets and eliminating fuel poverty – political will (and resourcing) swiftly diminishes. We only have one planet and, according to the latest Intergovernmental Panel on Climate Change report, a limited time frame to prevent the irreversible impacts of climate change upon it.

The mandate is clear and urgent, and successive governments have gone to great lengths to be seen as Green. But when it comes to driving through substantive change, the appetite evaporates.

When Prime Minister David Cameron dubbed climate change 'the biggest threat facing Britain and the world' during the 2013 winter floods – it continued to be unapologetically disregarded as the domain of anti-business types, madcap revolutionaries, idealists – and feminists.

I think of the wonderful marine biologist Rachel Carson, whose groundbreaking book *Silent Spring* was one of the most influential ever written on the environment and ecology. Which inevitably incited the wrath of the major chemical corps it challenged. Carson was publicly ridiculed, threatened with legal action and labelled 'a spinster' and 'hysterical'.

But the undeniable quality of her peer-reviewed research withstood the predictably gendered smear campaigns and it's hard to overstate the book's legacy.

Part fairy story and part meticulous study, *Silent Spring* breathed life into science, making academia not only accessible but *unputdownable*. Its message went viral (or the 1960s equivalent of), tangibly shifting the public (and eventually political) perception of environmental concerns.

In the UK alone, it helped spark the creation of PEOPLE, which, in the 1970s, developed into the Ecology Party, which grew into the Green Party. It has informed much of my own work – as an activist, an MEP in Brussels and an MP in my Brighton constituency and Westminster.

In the male-dominated fields of politics and science, Petra Kelly and Rachel Carson influenced – even shifted – entrenched patterns of thought. They didn't 'step outside the box': they re-formed it from within.

In her narrative Carson irrevocably altered our understanding of the fundamental yet fragile connection between person and planet. Kelly, with incredible passion, connected planet and person with politics. Their ideas and uncompromising courage of conviction challenged the status quo and, in time, altered minds and hearts globally.

They were creative, innovative, dynamic forces to be reckoned with. But they had to be – their gender compelled it – as women in their fields, they had to work harder, and their work had to be flawless. They were human, humble, passionate about people and planet – qualities which, I believe, helped capture public imagination, ensuring their theories took flight and their legacy endured: and environmental sustainability took a determined step forward.

Both were unique talents. But one might argue that gender played a role in their success – that their very experiences as women contributed to their worldview and thus their work. Were they simply brilliant women, or did their brilliance stem in part from being women?

And if it's the case that the hand we're dealt as women – our unique experiences – can be a tool to our advantage, can we do more to harness that, develop it, as politicians and activists for the environmental cause, to stand on equal footing in our so very patriarchal halls of power and further our cause?

Women and leadership

Kelly's thoughts on women and power have deeply influenced the way I approach my work in Westminster. I love this quote from her, connecting feminism, activism and leadership:

> Feminism seeks to redefine our very modes of existence and to transform non-violently the structures of male dominance. I am not saying that women are inherently better than men. Overturning patriarchy doesn't mean replacing men's dominance with women's dominance. That would merely maintain the patriarchal pattern of dominance. We need to transform the patriarchal pattern itself.
>
> The work of feminist women and pro-feminist men is to liberate everyone from a system that is oppressive to women and restrictive to men, and to restore balance and harmony between women and men, and between masculine and feminine values in society and within each of us. Feminists working in the peace and ecology movements are sometimes viewed as kind, nurturing Earth mothers, but that is too comfortable a stereotype. We are not meek and we are not weak. We are angry – on our own behalf, for our sisters and children who suffer, and for the entire planet – and we are determined to protect life on Earth.
>
> There is a saying: Where power is, women are not. Women must be willing to be powerful. Because we bear scars from the way men have used their power over us, women often want no part of power.
>
> But playing an active part in society, on an equal footing with men, does not mean adopting the old thought

patterns and strategies of the patriarchal world. It means putting our own ideas of an emancipatory society into prac- tice. Rather than emulating Margaret Thatcher and others who loyally adapt themselves to male values of hierarchy we must find our own definitions of power that reflects women's values and women's experience […] This is not power over others, but power with others, the kind of shared power that has to replace patriarchal power.

I think that applies across the board – from Parliament to grassroots environmental campaigns.

It's undeniable that women have to work harder to get heard. And we cannot hope to be heard, to change climate policy, if we are unable or willing to embrace power. And I don't mean mimicking the old structures designed to oppress rather than liberate, much less empower, us – but embracing that which sets us apart, those uniquely female experiences which contribute to our view of the world and our place in it.

Our political power structures are patriarchal. Just watch Prime Minister's Questions (it's even worse in person); saturated with sexism, with audible comments about the way women look.

What it if were more gender balanced?

More female MPs wouldn't necessarily make for a more compassionate, friendly Parliament. But it would diversify politics and (as any ecologist will tell you) diversity is the key to strength, and survival. And such a change is long overdue.

I don't necessarily think women are better at selfless giving, but perhaps there really is something born of our unique experience which is advantageous in using power well and in furthering the environmental cause.

Perhaps the extent to which women have had less power – or, as Kelly says, because we 'bear scars from the way men have used their power over us' – we're more aware of the sensitivities in using it over others, over nature. Furthermore, perhaps the female expe- rience of fighting for the right to be heard in politics – national, local, grassroots – makes us naturally better equipped to fight for a cause that has also traditionally been neglected, ridiculed even, in politics. I don't suggest that we are innately or inevitably (or always – think Margaret Thatcher) programmed this way, but that as a result of our experience in a patriarchal world, we can empathise with a neglected cause – and, one might argue, will more naturally be drawn to it in the first instance.

I'm reminded of a conference I attended, on the subject of climate change. It'd been organised by a woman and every speaker was female. She said to me at the time, 'I got so fed up with going to meetings where the best person to speak on merit would have been a particular woman who, often, would be sat in the audience.'

Speaking at that conference was great. It felt less competitive, more honest – with people saying much more about what they felt about the subjects, not just what they thought – and as a result it felt more balanced. None of those things are intrinsically tied to the fact the event was dominated by women but, given our culture, it's more likely that a high proportion of women will shift the nature of any dialogue or debate.

Women were not being favoured as speakers simply because of their gender – they were given a platform because they were the most capable, most compelling and probably the most over-looked too.

Perhaps a more gender-equal Parliament would make politics more like a public service, less self-serving and elitist. Perhaps one of the reasons more women don't stand for election to Parliament is because politics has become something all too many people consider as a career – rather than a way to make a difference.

Collaboration

When I was a member of the European Parliament (1999–2010), where a third of MEPs are women, I virtually forgot about gender. The work culture was far more conducive for a woman – far less grandstanding, more cooperation. Compromise wasn't a dirty word but a noble pursuit of common ground. In Westminster, you're in a noticeable minority in every committee, in every debate.

We have some fantastic female voices there, but they're woefully under-represented.

We won the right to sit in the House in 1918 but since that time just 369 women MPs have done so – yet in Parliament right now, there are over five hundred male MPs. Ours is supposed to be the mother of all parliaments: yet just 28 per cent of MPs are women. Afghanistan tops us in that poll.

Green politics sets store by gender balance and advocates a different ethos of leadership and power that, I think, sits far more comfortably with the European Parliament than our own patriarchal version – and I think Westminster can learn a great deal from it.

It stresses collaboration over competition. It's about making a difference, not climbing ladders. It emphasises balance.

To be alone and in conflict with all would be hopelessly ineffective. I collaborate across parties very well, and perhaps that's down to a number of things – my politics, my own ethos, my experience in the European Parliament, a sense of urgency in the face of climate change, my gender.

But the culture, vested interests and workaday rules of Westminster are rigged against women – against anyone, in fact, trying to do things a bit differently.

Politically independent community leaders are disadvantaged because we don't have a proportional voting system.

And without state funding for political parties the 'old boys' networks continue to thrive along with every other bloated symbol of the status quo – a status quo that has been built by men and, I'd argue, depends upon the continued disenfranchisement of women.

Changes are creeping in – prior to 1987 women had never made up more than 5 per cent of MPs.

But Westminster has always dragged its feet. We need to keep fighting for reform, challenge the establishment and make the system fairer, more balanced.

And politics isn't confined to Parliament. It's everything we do, and something we are. Grassroots activism in the UK is blooming: creative, dynamic, resilient, resourceful, passionate – and highly influential.

Like Petra, my own involvement in party politics was sparked by activism, particularly around the Campaign for Nuclear Disarmament (CND) in the 1980s, and I was involved in the CND protests at Molesworth and at Greenham Common. I supported other causes too, but it was reading *Seeing Green* by Jonathan Porritt in 1986 that suddenly made clear to me how all these issues were underpinned by the political process. The Green Party offered a political solution which recognised the connections and stood for real and necessary change.

But one of the things I love most about the Green Party is that it has never broken from its activist origins. It embraces grassroots and established political systems as complementary – their collaboration as necessary to achieving real change.

Parliament can learn much from that; from the best examples of grassroots democracy and non-violent direct action, historic and contemporary.

Deeds not words

Were the suffragettes a group of unusually brilliant, creative women – or did their experiences as women influence the movement and make them brilliant?

They knew all about being ignored and excluded – and all about fighting back. True experts of direct action, on one occasion two women posted themselves as human letters to Downing Street; on another, they boarded a boat and unfurled banners opposite the terrace of Parliament. They boycotted the census, on the grounds that 'if women don't count, neither shall they be counted'.

They taught us how to find our voice, and use it. To constantly speak up and speak out.

To be courageous.

But perhaps, more than anything, we can take from them a passionate commitment to never give up.

The fantastic Tamsin Omond, a founding member of activist group Climate Rush, has been heavily inspired in her work by the suffragette movement. What a great example of an exciting and influential political independent trying to do things a bit differently.

And she's not alone – just skimming the landscape of grassroots campaigning shows the influence women have – from Anita Roddick, founder of the Body Shop, to the EveryDay Sexism and No More Page 3 campaigns.

The suffragettes won us the vote. We can sit in the House. The Commons belongs to us – but still it's controlled by a privileged male elite and their vested whims. We need to change that. To make it easier for voices like Tamsin's – and others – to be counted, and make Parliament truly representative and accountable to the people.

A hundred years ago, Emmeline Pankhurst said, 'to be able to be militant is a privilege'. She was right, and now is the time to use our voices, collectively, to speak out to prevent our government from sleepwalking into climate catastrophe.

Too often our efforts are disjointed, and we're the weaker for it. We must collaborate much more.

Canadian author and social activist Naomi Klein – a bona fide rabble-rouser for change – consistently and convincingly connects the dots: between politics and people, financial chaos and climate chaos – and advocates a joined-up strategy for change. Campaigners should unite, she says, because the root of our problem is the same: unrestrained corporate greed. There's an urgency to this fight and it's a battle we must win. To do so, we must recognise and respond as one, 'weaving' our fights into 'a common narrative'.

Her fuss-free, commonsense take on people, planet and politics captures imaginations and wins debates hands down.

Feeling as a catalyst

And – simple though it may sound – I believe a great deal of what we're seeking boils down to something so simple, it's almost counter-intuitive: feeling.

Why is it that we're so squeamish about discussing how we *feel* about the climate crisis?

Perhaps it's that such a traditionally female attribute is equated with weakness; and emotion as an absence of reason – another legacy of a patriarchal power structure.

But only by talking through how we feel will we manage to dig deep enough to find the creativity and innovation that are needed to respond effectively to what many now recognise is the biggest threat facing humankind.

We need to find the courage to look the crisis in the face and genuinely connect with it on an emotional basis, without flinching.

I remember how, when I first heard that there had been a record loss of summer sea ice, and that greenhouse gas concentrations in the atmosphere were at their highest point for possibly 800,000 years, it felt like a physical kick in the stomach. I felt literally winded, short of breath – and very tearful.

There is such a thing as too late, and the idea haunts me.

But if facing the true horror of what we are doing to our climate is a prerequisite to generating the political will to act – to move from the elegiac to the practical – how do we equip ourselves to do so?

Not without hope.

Hope is a potent catalyst, far more so, I'd argue, than fear. And while our failure to adequately appreciate and guard against ecological destruction fills me with frustration – and sometimes despair – my hope, as Petra Kelly might say, is not meek or weak. It is urgent and raging, and I think that's helped, rather than hindered, me in getting heard as an MP and campaigner.

It's a hope that believes a better world – away from cyclical war, the annihilation of the earth's treasures and the grinding down of the poor and marginal – is possible.

And in my book, that's worth a fight.

We need to actively choose a better future – and make it happen. Martin Luther King had a dream, not a nightmare, and we need that same vision today. We need to harness the transformative power of hope, so it can be turned into creative and innovative solutions.

Nature is full of inspirations, and not for nothing did sunflowers fill Petra Kelly's arms as she entered the German parliament. The most powerful ideas grow in strength with the right energy, motivation. Heads turned to the sun, these flowers reach sturdily up, improbably high, towards a promise of something better.

It's a simple idea, but remains a deeply radical one: that if we decide we want a different kind of future, we can reach it. That just making the commitment can be the catalyst we need.

But every voice counts. We must reclaim politics as everything we do. And – lobbyist, activist, international NGO or MP – cooperation between us is crucial. Being powerful *with* one another – living out the wonderful words of Robert F. Kennedy:

> Each time someone stands up for an ideal, or acts to improve the lot of others, or strikes out against injustice, she sends forth a tiny ripple of hope, and crossing each other from a million different centres of energy and daring, those ripples build a current which can sweep down the mightiest walls of oppression and resistance.

Or, to quote the wisdom of Dr Seuss, in his excellent book *The Lorax*:

> Unless someone like you cares a whole awful lot, nothing is going to get better. It's not.

16

JULIE A. NELSON

Economist, University of Massachusetts Boston

Empowering a balanced and useful economics of sustainability: the role of gender[1]

A more subtle relation between gender and sustainability

The issue of gender and sustainability does not end with the issue of the empowerment of women, although that is certainly important. Feminists have sometimes made a crude but useful distinction between 'sex' and 'gender'. Biological distinctions among male, female and intersex persons are referred to as 'sex'. So, for example, gathering and analysing information about women is an analysis at the level of sex. 'Gender', on the other hand, is used to refer to the cultural expectations, biases, beliefs and practices that are created on top of these distinctions. The discussion of societal *gender* norms – for example, whether it is considered appropriate for women to take leadership positions – is also important in efforts towards sustainability.

This chapter, however, takes gender analysis to a different, more subtle but yet more permeating, level. Human thinking – across the sexes, and apparently also across many cultures – has a tendency to be *cognitively gendered*: that is, as humans with limited brainpower, we have a well-documented tendency to simplify the world by splitting it, in our minds, into simple binary categories such as 'masculine' versus 'feminine'.[2] We find it very easy to think in dualistic terms. We even create beliefs about transcendent 'essences' based on this handy (and largely unconscious) organisational strategy.

Meanwhile, discussions of sustainability – and, in particular, of climate change – have increasingly focused around economic questions. Should we have carbon taxes? Can we 'afford' mitigation? Can economic growth continue? Who should bear the costs of adaptation? Do we need to invent an entire 'new economy' to achieve sustainability? This chapter explains how these discussions have been distorted and limited by unexamined – and deeply cognitively gendered – assumptions, and how a re-examination of these assumptions opens new doors.

The mainstream discipline of economics is, as I will describe below, strongly *cognitively gendered* as masculine. As a result, it takes only the most partial and incomplete view of economic realities. Although economists have a strong voice in current national and international policy-making, contemporary mainstream economics makes a very bad guide.

Furthermore – and here I depart from many other critiques – much of the distorted view preached by the mainstream is also uncritically accepted by many who propose 'alternative' or 'new' economies. As a result, these visions also offer unnecessarily limited and biased guidelines for action. Understanding the role of gender is therefore crucial to the project of improving analyses and motivating more effective action, no matter what your starting point.

The state of mainstream economics

My own training in academic economics (I hold a PhD) was of the thoroughly mainstream (also referred to as 'neoclassical') sort. Teaching at European and North American universities, and in many other parts of the world as well, is dominated by this approach.[3]

'Production' is a major focus of mainstream economics. This is true at the micro level, where models of production choices made by profit-maximising businesses are central. At the macro level, economists are fixated on gross domestic product (GDP) and its growth rate. But the definition of 'production' is narrow. The core models look only at the production of goods and services destined for sale in markets. And production is assumed to require two (and only two) factors: 'capital' (variously, machinery or finance) and 'labour' (the time and skills of adult – traditionally male – workers).

While micro-theories of production focus on business, micro-theories of consumption focus on households. Households, like businesses, are considered to be unitary, rational, autonomous, self-interested decision-making economic agents. Households, in mainstream theory, have three (and only three) roles: they consume goods and services purchased on markets, supply adult workers to labour markets, and enjoy leisure.

I noticed, over time, that women and nature share similar treatment in mainstream economics. They are largely invisible. Women's traditional, non-marketed, production of provisioning and care in homes and communities is completely ignored. Similarly, the productivity of nature is pushed into the background. When considered at all, women and nature are treated as passive 'resources' for the satisfaction of male or human desires, and treated as totally subject to male or human control. Explicit attention to, or appreciation of, them and their activities is deemed unnecessary, as they are assumed to possess an infinite capacity for self-maintenance and self-regeneration.

One would search in vain in the core models of economics for any inkling of where the materials used in production came from, or where the waste from the production process goes. Similarly, one would search in vain in most descriptions of economic agents for a discussion of where people come from, or where they go when they are broken or used up. The bearing and raising of children, and the care of the aged and sick – traditionally women's responsibilities – are, like nature, considered too unimportant to mention.

Another odd bias that became obvious to me had to do with the methods of analysis preferred in mainstream economics. As an undergraduate student, I was exposed to some discussion of real-world issues, as well as simple mathematical models meant to represent the behaviour of economic agents. Business firms were modelled as though each consisted of only *one* decision maker, who had only *one* goal (profits), and produced only *one* good, for *one* market. This was convenient, since 'maximising profits' could then be easily expressed in graphical and calculus terms – one just solved for the high point on the mathematical 'profit function'. I expected that in graduate school we would study more real-world issues by, for example, doing some hands-on investigating of how business boards and managers actually make decisions about their goals and their products and locations, and how they manage to get their decisions implemented by motivating workers and negotiating with suppliers and communities.

Instead, I was surprised to find, we started with the same extremely simple models, and merely went deeper and deeper into elaboration of mathematical fine points. I discovered that prestige in the profession came with being as abstract, technical and quantitative as possible, while disavowing hands-on research, concreteness, engagement, discussion of ethical issues, and anything else that smacked of softness or messiness.

This biased approach is reflected, for example, in the way the economics of climate change tends to be analyzed in US academic and policy contexts[4] and (although with *slightly* greater attempts at nuance) in the reports of the Intergovernmental Panel on Climate Change.[5] These assume that human well-being can be numerically measured, and that well-being is based purely on consumption (GDP). Furthermore, the changes in well-being related to climate change are assumed to be of a small, marginal nature suited to evaluation by standard calculus tools. People are assumed to think about future generations in the same way we think about short-term financial investments. Consideration of the ethical issues related to global inequalities is often eliminated through assumptions that are disguised as being merely technical.[6] Technology and machinery are generally assumed to be so easily substituted for natural resources that economic growth can continue unfettered for ever.[7] In this way, consideration of the foundation of economic life in society and nature, as well as consideration of moral responsibility and the possibility of uncontrollable change, are assiduously avoided.[8]

My two musings – about the content of economics, and about its methods – came together for me in the 1980s when I discovered feminist scholarship on the history and philosophy of science.

Feminist critiques of (social) science

In the 1980s, a number of feminist historians and philosophers, including Evelyn Fox Keller[9] and Sandra Harding,[10] brought to light the strong binary *gendering* that underlay the historical development of science. They pointed out how imagined binary oppositions between 'man' and nature, mind and body, order and chaos, and males and females strongly influenced the Western conception of where people fit into the order of the world. From Plato and Aristotle, through Descartes and Bacon, the image of scientific knowledge as the masculine means to firmly control a dangerous feminine Nature emerged.

In the early 1990s, feminist economists began to notice that the definition, models and methods of mainstream economics followed just such a cognitively gendered pattern.[11] The choice of economists to one-sidedly favour, for example, the analysis of production for markets over production for own use, mental decision-making over bodily needs, control over interdependence, and reason over emotion follows point by point the typical cultural associations of masculinity with high status, 'hardness' and power, and femininity with low status, 'softness' and weakness.

The elevation of quantitative and technical work in the profession, to the neglect of more engaged methods and consideration of normative (that is, ethical) concerns, likewise reflects gender bias. A look back at the history of the discipline reveals that the methods were chosen not because they portrayed the world most accurately, but precisely because they gave the discipline of economics the aura of being a 'hard' science.[12]

The myth of the machine

This 'physics envy' demonstrated by the economics profession has led to a very odd result, but one that has permeated contemporary society: people have come to believe that market-using economies are machine-like 'engines', 'driven' by self-interest, blindly following 'market logic' and 'imperatives of growth'. We have come to believe that economies somehow operate in a realm set apart from dependency on the natural world. (Economists left those considerations to the natural sciences.) We have come to believe that they somehow operate in a realm set apart from human sociality, interdependence and moral consideration. (These were left to sociology and philosophy.) How bizarre.

This problem has been accentuated by the recent ascendance of neoliberal thought, which takes the core assumptions of mainstream economics to an ideological extreme. Neoliberalism suggests that market-using economies (should) have only one possible kind of institution – unregulated businesses – and one norm – 'greed is good'. Not only does neoliberal thought suggest that such a 'pure market' economy is possible, neoliberalism presents this view as a true understanding of the deep underlying essential nature of capitalism.

In fact, as a number of (dissident) economists, business theorists, legal theorists, economic sociologists and business leaders are increasingly pointing out, real economies – even capitalist ones – are actually *part of* nature and society.[13] Economies are actually deeply entwined and co-constituted with the natural environment, public regulation, cultural beliefs, real human emotional motivations, social practices and complex ethical norms. A 'pure market' has never, and can never, exist: markets and business are thoroughly shaped by norms and institutions.

Mainstream economists' claim that firms *should* 'maximise profit', for example, is dangerous not only for humans and the environment, but for businesses themselves and the system in which they function.[14] Real businesses find long-term success by balancing multiple goals, and organising cooperation among shareholders, customers, suppliers and workers to achieve them.

A single-minded focus on short-term financial outcomes is, in contrast, behind many of the corporate and financial scandals and crises of recent decades.[15] The idea that firms (not only 'should' but) *do* aim to 'maximise profit' has likewise been exposed as a myth from commentators within the corporate sector itself. While short-sighted firms may adopt only financial goals, these days such goals tend more towards ridiculous compensation of top-level executives than towards profits for shareholders.[16]

Unfortunately, many 'alternative' economic views put forth in the literature on sustainability suffer from a failure to distinguish between (1) how market-using ('capitalist') economies *actually* operate and (2) how the masculine-biased core models of mainstream economics have *told us* they operate ('neoliberalism'). Accepting that mainstream dogma about markets and businesses being mechanical, inhuman and separate from 'society,' they suggest alternatives that are merely reactive instead of transformative. This is a tragic error.

If advocates of capitalist economic systems believe profits and markets to be 'engines of growth', these opponents adopt the same mechanical image to characterise them as destructive juggernauts, intent on destroying more socially oriented values.[17] If the conventional approach is pro-globalisation and large-scale, then these critics are diametrically pro-local and small-scale; if current elites are pro-technology, these critics are diametrically Luddite and anti-technology; if policy debates focus on humans in industrialised societies, these critics diametrically venerate the untouched wilderness, indigenous cultures and non-human species; if those in control praise profits and private property, these critics advocate a complete disavowal of both.

Such critics' strong voices have often served an extremely useful role in bringing attention to processes of environmental destruction and the need to dramatically change course. But such analysis is insufficient radical. 'Radical' means 'going to the root', while such prescriptions leave the root assumption about the nature of economies unexamined.

A necessary intervention: reinventing economics

The widespread belief that 'the economy' and 'society' are some-how separate and opposed realms was invented by mainstream economics. Letting cultural biases about the relative values of things culturally coded as masculine or feminine hold sway, main-stream economists ended up by 'playing with half a deck'. The result is economic advice that contributes to the neglect of the environment by fixating on markets and economic growth. When not informed by a gender analysis, however, 'alternative' analyses too often merely switch to the other half of the deck. By blindly rejecting capitalism and large-scale activity, they also become inade-quate for guiding us in the direction of sustainability.

A balanced view of market-using economic life, on the other hand, recognises that real-world economies are social creations. They run on both competition and cooperation, both reason-able self-interest and socially oriented norms, both innovation and conservation. We recognise that we create our economies through our individual expectations, beliefs and actions. We create them in our homes, communities, civic activities and workplaces. We create them through our collective actions, whether through 'outside' action such as boycotts or demonstrations, or 'inside' action such as shareholder resolutions or effective organisational leadership. We create them through lobbying, legislation and regulation. A 'provi-sioning' approach to economics frames it as the study of how societies organise themselves to provide for the survival and flourishing of life.

Or, unfortunately, about how they *fail* to do so.[18]

Such a realistic and pragmatic view opens the door to a wide range of action. The image of an inescapable mainstream 'market logic' stifles any initiative towards sustainability. An idealised vision of a purely cooperative, non-monetised, local economy of sharing motivates action, but does not seem to appeal to more than a smallish cadre of true believers. The pragmatic view, in contrast, suggests actions that can be taken here and now – not only by inventing new institutions, but by dedicating ourselves to making the economic institutions we already have, and in which the vast majority of us already function, respond to the realities of social and environmental needs.

One need not, for example, dogmatically limit oneself to, nor dogmatically oppose, market-based environmental policies such as carbon taxes or licences to pollute. We will obviously need far more than just a carbon tax to ameliorate the problems arising from climate change – especially among the most vulnerable populations. But if a well-designed, sufficiently large carbon tax could encourage conservation and conversion to more sustainable energy sources, can we really afford to miss this opportunity? Likewise, one need not have blind faith in, nor entertain blind opposition to, technological innovations or global-scale economic activity. A pragmatic and balanced economics approach goes with what can work, not with what is ideologically pure. It requires far more non-dogmatic, hands-on research and experimentation, and far less armchair theorising.

One more note on gender

Is this 'ecofeminism'? While I work on both feminist and ecological issues, I reject the close association of women with carefulness, community and connection with nature that can be found in some of the ecofeminist literature. I see that as simply the flip-side of the image of the association of men with agency, individualism and control of nature that got us into all this trouble in the first place.

It may be that, owing to positions in the power structure and common experiences, women and men may sometimes, on average, have different views or behaviours. But women *and* men (and anyone else) are fundamentally and equally embodied. Women *and* men (and anyone else) are individual; are connected; are rational; are emotional; are moral beings. An essentialist view that identifies women with nature and morality has the dangerous side effect of letting men morally 'off the hook' for action on sustainability. Yet, given the urgency of the environmental crises facing us, we all need to pull together.

Last words

Our habitual dividing up of the world into 'masculine' and 'feminine' camps has contributed to the creation of a belief that market-using economies are 'economic machines'. Moving us past that fundamental trap, a gender-balanced way of thinking opens new vistas. It avoids the trap of seeking a non-existent 'man versus nature' state of security, control and infinite economic growth. And it avoids the merely reactionary trap of retreating from commerce into a romanticised vision of a strictly local, cooperative, Earth Mother, no-growth society.

Of course, such an intervention will not be easy. We have centuries of deep-seated old habits of thinking about (and thinking *using*) gender, and thinking about economies, that need to be overcome. Ideological neoliberalism and ideological anti-globalisation make much simpler bumper stickers and rallying flags than does a pragmatic and nuanced 'provisioning' approach. Empowered people need an empowered economics, however, if we are to move in the direction of sustainability.

17

VANDANA SHIVA

Philosopher, activist and co-author of *Ecofeminism*

Hand in hand: women's empowerment and sustainability

What would you say to those people who say 'save the planet first and talk about equality later'?

I would say that you can't save the planet without equality. I started my own journey in activism forty years ago and in the last half-century of ecological movements, it is women who have been leading at the grass roots. Women have knowledge from their experience of being the providers for societies, the custodians of biodiversity, and that experience is vital for us to understand why the planet is being so rapaciously destroyed, as well as to understand how to save the planet.

Ten years ago, as you travelled on a train from the Punjab, you wrote an article about empowering women. Can you remind us of the main issues that you were trying to raise at that time?

This was about Punjab – where I did my physics honours and which I saw as prosperous country. I saw it erupt into deep violence, killing 30,000 people in extremism, six times the scale of 9/11. I saw that women had disappeared from the farms of Punjab; they had been replaced by chemicals and tractors. In a society where women are made disposable in the economy, they are then made disposable in their lives. In the early days I saw billboards talking about sex-selective abortion, which then became the epidemic of female foeticide. States like Punjab lead in it – 50 million girls haven't been allowed to be born in India. My sister, a medical doctor, helped to draft the law to stop female foeticide. She had a map of areas where the disappearance of girls was highest and these were the same areas where the green revolution and chemical agriculture have spread most.

What do you think, if anything, has changed over the last ten years, since you wrote that article – for better or for worse?
We are living in times where in everything there are two trends. There are two trends in terms of the destruction of the planet and the protection of the planet. There are two trends in terms of increasing violence against women – and India has become an epicentre of violence against women – but there are also trends of the empowerment of women; and it is not linear phenomena, it is very much pluralistic trends; and quite clearly the trends that protect the Earth and protect women's rights are the trends that create a decent society, a liveable society, a sustainable society.

Do you see anywhere that progress on gender equality is moving steadily forward, rather than one step forward and two steps backwards? Do you see a general trend in progress, or do you think it's circular?
I think that where gender equality is directly addressed, wherever there are bodies created to empower women directly, in law and in policy, we are doing very effective work. For example, in India we have the National Commission of Women – a statutory body for gender equality. That's the commission for which I was travelling across the country – in Punjab, in Bengal, in Tamil Nadu – to assess the impact of globalisation on women. But because globalisation, like so much else in the economy, is based on a blinkered and fragmented vision that really has been shaped by capitalist patriarchy, it defines things in a very narrow way: GDP being one of them. If you produce what you consume, you don't produce. But most women produce for the family and the community, and what they produce is consumed there, so they don't contribute to the GDP.

The increasing violence against women we are witnessing is because of the way the economy has excluded women, marginalised women, but most importantly created a world in which everyone is made to believe that everything is for sale. Your biodiversity is for sale, your water is for sale, your land is for sale – everything can be grabbed, and into that commodification fall women's bodies. All these crazy advertisements, whether selling a car or a phone, are all about the commodification of women's bodies.

So when an economy starts to touch on the devaluation of women's role and status, it brings an increasing problem of violence against women. We must redefine economic arrangements to include social externalities, like the impacts on women and ecological externalities. We're just finishing a report on the true cost of industrial farming which concludes that it is an unaffordable enterprise if you really count the costs of soil degradation, pollinator extinction, the death of our farmers. We need new economics informed by the larger picture, an economy that puts women and the Earth at the centre.

You've written and spoken about how male dominance in power relations and male-dominated viewpoints can translate into female deaths, into violence against women, into poverty for women, and into environmental degradation – especially, but not just, in agriculture. Do you see this dominance being eroded anywhere in the world, in developing or developed countries?

We see both an intensification of patriarchal signs, blinkered by the visions of men with economic and politics power, and a patriarchal economics. And the two are converging, in terms of globalisation and corporate rule, where corporate rights have higher status than the rights of people (especially women). But we are also seeing a shift, a major shift, because the crisis has become so deep that ecosystems are collapsing, economies are collapsing – not just in poor countries but in Europe; look at southern Europe, where half of the young don't have work. When you look at the big picture, people are realising that the system is only working for very few people: as the Occupy movement put it, it's a 1 per cent model. Shifting to the 99 per cent, it is the experience of women, their knowledge and wisdom, the alternatives they have in terms of what defines an economy, of what is knowledge and science – those trends, I believe, are growing very, very fast.

As a female international activist yourself, do you hold out much hope from the myriad of international negotiations on climate change, on sustainable development goals, on bio-diversity? Or is there a better way to get agreements?

Those of us who were working, especially on the Convention on Biological Diversity, and also on issues of free trade and the WTO, organised very much as women. We created a movement called Diverse Women for Diversity, which was launched in Bratislava at a Convention on Biological Diversity Conference of Parties. We created this movement for two reasons: firstly, we realised that it was only women who were left to fight the long fight, because we are not part of privileged clubs, we are excluded; but when we've crossed the boundaries, the boundaries don't matter beyond a point. Secondly, we knew that we were bringing something different into play, and I remember at Seattle we had the raging grannies, we had amazing women chefs, and we made the slogan 'WTO means Women Take On, Women Take Over'.

The work we did with the Convention on Biological Diversity, the fact that we even have a Biosafety Protocol, is because I stuck to my ground there with Article 19.3, I was appointed to the expert group to shape the protocol – it wasn't an easy job, but I don't ever give up because jobs aren't easy. At the convention negotiations in Madrid, the US government stood up, as they stand up every-where today, and said they're bringing us into the Transatlantic Trade and Investment Partnership (TTIP), saying there is no proof of harm in GMOs, it's all safe. Then a women scientist called Elaine Ingham stood up and said 'no, my government's lying to you. I've just finished research for the Europeans.' It was research on GM organisms that were meant to convert biomass into ethanol, and her research showed that all the wheat plants died with this genet-ically engineered Klebsiella even though the normal Klebsiella is fine in the soil.

So at the international level, when we were organised, we had a major impact. Women's presence wasn't big in the early days of the climate negotiations but now the women's ecology movement is becoming very active on the climate issue, both internationally as well as locally.

Your work also takes you to the grass roots, where you see immense hardship and poverty. But also I'm sure you see many inspiring cases and stories of women making real progress against the odds. Can you give us some examples of what has inspired you in recent times?
Most of my work is actually at the grass roots, especially through building the movement Navdanya, for creating seed sovereignty and food sovereignty. When it comes to seed and food, women are the primary actors; they are the main savers of seeds, they have the knowledge on seeds. We've created a very large network of women's food sovereignty. I've been so inspired by the fact that women have been able to take knowledge that is theirs, adapt and evolve it to the new context. They've organised and created producer crops and, through saving their traditional seeds and doing ecological agriculture, and shaping fair-trade markets, determining the price, they are earning ten times more than farmers chasing cash crops. We have the experience of the Bt cotton in India and the dependence on seed. That dependence, a death trap, has pushed 300,000 farmers to suicide.

I can give you particular examples: women growing millets are then making products from them. The millets see them through a bad drought year, they don't need irrigation, they're good nutrition for their own family, and they're good income for when they sell it. Compared to the soya bean, the round-up ready soya – in the Himalaya, where I come from, we have a very beautiful ancient kidney bean, whose taste is so good that it sells for much more – farmers who save the [kidney bean] seeds are now using that seed to grow the crop, to use locally themselves. We work on the principle of 'first for the soil, then for the family, then for the local market, then for the national market' (then tiny bits can be exported, but authentic surpluses). So the real economy, the true economy, benefits the Earth, the women and the children, and creates well-being for all throughout the food chain.

Does the seed ownership issue influence the Fairtrade schemes? Is it a requirement of some Fairtrade schemes that the self-seeding issue comes in there?

No, all of the Navdanya programmes are based on open-pollinated, open-sourced seeds, from community seed banks, seed as a commons. It is redefining the patriarchal construction, which Monsanto put into the WTO, of seed as intellectual property. Monsanto admitted that they wrote that agreement and they were the patient, diagnostician and physician all in one. In contrast to that, seed is a commons for the women's groups. Knowledge of how to do agriculture does not lie with five biotech companies – who actually don't know anything about farming, they just know how to shoot genes with a gene-gun. It lies with the women, particularly the elder women. One of the really inspiring aspects of my work at the grass roots is we realise that the older women have more knowledge. We run a grandmothers' university to transmit that knowledge from older women to younger women as well as children.

How does that actually work in practice? Does that have to be very localised, face to face, or can people learn from a distance?

It's both. A large part is to build community biodiversity registers, through which the young who know how to write but have lost the knowledge of biodiversity get it from the grandmothers, who have all the knowledge but don't know how to read and write. If their knowledge is not documented it will be lost for ever. This transfer of knowledge happens very locally, very intimately. But the wider reach has been a very important aspect of climate adaptation.

For example, Orissa on the Bay of Bengal has always had cyclones, but the cyclones are becoming more frequent with high velocities, reaching further inland. The seeds of the climate-resilient crops, like salt-tolerant rices, have been saved by the women and are used to grow in these coastal areas. These have not just allowed agriculture to continue in spite of the cyclones, but farmers of Orissa gifted two truckloads of seeds to Tamil Nadu after the tsunami. So the open-source seed means both that the seed can become seed and is open-pollinated, but it also means that the seed gets exchanged across farming communities.

How transferable are the lessons that you're producing through your grassroots project, either in specific detail or in terms of general lessons, to other countries and other cultures?
In terms of principles they are totally transferable, because they are the principles of biodiversity intensification. To intensify bio-diversity you have to turn to women. When I started to do seed collections I'd go to the village and I'd ask the men 'do you have the seeds of this, this, this?' and they'd say 'no, we only grow soya' or 'we only grow potato'. Then I'd go into the kitchen and talk to the women and they'd say 'of course we grow it', back in the kitchen you see this and this and this and this, because women have to take care of the children's health, and they are growing those crops that in the marketplace have disappeared. So the principles of biodiversity intensification, intensification of women's knowledge in agriculture, which is what then leads to the broader frameworks of agro-ecology, of the links between biodiversity and climate resil-ience, these work across the world. The varieties of particular crops might be different, and therefore the particular knowledge might be different, but the principles are the same around the conver-gence between sustainability, protecting the planet and women's empowerment, especially through the knowledge of the land, of biodiversity, of agriculture, of health. That convergence, I think, is common everywhere in the world if we look for it.

How does this dynamic play out in the cities – globally we're urbanising very quickly. What's the role of this kind of knowl-edge in a massively urban culture?
We are in such a deep food crisis, even though we don't realise it, as well as a deep planetary crisis, and, I would say, a political crisis of a handful of corporations trying to control the planet, its resources,

our food supply and our seeds. We've been given a model of agriculture that grows about eight globally traded commodities. In these multiple crises the city must, quite clearly, begin to look more like a village in the sense that it must conserve its water, it can't just be a consumer of water; cities must stop dumping their waste into rivers; cities must become food producers – in very little space, you can produce a lot of food. In some parts of the world – the Midwest of the USA, the Punjab in India – every part of the earth is fertile and you can make your balcony fertile.

We started a very inspiring programme called Gardens of Hope. These Gardens of Hope are for those who lost their land and their husbands, in the areas where the farmer suicides have become very intense like Maharashtra, Bihar or Punjab. But these Gardens of Hope are also spreading in schools and in urban areas, and we are encouraging people in the cities to use every bit of space to work with the soil, work with the seed, grow your own food. This works as a solution to climate change, because if we can get rid of industrial agriculture and long-distance transport, which accounts for 40 per cent of the greenhouse gases, in your little balcony with five pots you've already made a contribution. We need a mind-shift because people are feeling so helpless, that climate change is too big a phenomenon and we can do nothing about it, but when you look at 40 per cent damage and that you can have a role in reducing that, then you suddenly have power. Every citizen – women, children, everyone – needs to participate in turning the city into a producer of food. Let's not forget that in other emergencies this has been done – during the war, most food eaten in England, most food eaten in Germany, most food eaten in the USA, came from gardens.

You've campaigned personally on the issue of women's empowerment and sustainability for many years, and there's no sign you're about to hang up your boots, as they say in football. So, what keeps you going? Is it anger, is it hope, or is it something else?
It's the experience of the inner power of women and the inner power of the Earth, to produce abundance on the one hand and burst back with resilience on the other. It's that inner resilience,

that inner power, for which we have a beautiful Sanskrit word which is called *Shakti*, the power from within. It's both the power from within that I witness in women and the power from within that I experience as a women.

Who are your heroes? Do you have any role models?
Most of my role models are from the grass roots; women of Chipko, they were such an amazing inspiration for me. Peasant women who teach me so much today; I keep learning more and more from them. Most importantly, they can go through the worst of hardships and yet women don't give up, such as in the terrible climate disaster in our region last year – we've had more intense rain than we've ever had, a glacier lake burst, the hydroelectric dams aggravated the damage, and 20,000 people died. Yet women don't give up.

Do you think there's any chance of achieving a healthy planet, environmental sustainability, without gender equality? If not, why do you think gender equality is largely absent from the narrative? Not just governments and corporations, but not many environmental groups actually major on gender equality. Why do you think that is?
I don't think true sustainability is possible without gender equality. The two go hand in hand. Because the same paradigm, the same mind-set, the same worldview, that has allowed humanity to destroy the planet, is the mind-set that treats women as the second sex. One defines nature as dead matter to be exploited, the other defines women as passive, as non-creative and non-productive.

The entire challenge of protecting and defending the planet is about recognising that in the final analysis, it's the Earth that has creativity, not capital; capital is a dead construct. We have created an amazing illusion to fool ourselves that capital creates and nature is dead. When we have that switch, in that same switch is the shift that women are, actually, amazing in terms of their productivity and creativity, if their productivity was counted. So, you can't have protection of the planet without the recognition of women's contributions and women's rights.

Why is it that this has been so neglected? One, most of the grassroots movements are women-led, but by the time you get to higher levels, including in environmental organisations, they become male-led. That's in the nature of dominant power in today's world. The second reason why the issue of gender equality gets forgotten is many of those people live in very distant places, they live in their heads, in constructions, in imagination, they don't have experience. In the absence of experience, they continue to reproduce the exclusions and biases against women that those on the destruction side enjoy, and that's why there is a common agenda of patriarchal domination.

So, when you travel to Europe and talk with environmental groups here, are you aware that it's a very male-dominated milieu? The difference between my going anywhere and others going anywhere is the minute I come I get farmers attending, I get lots of women, lots of babies howling in the back; the nature of the mobilisation changes.

If you could change one thing in what remains, hopefully, a very long career, what would it be? In my life? No, I wouldn't change anything, because even the nasty experiences have been lessons of learning. I'm going through this amazing focus by the PR industry of the GMOs, who, of all the 7 billion people on the planet, can only find me to attack. But, you know, every time they attack I learn a little more. I've responded with my deepest consciousness, with the highest of intellectual integrity and very deep compassion, in everything I've done. Whichever turn my life has gone, that's the turn I took, and I have no regrets.

Looking forward, if there's one thing you could make happen, what would that be? I'd change patriarchal science, its reductionist, mechanistic assumptions; the whole GMO assault is based on this idea of master molecules commanding the rest of life how to behave. The world doesn't function like that, the world is a democracy of life. Second is GDP, which was created during the Depression and for the war to mobilise resources. It's time to give up GDP, it's time to give up mechanistic science, and shift to ecological economics and to ecological science – and that is where women lead.

18

CELIA ALLDRIDGE

Activist with World March of Women

How the defence of the commons and territories has become a core part of feminist, anti-capitalist struggles

Women on the march for autonomy over our bodies and self-determination of our territories ... until we are all free

The World March of Women (WMW) is an international, feminist, anti-capitalist movement bringing together organised grassroots women – as individuals or as part of groups, collectives, trade unions, social movements, etc. – in the struggle against all forms of inequality and discrimination against women. WMW actions are founded on anti-systemic analyses of the patriarchal, racist, lesbo/homophobic, neo-colonialist, capitalist system, with the aim of transforming women's lives through international solidarity, the strengthening of women's resistances and the construction of feminist alternatives. We carry out our struggles in our urban and rural communities, workplaces, families and public spaces, and in alliance with other progressive social movements.

This chapter looks at how the defence of the 'common good' and of our territories has become an organic part of WMW analyses and actions. It begins with a brief look at key WMW documents in order to illustrate the evolution of internal debates and continues with a reflection of the 4th WMW International Action in 2015 and the formulation of a working concept of women's territories. It ends with the ongoing feminist fight against the corporate control of women's bodies and labour force.

During this period, at both the local and international levels,[1] the WMW has highlighted the relationship between the exploitation and commodification of nature and of women's work and bodies as infinite resources within the current phase of capitalist accumulation. This chapter will show how the WMW continues to defend and strengthen feminist alternatives towards the building of societies in which the harmonious relationships between women and their bodies, between peoples, and between people and the environment, lie at the heart of the production–reproduction model.

Women reflecting on and strengthening their relationship with nature and the environment

The first key WMW document was collectively written in 2000 to accompany the 1st WMW International Action, and comprises seventeen demands for the elimination of the causes at the root of poverty and violence against women, one of which mentions the need for food security for women.

In preparation for the 2nd WMW International Action, the 'Women's Global Charter for Humanity' was collectively discussed and constructed by WMW activists around the world and officially adopted at the end of 2014. It describes the world women want to build, based on five values – equality, freedom, solidarity, justice and peace – and includes references to equal and fair access to natural resources, environmental preservation and sustainability and food sovereignty. This charter was physically and politically taken around the world during the 2nd WMW International Action in 2005, inspiring and strengthening grassroots women and their groups in urban and rural areas.

It was in 2006 that WMW activists really began to engage with the environmental debate, following the lead of the WMW–Philippines in relation to the concept of biodiversity, and from allied movement La Via Campesina in relation to the struggle for food sovereignty. At the 6th WMW International Meeting in Peru in the same year, four WMW Action Areas were proposed, with a strong debate taking place around environmental issues, which was the first step towards the definition of the Action Area – 'The common good and public services'. Delegates discussed women's role in the protection of biodiversity, seed diversity and cultivation, the use of medicinal plants, and the struggle for continued access to land and water, among other issues.

WMW international actions and activities are shaped by local struggles, and at the 7th International Meeting in Galicia, in 2008, local WMW activists organised two days of food sovereignty activities – a local produce market, a public conference and cultural activities – and environmental issues were a prominent part of political debates. Delegates also progressed significantly with the final versions of the four WMW Action Areas, including 'The common good and public services', which affirms the principles of food and energy sovereignty, the struggle against the privatisation of nature and the highly polluting capitalist production–consumption model, and our commitment to strengthening the bonds of exchange and knowledge between rural and urban women.[2]

In 2010, almost 150 WMW activists from forty countries concretely demonstrated their solidarity with women from the Democratic Republic of Congo (DRC), during a five-day programme of public debates and actions in Bukavu, South Kivu, including a women's march with 20,000 women (and men) on 17 October. We supported the protagonism of our DRC sisters as they lifted their voices and expressed their demands and solutions for long-lasting peace, and we suffered together with them as they shared their horrendous experiences of an armed conflict provoked by the fight for control of mining and forest resources that has devastating consequences for women and their communities. The control of women's bodies through mass rape and sexual and physical violence continues to be used as a weapon of war in the struggle for the control of the South and North Kivu territories and the rich mineral resources they contain.

The People's Summit 2012: feminist resistance against the green economy and false market solutions

> Women and men around the world are resisting the fact that nature is considered as a resource at the service of corporate profit, that is unlimited or just another product, and that becomes increasingly expensive as it becomes more and more scarce due to improper use. We women, in particular, are very active in these struggles. Our experience of being made invisible and with the devaluation of the work we do to care for others is very similar to the invisibility and devaluation of nature.[3]

Seven hundred national WMW grassroots activists as well as a small international delegation joined thousands of other civil society activists for the People's Summit in June 2012 to denounce market solutions to climate change, the 'green' economy and the commodification of nature. For seven days, the streets of Rio de Janeiro, Brazil, were occupied by banners, slogans and the WMW feminist *batucada*[4] that accompanied cries of 'No to patriarchy and green economy. Yes to feminist, solidarity economy!', 'Climate justice with equality for women!' and 'Eco-capitalism does not resonate with feminism!'

As part of the summit programme, WMW activists took part in several demonstrations (including a People's March with 80,000 participants), plenary sessions, self-organised workshops/conferences and people's assemblies. From within these spaces we affirmed our feminist struggle for social and environmental justice and against the commodification of nature, life and our bodies. Although the WMW did not take part in the official conference, our strong physical and analytical presence at the People's Summit contributed to the weakening of other, institutional, feminist discourses that promoted the REDD++ forestry mechanism and other false solutions to climate change without debating their impacts on women and their communities, nor challenging the hegemonic economic model promoting them.

The WMW is constructing its feminist critique of the green economy and of false solutions to the current environmental, food and climate crises from the grass roots upwards. Women know from personal experience that the market 'solutions' offered by transnational corporations and governments are causing these crises in the first place. These market mechanisms – for instance, monoculture agricultural production for export, genetically modified seeds and the enclosure of communal land for 'environmental preservation' – exclude indigenous and local communities and intensify environmental destruction and climate change.

Owing to their socially constructed responsibility for sustaining their families and communities, it is women who feel the main effects of the corporate exploitation of their land and the 'common good' (water, seeds, knowledge, etc.) and whose work and bodies are controlled through commodification, economic dependence on husbands and families, violence and excess medicalisation. From a young age, girls and women are prepared for their 'natural' tasks as non-remunerated caregivers and wives primarily in the private sphere – the home and family – and as low-paid employees in the public sphere – in the service industries, as health or education professionals, as domestic workers, etc. In this way, women are considered responsible for the reproduction of the labour force both in terms of household chores (cleaning, cooking, washing, etc.) and the emotional care of family and community members (showing love, affection and commitment).

Women's time, energy and (re)production capacities are considered infinite resources and are thus at the same time invisible (considered outside the sphere of the market) and appropriated by the capitalist patriarchal system. Faced with the current crises mentioned above, the system relies on women's work to 'make up for' the destruction and privatisation of the common good and the increasing precariousness of paid employment. Women take on multiple exploitative jobs or intensify their agricultural labour in order to continue feeding their families in the face of rising food prices. Women walk further and further to collect firewood or water, and they pick up the emotional and physical pieces of their homes and communities when they are destroyed by 'natural' disasters provoked by climate change.

On the other hand, it is also women who – from within their communities – are constructing concrete alternatives as part of the struggle for a radical transformation of the production, reproduction and consumption model. We struggle for the deconstruction of the sexual division of labour – which considers women uniquely responsible for care work, as seen above – and demand the reorganisation of domestic and care work with shared responsibility between men and women and state support. Initiatives in the areas of the solidarity economy, food sovereignty and agroecology are challenging the dominant economy, as is the priority given to building solidarity between women at local and international levels and between rural and urban women. To confront the multiple crises faced by women and our communities, it is essential that these bottom-up alternatives incorporate women's contributions and anti-patriarchal, anti-racist and anti-capitalist analyses and actions.

WMW activists are guided in this struggle by feminist economy and ecofeminism analyses, particularly where they converge around social and material relations. Ecofeminism analyses strengthen our understanding of exploitation within the system, such as Ariel Salleh's explanation of capitalism as 'built on a social debt to exploited workers; an embodied debt to unpaid women for their reproductive labour; and an ecological debt to peasants and indigenes for appropriating their land and livelihood'.[5] In dialogue with ecofeminists who have developed a radical critique of the hegemonic development model – such as Maria Mies, Ariel Salleh and Vandana Shiva – feminist economy analysis affirms the need to establish a model that prioritises the 'sustainability of human life'. This model is envisaged as being based on 'a harmonious relationship between humanity and nature and between human beings'[6] and on the relocation of collective well-being at the centre of economic and territorial organisation.

4th World March of Women International Action: a year of feminist struggle for bodily autonomy and territorial self-determination

> We are indigenous women,
> We are peasant women,
> Daughters of the land and of life,
> Struggling for our territories and sovereignty.[7]

As part of the preparation process for the 4th WMW International Action in 2015, activists dedicated time at the local and international levels to analysing the current phase of capitalist accumulation known as 'accumulation by dispossession'.[8] This process is dependent on the 'same violent mechanisms of accumulation that were at the system's origin', including 'the appropriation of nature' and 'control over women's bodies and lives'.[9] During debates at the 9th International Meeting in Brazil in August 2013, delegates and allied group guests from forty-two countries debated the current context of multiple crises and exchanged experiences of 'accumulation by dispossession' in their communities. Many of them shared very similar stories of struggles related to the defence of their land (rural and urban spaces) and for bodily autonomy; however, they had different understandings of the concept of 'territory', depending on their local realities.

In the European region, there are countries (for example, France and Switzerland) in which nationalist and/or right-wing groups have co-opted progressive discourse and thus the idea of territory has become a concept associated with the defence of 'our' borders from outsiders, xenophobia, anti-immigrant violence, exclusion, sexism and hate politics. In the Asia-Oceania and Arab regions, we have heard the experiences of sisters from New Caledonia and Palestine, for example, for whom 'territory' is a colonial term representing the 'possession' of their country by another.

On the other hand, in the Americas region, WMW activists relate strongly to the 'defence of territory' as defined by our Guatemalan sisters, who have spent many years collectively discussing and defining this concept. We have learned from them that territory is where we live, we dream, we decide, we do, and we define belonging, symbolism, spirituality and culture, and that there are four defining features: our body (our primary territory), our land, nature that gives us life, and our collective history. In the Americas, as in other regions, women personally and collectively experience a direct relationship between the violent exploitation of our land and the 'common good' (through large-scale mining, hydroelectric dams, monoculture agricultural production, etc.) and the violent exploitation of our bodies (through prostitution, sexual violence, trafficking) and the appropriation of our labour.

In Cajamarca, northern Peru, corporate mining megaprojects are destroying women's relationships with their territories (land, water, bodies), as expressed in the destruction of their means of subsistence (family farming, rearing of livestock) and a marked increase in sexual violence. Prostitution and trafficking have become much more widespread – as women's bodies are made available to male mining workers – and HIV and sexually transmitted diseases are on the rise. Women and their communities are attacked by sickness caused by contaminated water and by the state, which uses extreme physical violence to protect the interests of the transnational mining corporations.

In Altamira, the town closest to the Belo Monte hydroelectric dam construction site in northern Brazil, the impact on women's lives is very similar. Women's work is exploited through very low wages (for example, as cleaners in offices and workers' accommodation), while prices have risen significantly in accordance with the wages of Belo Monte educated technical staff. Women are no longer able to afford to pay for collective childcare (which used to be organised among themselves). Sexual violence, prostitution and trafficking have risen significantly, particularly among vulnerable teenagers. 'Women's bodies, through prostitution, are used as a mechanism to pacify tensions between [male] workers'[10] and as part of their right to leisure time, with whiter-skinned women reserved for better-paid workers, and the 'cheaper' bodies of local women of colour swapped for drugs.

Although she does not use the expression 'territory', Federici[11] describes an identical appropriation process in relation to 'the commons'. She explains how, through the process of capitalist accumulation – in its original, primitive form and now in its 'accumulation by dispossession' phase – the commons have been fenced off, expropriated, privatised and over-exploited for market profit. As part of these enclosure processes, women not only lose access to the commons, but *women themselves become the commons*,[12] as we have seen in the examples above. Women's bodies become the commons of men and the market for sexual exploitation. Parts of women's bodies become the commons for reproduction of the workforce – wombs and vaginas for giving birth, hearts and hands for care work. Women's labour becomes 'a communal good [...], a natural resource'[13] available for unpaid domestic and care work, for unpaid professional 'help' to families and communities.

For Federici,[14] feminism is fundamental to defining the commons as sites not only of collective production and consumption but also of the social reproduction of life. Efforts to collectivise domestic and care work are led by women for whom community relations promote the valorisation of their labour and the survival of their families and territories. WMW and other activists around the world are demonstrating that it is we women who 'are the main social force standing in the way of a complete commercialisation of nature' and who have 'joined hands to chase away the loggers, made blockades against mining operations and the construction of dams, and led the revolt against the privatisation of water'.[15] Women are resisting the violent attempts to destroy their relationship with their territories and actively constructing the alternatives and elements that they and their communities need in order to live well within those territories.

The feminist fight against corporate control of our bodies, commons and territories

As validated by the 10th WMW International Meeting in Mozambique in October 2016, we identify our feminist fight not only as anti-capitalist but also as anti-colonialist,[16] and we strengthen our resistance against neo-colonial forms of territorial occupation and control by transnational corporations through large-scale mining, agribusiness, mega projects ('clean' energy, infrastructure, and others) and the privatisation of social services.

In this current context of neo-colonialist territorial occupation supported by militarisation and conflict, criminalisation of social movements and activists,[17] the conservative offensive against women's bodily and economic autonomy and the rise of populist right-wing governments, women are (re)claiming the streets and urban spaces and creating feminist alternatives to the xenophobic, nationalist discourse. This was the case in Switzerland in November 2014 when WMW activists occupied the streets to say no to the 'Ecopop' initiative that aimed to drastically reduce immigration levels on the basis of 'protecting the Swiss environment and natural resources'. In Mozambique, activists from the WMW and allied organisations took to the streets of Maputo in March 2016 to protest against the nationalist-xenophobic discourse adopted by the Mozambican government to justify the expulsion of WMW International Secretariat team member Eva Moreno, a Spanish citizen who was working legally in the country. Eva was supporting and photographing a national women's demonstration against a government ruling obliging girls to wear long skirts to school to 'protect' them from sexual violence when she was illegally detained and deported.

Popular feminism is constantly being (re)created as 'a tool that gives us visibility and allows us to be protagonists of our histories and of our country',[18] built on the unity between rural and urban women. Women are struggling against the capitalist appropriation of our territories, such as in Paraguay, where indigenous and peasant women are protagonists in the struggle against an agrobusiness model of land privatisations. In a similar way, in India and Brazil, two countries that have hosted international sporting events in the last few years, women continue to say no to the commodification of their bodies for sex-tourism profit and to resist forced evictions from their urban territories. In countless places and spaces, women are self-organising in the face of intense state violence to defend their commons and reconstruct their harmonious relationship with nature and its rhythms.

We are (re)occupying territories that were once under the control of foreign or national armed forces or groups and (re) constructing territories that promote new social relations based on equality and allow the free movement of people and knowledge without frontiers or restrictions based on race, colour or sexuality. The European launch of the 4th WMW International Action in March 2015 was organised by Kurdish and Turkish women in Kurdistan on the border of Turkey and Syria. During this solidarity action, and during the 10th International Meeting in October 2016, we learned of women's key role in the organisation of the Rojava Revolution and Kurdish autonomous zones, based on radical democracy, women's liberation and eco-socialism. From Kurdistan, a European Feminist Caravan of young activists travelled across Eastern and Western Europe throughout 2015, getting to know and supporting women's resistances against territorial occupation by neo-colonial, conservative and fundamentalist forces across the continent and giving visibility to the Rojava Revolution. As our Kurdish sisters have taught us, 'no woman should be left unorganised'.

Women are self-organising against the corporate control of our lives and labour and as experienced workers in their own right, in order to give visibility and value to our labour. Women working in the fisheries and artisanal fishing sector in the Azores, for example, have created their own associations and networks across the different islands and now have a growing role in the sector and are taking part in fishing industry events that were once considered men-only. Since the Rana Plaza massacre in April 2013, women textile workers in Bangladesh have denounced the highly exploitative labour conditions to which they are subjected, and have successfully fought for higher wages and safer working conditions.

On 24 April 2017, the fourth anniversary of Rana Plaza, WMW activists across the world mobilised and occupied the streets once again – as they did on 24 April 2015 during the 4th International Action – under the slogan 'Rana Plaza is everywhere'. They united in solidarity to denounce the capitalist expropriation of women's productive labour and the patriarchal control of women's bodies in Bangladesh and around the world.[19]

Urban and rural women in all countries – especially working-class women, women of colour and indigenous women, lesbian, bisexual and transsexual women and women living with disabilities – experience the exploitative impacts of transnational and national corporate control. In the struggle for an end to corporate abuses, impunity and human rights violations, to guarantee access to justice for their victims and to oblige corporations to respect rights within international human rights law, the WMW is part of the global campaign for a United Nations binding treaty on transnational corporations and human rights.[20] Together with our allies, and in international, regional and national spaces, we, World March of Women activists, continue to march for autonomy over our bodies and the self-determination of our territories: Women on the March until we are All Free.

WMW key documents

» 'The common good and public services' (2009), www.marche mondiale.org/actions/2010action/text/biencomun/en
» Goals (revised in 2006), www.marchemondiale.org/qui_nous_ sommes/objectifs/en
» Declaration of values (2003), www.marchemondiale.org/qui_ nous_sommes/valeurs/en
» Demands (1998, 2001), www.marchemondiale.org/revendi cations/cmicfolder.2006-01-13.7149178479/cmicarticle. 2006-01-13.8582817191/en
» Rules and by-laws (revised in 2011), www.marchemondiale. org/qui_nous_sommes/statuts/en/base_view
» Women's Global Charter for Humanity (2004), www.marche mondiale.org/qui_nous_sommes/charte/en/base_view
» Call to Action: Women on the March until we are All Free! 3rd International Action (2010), www.marchemondiale.org/ actions/2010action/call-2010/en

» Women in resistance, building alternatives for a better world. Declaration of the 10th International Meeting in Mozambique (October 2016), www.marchemondiale.org/news/mmfnewsitem.2016-10-28.0582816348/en

19

MARIA MIES

Sociologist, activist and co-author of *Ecofeminism*

Mother Earth

To clarify my position regarding the concept of *gender equality*: as it is commonly used, this concept is not adequate to overcome the current man–woman relationship, which I criticise in this chapter. Because, historically, 'man's nature', his dominance over women, is not based on his physical strength but on the invention of arms – *man the warrior* – should gender equality now mean that 'women's nature' should be *woman the warrior*?

For Indians and in fact for many people in the world the idea that the Earth is our Sacred Mother is still alive. As Vandana Shiva says, '*mati*' – soil – reverberates in the songs and slogans of Indian people struggling against 'development'. 'Mati Devata – Dharam Devata – Earth Goddess' were the words of the Adivasi women in the 'Save Gandhamardhan Movement' as they embraced the earth while the police tried to drag them away from the blockade of the Gandhamardhan Hills.

> We will sacrifice our lives, but not Gandhamardhan.
> We want to save this hill which gives us all we need.

'Modern development' means the 'ecological and cultural rupture of bonds with nature'.[1] It means the transformation of the living earth, of the soil, into a dead resource for industrialisation.

In India this Earth Mother can still be seen in thousands of images, representing her many manifestations. In modern Europe, however, the idea that we are not only with our body but also spiritually directly connected to nature, to the soil, is almost forgotten.

And yet there was also a phase in European history when Mother Earth was venerated as our Sacred Mother, the source of food and life, of biological and cultural diversity and also of society. The Earth was female and sacred. This idea found expression in numerous old small clay statues which archaeologists found all over Europe. They called them 'Mother Goddesses'. As in India, they were conceived as the power who creates and regenerates all life forms by herself. As the All-Creator she would take her children back to herself in death and transform them again into new forms of life. Although she was one she was called by many names and appeared in different manifestations: as the 'Mother of Grain', the 'Mother of Animals' (birds, fish, cattle and other animals). But she was also the Mother of Water, because all sources, brooks, rivers and finally the sea, were goddesses.

As Marija Gimbutas, the late archaeologist, discovered, the 'Gods of Old Europe' were practically all female. Through extensive excavations in the Balkans, Greece, Crete and Anatolia, and her studies in central Europe, she was able to prove that the 'World of Old Europe was a civilisation of the Great Goddess'. Among the thousands of excavated images of gods there were hardly any male deities.

In her book *The Civilization of the Goddess – the World of Old Europe* she shows convincingly that the world of Old Europe was not a primitive world of poor peasants, hunters and fishermen who had to fight day in, day out against scarcity and the threat of hunger, having no leisure to create art, beauty and 'culture'. On the contrary, she calls the civilisation of Old Europe a 'true' civilisation because it was not based on violence, warfare, conquest and male dominance.

Neolithic Europe was not 'before civilization' [...] It was, instead, a true civilization in the best meaning of the word. In the 5th and early 4th millennia BC just before its demise in east central Europe, Old Europeans had towns with a considerable concentration of population, temples several stories high, a sacred script, spacious houses of four or five rooms, professional ceramicists, weavers, copper and gold metallurgists and other artisans producing a range of sophisticated goods. A flourishing network of trade routes existed that circulated items such as obsidian, shells, marble, copper, and salt over hundreds of kilometers.[2]

In fact, it was a civilisation of abundance, not of scarcity.

Old European civilisation was not the creation of nomadic warriors, who, with their swift horses, their war chariots and their far-reaching weapons such as spears and bow and arrow, were able to invade the lands of the early Europeans, who were regular agriculturists. In such societies the main mystery and wonder is the regeneration of life.

> [...] with the inception of agriculture, farming man began to observe the phenomena of the miraculous Earth more closely and more intensively than the previous hunter-fisher had done. A separate deity emerged, the Goddess of vegetation, a symbol of the sacral nature of the seed and the sown field, whose ties with the Great Goddess are intimate.[3]

In her study of the *Goddesses and Gods of Old Europe*, Gimbutas shows that there were hardly any male deities among the thousands of excavated images of gods. Old European religion was a religion of the goddess. There was no Father God. The role of men in human reproduction was not yet known in the Neolithic. But there was also not the division and polarisation between female and male and the subordination of the female to the male element which we have learned to accept as 'natural' – 'Both principles were side by side.'[4] Also, the Old European civilisation does not reveal traces of a society based on warfare and conquest. In the excavations of tombs and cities no weapons to systematically kill humans – such as swords, spears, bows and arrows – were found. There were no strong fortifications of the cities or towns or villages to protect them from enemies. According to Gimbutas, Old European civilisation 'was in the main peaceful, sedentary, matrifocal, matrilinear and sexegalitarian'.[5]

Images of the Earth Mother

The earliest European image of the Earth Mother is the 'Woman of Willendorf', found in Austria. It is dated to a period around 30,000 BC. Archaeologists found such figurines at many sites in Europe. All Palaeolithic and most later Neolithic images are characterised by similar features to those of the Woman of Willendorf: big round breasts, symbolising the giver of food, a big round belly and a pronounced vaginal triangle – the source of the generative powers of the Big Mother. She is the giver of all life. The forms of her body mean that she is not only the creator and regenerator of human life, but of plant and animal life as well. Moreover, in her body the cyclical unity of the cosmos, of the interconnectedness of all life forms, even of time and society, is expressed.

After the advent of regular agriculture (which is usually dated in the Neolithic era, c. 10,000 BC) the religion of the Old Europeans was based on the agricultural cycles: sowing, growing, harvesting, resowing. These cycles are expressed still in historical times in the names of many Greek and Roman goddesses. Thus Ceres (Rome) was the goddess of grain, Flora protected the blossoming grain, Diva Angerona was in charge of the solstices, Anna Perenna ruled over human and vegetative regeneration. Juno was the goddess of birth, Kybele, the Magna Mater, was the Mother of all life – she protected the fields.[6]

In the Rhineland (Germany) the Three Matronae were venerated till long after the beginning of the Christian era. As Young Woman, Mature Woman and Old Woman they symbolise the trinity of life, death and rebirth.

This civilisation lasted for at least 4,000 years until it was violently destroyed by invaders coming from the steppes of Russia. Gimbutas called them the 'Kurgan' people, because they built huge tombs for their leaders: 'The gentle agriculturists were easy prey to warlike Kurgan horsemen who swarmed down upon them. These invaders were armed with thrusting and cutting weapons: long dagger-knives, spears, halberds, and bows and arrows.'[7]

The thrust of the Kurgan invasions went westwards, through Ukraine, Bulgaria, Romania and eastern Hungary, following the

Danube and other rivers up to the Rhine – and southwestwards into Macedonia and Greece, even reaching the Peloponnese.

The 'superiority' of the Kurgan horsemen lay not in their culture but in their control over more efficient means of destruction – arms – and better means of transport – namely the tamed horse. The armed man on the horse was a new war machine. He could not be used for any productive and peaceful purpose, only for attacking, killing, looting, invading, conquering and colonising. The civilisation which these warrior horsemen brought with them and built up in the course of their invasions all over Europe lasts till today. The latest 'inventions' of such long-distance arms are the atom bomb and the drone. These arms can destroy faraway 'targets' without fear that the enemy can retaliate. The civilisation of 'Man the Warrior' is the opposite of that of Mother Earth. It is aggressive, xenophobic, patriarchal, it creates social hierarchies based on the subordination of women, on slavery, classes and castes. Its economy is dependent on loot, tribute and on the exploitation of foreign peoples and their lands. Man the Warrior considers himself as the creator of life on Earth, of plants, animals, even of children. In all patriarchal societies, the 'father' is considered to be creator and the beginning of human life. Even today all genealogies follow the male line. Our family names are our father's, not our mother's. Thus our mothers are deleted from history. Here we see the dilemma of patriarchal men: if they want to have sons they need women, mothers. Without women they are sterile. To overcome this dilemma Man the Warrior invented ever more effective means of destruction. The new patriarchal civilisation that grew out of the killing of Mother Earth is based on the principle Creation out of Destruction. This principle was expressed most clearly by the Greek philosopher Heraclitus, who lived around 500 BC and wrote the famous phrase 'War is the father and king of all, some he has made gods, and some men; some slaves and some free'. And we can add to this patriarchal philosophy: 'Some he made men and others women'.

If we want to understand the ruling worldview on our planet today we have only to look at this sentence coined by Heraclitus. Everything is there: War is the Father and King of Everything. He has created the world and hence he is the ruler of this world. This means he who kills is the creator and king over humans and non-humans. War is the beginning of life on earth. War also creates the patriarchal and hierarchical social order of this world, which cannot be changed: once a slave, always a slave, once a god, always a god; once women are subjected to men they will always be subjected to men. This is the iron law of our patriarchal civilisation even today. Yet the secret of this civilisation is violence, not superior intelligence or creativity. Man the Warrior needs ever more destructive arms to keep his sovereignty over all things and life on Earth. Only by killing Mother Earth can he show that he is the true Father and King.

Yet we, the women, the daughters of Mother Earth counter Heraclitus by saying: 'But nature is the the mother of life'.

This truth is still accepted, or has been rediscovered, by a number of countries in today's world, particularly in South America, for instance in Bolivia and Ecuador, where Pachamama protects the Earth and all creatures on it.

Heraclitus must have known the mother goddesses of his time and region (Turkey). Therefore the main target of 'Father War' is not just human enemies but Mother Nature herself. Because the new wars are wars of conquest of new territories, populations and particularly of women. Mother Nature as the creator of life has therefore to be killed. Matricide is the most efficient 'mode of production' of patriarchy, and his latest son or avatar is capitalism. Today capitalist patriarchy is indeed considered the only source of wealth and of modern life. It can overcome the limitations of space, time and the limits of our planet Earth. The method of achieving this goal is the same today as it was thousands of years ago: kill Mother Earth, divide the parts of her body into separate bits and pieces. Thus our living Mother Earth is transformed into dead matter, material, raw material, which is necessary to produce new 'things' .The new warrior-engineers recombine these dead parts into new machines, new engines, driven by new energy. Heraclitus would be happy: destruction as creation by Man the Warrior. War unlimited[8] is the father of progress and and of life on Earth.

Yet today many people in the world realise that this victory of 'Father War' over Mother Nature also threatens the lives and the sheer existence of all creatures on Earth. Therefore the most burning question is: How can we stop this war against nature? How can we stop the ecological destruction by our modern civilisation? How can we stop climate change, atomic pollution, air pollution, the disappearance of forests, of a number of species, of clean water and air, the poisoning of the soil by huge chemical industries like Monsanto, the destruction of biological and cultural diversity and its replacement by monoculture – in short: How can we stop those who sacrifice Mother Earth for the accumulation of money and capital?

Women, mothers, were among the first to recognise these dangers, because they ask: What future will our children have in such a world? They were also among the first who fought against the enemies of Mother Earth. But today many men and many organisations are also fighting against this ecological warfare. Many, however, believe that this is possible within the framework of capitalism. Even the German government passed laws to replace destructive energy sources with renewable ones. Like most people they want to have their cake and eat it too. Yet this will not be possible because some of the damage done to nature cannot be repaired – witness climate change and its consequences for the entire world. The only way to save life on Earth is to stop the war against nature and create a totally new civilisation, based on love and respect for Mother Earth.

20

JUDE KELLY
Artistic Director of Southbank Centre, London

From icebergs to climate refugees

Jude Kelly joined Southbank Centre in 2006 and set up the Women of the World festival, held each March, in 2011. She's well known for fitting in a great deal to each day, so this Q&A took place at 8.30am in a café on her route to work – and just after she'd finished a phone meeting with participants, based in a very different time zone, planning next year's WOW.

What made you alert to climate change?
It grew slowly but the pivotal moment was one that most people sadly wouldn't have access to. I went to the Arctic on the second Cape Farewell trip, with a group of twenty scientists and twenty artists. The whole purpose was to watch the scientists measuring climate change in the Arctic and then to consider as artists how you would tell that story that would alert the public to it in an emotional way, through the heart rather than only in a factual way. We did indeed measure glaciers and sea depths and temperature of the water but the thing that most stuck in my mind was actually seeing an iceberg. It was so close that I felt that I could almost touch it. The ominous scale of it was just extraordinary and also the overpowering beauty. The visible reality of it – and knowing that the melting of that area couldn't help but have this incredible effect on other parts of the world – made me think about climate change profoundly.

What did you learn about talking about climate change?
At the time I was running the Southbank Centre – still am – and in 2009 I invited Cape Farewell to be artists in residence in order to build that conversation. In preparation for that, I had so many conversations with scientists and realised their struggle to communicate is actually very similar to many stories where you're trying to alert people to a problem –whether that's a health problem, an issue of poverty, homelessness, whatever it is. It's why people create adverts about an individual. It's because as humans, we connect to identifying with our own pain, our own loss, our own happiness, and we can extend that to animals. It's harder, because we're less practised at it, to extend it to this idea of The Planet, The Environment. Obviously when you talk to indigenous communities, their world includes an idea of an indivisibility between ourselves and the Earth and all creatures and all physical elements. They have that in their cosmology in a particular way, and we don't.

Going to the Arctic was a luxury. We have to think of other ways to understand climate change and that's what it made me think about. When I grew up in Liverpool, at school you sang *All things bright and beautiful, all creatures great and small* ... in the Christian tradition. The Bible describes what God made first and then the human was the finale, so we've been taught that we are more important than the Earth and other living beings.

There is a reductive way that humans have come to think of themselves. Even if you're not religious, you have a residue of all of this thinking that this Garden of Eden was in order that humans could then have a fantastic time. When they were rejected from the Garden of Eden, then their job, in a way, is very focused on human behaviour, and how humans can get back into the Garden of Eden. There's no real discussion about being looked after or being equal in the Garden of Eden, is there? Now, I'm not a religious person, but really what I'm saying is that this idea of the cosmology is hierarchical with humans at the top. So I think it's hard for people imaginatively to reposition themselves into a place that isn't just a sort of 'Well, we ought to look after our planet' ... Other religions deal with cosmology differently – few, though, are giving equal weight to the planet as a whole.

How did you take the environmental conversation to colleagues?
Some members of the staff were further ahead than I was. I don't feel that we are having a conversation in the creative industries that's fully joined-up yet, but in the past ten years the conversation has definitely accelerated. Because if you're interested in community welfare, in the impact of how expressiveness releases people, how expressiveness is a key agent for people to be able to speak about who they are and share who they are, and build empathy and understanding, then you're propelled towards ideas of what's a caring framework for an individual, what's a caring framework for communities of all different kinds, and therefore what kind of world do we want to live in? You're already in the territory of 'What kind of world do you want to live in?' because you're thinking about equality, inclusion and about individuals having agency. So that conversation is already taking place among all my colleagues and now is extending to climate issues.

We really have to be prepared to face the impact of climate change on communities, whether it's flooding in some parts of the world or drought in sub-Saharan Africa. Whatever it is, you can look at the facts and you can start thinking about the appalling impact climate change has on communities. As a human, you can empathise with that and be frightened on everybody's behalf. People understand oil spills and they're horrified. They understand Chernobyl and toxic wastelands, but an abstract idea of the Earth fading in some way, or the atmosphere being harmed, I think that's harder for people. I don't feel like I'm leading these conversations. I'm including myself in them.

What are your thoughts on gender equality?
In the process of gaining gender equality, you have to begin from a premise that equality is a human justice, not because one gender is nicer than another or more deserving than another, or one is more equipped than another or more intelligent than another, because

that's just a reversal of where we are with patriarchy. But what I observe is that women have roles ascribed to us about caring, nurturing, watching and observing. We've had thousands of years of observing. That, I think, has given women an intelligence about what happens if a society becomes dominated by selfishness and what happens if a society does the reverse and is more egalitarian and shares more. Because I think that the model of a good loving home is one that has a place for everyone, a voice for everyone. This is something that women have been steered towards and therefore are very practised at, though I'm not saying that they always succeed. It's a different model to the war-like 'kill or be killed', which is what a lot of male education has been geared towards.

For the survival of the planet in a good and healthy way, you have to include the planet in your set of thinking – in your family, as it were. It has to be part of that conversation. And I think women understand that and are less embarrassed about the idea, or are more inclined to feel that is instinctively correct. That seems to be borne out of the conversations you have in indigenous communities. For example, we do a Women of the World festival in Katherine, north-west Australia, run by indigenous Aboriginal women. They are extremely matter of fact about the way that they are absolutely bound into the Earth and with the earth. Men may hold all those philosophies too, but my observation is that women are the ones who somehow feel they are the guardians of it

What's special about WOW?

It's the idea of women and girls telling stories to each other in language that is *their* language – not academic, not party political. Of course it can be, if that is how the woman chooses to frame her story, but it's really about trying to get girls and women to celebrate their history, their present and their future, and be courageous about any obstacles that prevent them from realising fully who they could be. The festival covers all subjects and it covers all kinds of women – it is hugely intersectional. I don't believe there's any other way of understanding the world unless you see it as a massive jigsaw made up of so many different intersections, and you try to understand those intersections and believe that your world will be so much less if you didn't have these great varieties of voices.

We do WOWs all over the world. There are twenty-one countries now. What I find is that women and men want a shared platform for many different kinds of people. In the end, they don't want to say, 'This is our version of the tribe and we'll just talk with each other.'

Do you have any leadership tips?
First of all, be your whole self. There's no way you can pretend to be somebody else anyway. And I think some of the things that have been thought of as leadership in the past – the ability to be ruthless, the ability to be single-minded – are all to do with the notion of being 'tough'. Good leadership is demanding, definitely, but there's no reason why you can't bring huge amounts of love and emotional identification (empathy) to leadership.

Leadership has a notion in the end about 'bucks stopping' and 'taking responsibility', but you can strive for greater collegiateness – and I think you should, because you're trying to give people more responsibility, more involvement, more self-realisation. I'm not saying that those things are innately female, but they are the ones that females practise. Instead of covering them up, I think women should enjoy them. They're great attributes in leadership. As long as you're not doing them because you're frightened of not looking authoritative. Besides, we all are frightened anyway, so that's just a given; most people are frightened quite a lot of the time about lots of things. The best of all of ourselves is brought out by more equal voices at the table. I think women struggle with being told, from when they were a little girl, to smile and be pretty. I think that wanting to be liked is often a stumbling block for women.

What's your take on climate refugees?
One of the problems we have with groups who need help, whether they're women in violent situations or people suffering from homelessness, is our instinct for going (a) 'Well, thank goodness I'm not them' and (b) 'Thank goodness I'm not like them.' We're somehow

encouraged to feel – or we let ourselves believe – that we're cleverer and more competent because we haven't ended up in that situation. We know it's absurd; we're an individual but refugees become lumps of people. It really prevents us hearing this huge amount of knowledge which they have individually. If you talk to any individual refugee, whether they're economic migrants or migrants of war or migrants of climate change, they have very particular stories to tell, and expertise about why certain things happened and the consequences, but we are really bad at listening to the narrative of each of those people.

The human brain and the human heart are capable of understanding masses of complications, but we're lazy and we kind of go, 'Well, just give me the elevator pitch.' The elevator pitch on refugees is: 'They're a problem. What should we do with them? Where can we put them?' As opposed to: 'How has the axis of the world been shifting?' We're all involved in that. Where do we start talking? How do we talk together to find answers? So I think that there are two different things with refugee communities. One is to push back the potential for hate, and the other is the really fertile space which is realising that refugees are people who have expertise that we don't. We need to flip the conversation.

What next?
In 2020, we are aiming to do a six-month festival that talks about climate change at Southbank Centre. We will use that to gather artists from around the world and scientists and thought leaders who are debating how to take the most effective steps about climate change.

21

NIDHI TANDON

Networked Intelligence for Development, Canada

From individual to communal rights: empowering women for sustainable use of natural resources

This contribution draws on time spent interviewing, walking with villagers and witnessing the eroding base of women's security and empowerment in rural and informal sectors in some African countries, a trend that has heightened in the last decade. The countries in question share some common features: a colonial legacy of peoples displaced from their ancestral lands; vast and valuable natural resources; high illiteracy rates among rural populations; patchy rural infrastructure; the vestiges of weakened traditional accountability systems; and investment policies that significantly favour the industrial commodity chain[1] over peasant-based food sovereignty.

Needless to say, rural women in these arenas are caught up in extremely challenging situations of feeding and providing for their families today while trying to plan for the future – a future fraught with unknowns. The narratives and experiences from women in Uganda, Tanzania, Malawi, Mozambique, Zambia, Zimbabwe, Ghana and Liberia all echo and reverberate to a common strain – their struggles are intensifying, their opportunities are limited and they are close to breaking point as their relationships with land, water, with natural capital[2] and with the public commons are weakened on multiple fronts.

In conversations with these women, it is apparent that they want their roles dignified, valued, recognised and supported. Where women are able to articulate their interests, or when their values and priorities are incorporated into policy-making and planning, more compelling demands are made for longer-term and holistic outcomes around health, education, food security and overall well-being for the community as a whole. In many senses, these are the bedrock factors of sustainable economies. Relative to men, women's immediate interests in these public services are especially high.

That said, rural women are *by no means* a homogeneous group. Some women are *so* disenfranchised, having no say in the decisions that affect their lives, that they will settle for hourly labour within the globalised production system at any price. In more desperate circumstances, they will rely on humanitarian and community assistance. A growing number of women and women's networks, however, are standing up to protect their version of sustainable or natural economies; their rights to public spaces; to seed, forest and water; to health, nutrition and secure food sources, despite the increasingly tenuous situations that they may find themselves in. More often than not, they are pushed to a point where they are prepared to lay their bodies on the line to prevent further displacement and disempowerment, at great personal risk. They are the 'shoot me first' constituency. Unregulated consumption, population growth, the commercialisation and privatisation of land and water, and a compromised political leadership that cares less about these women, all serve to heighten the stakes.

Between a rock and a hard place

Liberia has one of the highest land concession rates on the continent. The government of Liberia has a range of policies and laws for the community management of natural resources and has signed up to related international agreements. It is still in the process of defining its new land policy and, notably, has not passed the 2010 Gender Equity in Politics Bill. The concentration of plantation and mining interests is extremely high; one 2012 report puts the total land allocated to rubber, oil palm and forestry concessions at approximately 25 per cent of the country.[3] A series of recent studies warn that agro-investments[4] in Liberia have not met the expectations of all communities; and that some communities have lost access to land resources and their food security in the process.[5]

Public scrutiny is pushing big companies to comply with national laws and regulations. Under pressure in Indonesia and Malaysia for their part in widespread deforestation, Asia's leading companies in the palm oil industry are turning their attention to Africa. On paper, palm oil companies have access to over 622,000 hectares and an average market capitalisation of US$8.2 billion in Liberia.[6] There are four main concession agreements at the moment with a total investment of about US$2.56 billion. If the agreement with Sime Darby to plant on 220,000 hectares goes ahead, then this is more than the total land area that the company had planted in Indonesia in 2009 (even though Indonesia is more than fifteen times the size of Liberia) and ten times more than the total area of oil palm plantations established in Ghana.[7] This gives a sense of scale to the plantation expansion in Liberia.

Traditionally, palm oil[8] is primarily a woman's crop; it ceases to be so once it enters the global supply chain. In the domestic markets across the West African region, women are the majority stakeholders in a thriving local supply chain in palm oil processing, palm fruit marketing and palm kernel processing and marketing. On the international market palm oil is increasingly traded as feedstock for biofuel although its primary use is for human consumption.

These developments could become a steep price to pay for the promised benefits of revenue and employment, as the portion of land managed by rural Liberians decreases. If community engagement around land use decisions is not integrated systemically into government policy, the resulting societal tensions could be trigger points for local grievances, conflict and violence. The long-term implications of losing land and dignity are well documented and the particular impacts for rural women are acknowledged by the international community.[9]

At the same time, with costs of living rising, the need to earn becomes more pressing. Faced with few options, and with the reality of their low employment marketability, women and men in rural communities will look to new rural investments with some expectation of employment, infrastructure development and service provision. In one palm oil plantation nursery, women are engaged in short-term seasonal work to bag, weed and administer chemicals to the palm saplings for the equivalent of US$5 a day. In one community on the borders of an oil palm plantation, one man works as a security guard; his pay is shared among his three brothers and their families, none of whom are employed. In an interview he observed: 'There are very few jobs at the plantation. We have to pay to get the job.' In Malema town, none of the women interviewed worked on the plantation. They farmed on the fringes of the plantation, supplementing their needs with charcoal burning, and had relinquished farmland to the plantation.

Rural women in Liberia already play significant roles in managing natural resources for their food, fuel, shelter and water needs. They have central and multiple relationships with natural resources that are core to their day-to-day livelihoods. They might not recognise the value of this management function themselves, and they might not be drawing the links between their farming practices, deforestation and long-term water sources. Yet on a day-to-day basis, they fulfil a wide range of activities that are directly linked to natural resource management. Asked to describe their relationships with natural resources, women invariably talk about these activities and are less likely to refer to their extractive (aggregates and mining) activities, as these activities are perhaps more mercenary or opportunistic in nature – driven by market demand and the need to supplement income. Artisanal mining continues to be a critical aspect of resource extraction in this country, requiring gender-specific policies, because of the non-formal and highly exploitative nature of the sector.

When it comes to the formal commercialisation of natural resource extraction, women's involvement becomes invisible and is put at risk, primarily because women do not have control over the decisions taken on land and natural resource access and use. Their relationship with the production and processing of these natural resources is reduced to a purely transactional one. In the process of commercialisation of these resources, women and their productive activities are invariably pushed out to marginal lands – where the environmental impacts on the physical environment can be especially taxing.

Entry points for policy intervention and regulation

Using the UN System of Integrated Environmental and Economic Accounts as a basis to categorise and analyse natural resources (Figure 17.1), four areas emerge for policy development.

Public commons
Most of the country's water, land and air are held as community property in the public commons, with distribution of natural resources traditionally governed by male elders in the non-formal economy. Women access these resources for energy, home construction and for income.

Figure 17.1 Entry points for policy intervention and regulation

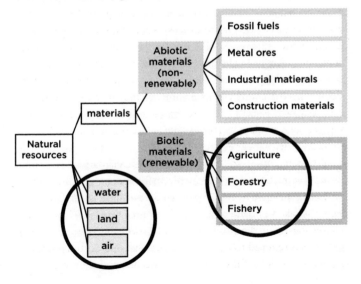

Food security

The circles superimposed on the figure highlight those natural resources that underpin formal and non-formal rural economies. The substantive basis for food security lies in agriculture, forestry and coastal and inland fishery, whose day-to-day management is predominantly undertaken by women.

Extractive activities

The extraction of non-renewable metal ores in the non-formal sector, artisanal small-scale mining (ASM) and plantation businesses all rely heavily on the support roles of women. The benefits they derive from these activities, however, remain largely peripheral.

Non-renewable materials

As the commercial exploitation of land and non-renewable abiotic materials intensifies and grows, women's access to the public commons and to biotic materials in the non-formal (communal) sector needs protection and strengthening, while enabling women to take engaged positions in the formal (private) sector.

Roadside markets showed a 'vibrant self-employment' informal economy based on the exploitation of natural resources. Neatly tied bundles of bamboo, wood and thatch for construction, sacks of charcoal, piles of rock and slate broken into different sizes, piles of wood for burning and hills of sand of various gradients speak to an entrepreneurial drive or need to earn cash. It is not clear what implications this may have for the natural environment from which these items are extracted, whether this is regulated in any way, or whether there should even be any control over these public commons. While these existing natural resources are community assets, a question needs to be raised about the replacement value of these assets and whether there are other, more sustainable alternatives to be considered as sources of income for the poor. The entrepreneurial spirit and drive need to be complemented by awareness and action to replace and regenerate what is being mined.

Empowering women to reclaim and advance community assets and rights

With population growth, competition for natural resources and growing inequalities, the empowerment of rural women needs to take place on multiple fronts. Empowerment is the process of enabling people to be actors in their own solutions to their issues. In the case of rural women, this will mean wresting back power to take control over the decisions that affect their domestic household security, in their informal and communal (public commons) spaces as well as in the formal and political arenas.

Policies that promote women's empowerment tend to lean towards 'economic empowerment', the assumption being that with expanded economic means come more and better choices. The more financial leverage one has, the more likely one is to project power: gain voice, respect, independence and the ability to negotiate terms and a more favourable hearing. In reality, in the course of earning income in mines, plantations or in the informal natural resource economy, women are systematically exploited, have decision-making choices taken away from them and are left with denuded natural environs – a heavy price to pay for so-called empowerment.

The empowerment goal will need to be to strengthen not only women's daily management roles, but also their capacity for directly engaging in community decisions around (i) how natural resources are developed, (ii) how the benefits from extraction of natural resources are fairly shared over time, and (iii) how they might themselves engage in supply chains. Given their societal status and relative lack of assets, women are more likely to lead change as a group than as individuals. They will need to build networks of solidarity with community members across gender barriers to articulate and act on collective interests. This becomes especially difficult in rural areas, where villages are relatively isolated from each other and where transport is a significant and expensive challenge.

Women's relationships with natural resources require transformative change to current practices and policies that discriminate against or undervalue women and their productive activities. Some fundamental bases for change include:

» **Correcting gender imbalances in landholding and use** through deconstructing, reconstructing and reconceptualising existing rules of property in land under both customary and statutory law in ways that strengthen women's access to and control of land while respecting family and other social networks.[10]
» Empowerment within the holistic agro-ecological **farming framework** – integrating organic farming practices with food security and natural resource management through **changing the mode of farm practice to a holistic agro-ecological system, including tried and tested models such as organic and permaculture farming which will integrate community management of natural resources with their food production activities.**[11]
» Enhancing the proactive contribution of women in defining and implementing alternative solutions to their local fuel needs, shifting towards clean and renewable energy systems.
» **Supporting the mobilisation, political consciousness and organisation of rural and urban women** to improve their situation, influence policy and realise their rights – at decentralised, local, national and political levels.
» Raising public awareness about rights and access to natural resources as both a **public service and a civil rights issue.**

From patriarchal traditions to gender-sensitive common regimes

Now more than ever, poor women and men must claim their rights of access to natural capital within the framework and cultural context of common property, community rights and community responsibilities and solidarity.

As in many African countries, the traditional management of forest landscapes in Liberia is made up of a complex hierarchy of gender relationships, knowledge and customs. An adult male 'bush manager' is appointed by the elders to manage access to forest resources, covering a number of villages, to prevent the over-exploitation of these resources. Women are not part of this group of elders, the suggested reason being that women are 'afraid' to make decisions and because they are excluded by the male secret society. Most sacred groves of the male secret societies[12] are associated with forests, with strong oversight by members. Taboos and sanctions prohibit the exploitation of forest resources for commercial gain. When it comes to land access, both men and women have equal rights to private ownership of the flood plains for sugar cane production, although capital availability limits women's investment relative to men.[13] With the demise of these local and hierarchical structures – through changing political space and the influence of Christian and Islamic teachings – this kind of localised forest conservation service is on the decline.[14]

The questions then arise: How can the appropriate aspects of traditional value systems that policed community use of natural resources be adapted to a gender-sensitive application of rules and procedures that empowers men and women in these communities? How can the empowerment of women within the collective framework secure their rights to natural resources? How can rural communities that sustained a non-formal rural economy be supported as they enter unmediated agreements in the formal economy that expose them to the risks of global markets? These are questions we need to address.

One response is offered by the Nobel laureate Elinor Ostrom, who argued that economic activity can be effectively regulated by *collective social activity*.[15] She applied the term Common Pool Regimes (CPRs) to categorise such forms of property. Her findings documented that collective community ownership of resources by rural communities may foster the evolution and adaptation of sustainable resource systems (or regimes). Along with clear rights and functioning policies for public goods and the commons, fostering collective rights to common property helps to secure the future provision of ecosystem services. Ostrom challenged the assumption that common property is poorly managed unless regulated by government or privatised, and proved that individuals can success-fully form collectives that protect the resource at hand. This way of thinking sits at the heart of the way pastoralists and rural women might measure the value of natural capital – where the idea of private ownership of part or all of an ecosystem runs counter to communal access to the biosphere.

The OECD Development Assistance Committee, the World Bank and international NGOs are renewing their focus on access to natural resources as a core component of poor rural people's entit-lements as citizens. Natural resources management and agriculture knowledge, technology and public services are of key importance to support natural-resource-based livelihoods, particularly in the face of environmental, climatic and market changes that require new solutions and adaptation.[16] These new solutions, behavioural changes and adaptive practices will need in the first instance to consider how women can be empowered to be community archi-tects for the future.

22

ANNA FITZPATRICK

Centre for Sustainable Fashion, University of the
Arts London

The role of fashion in bringing about
social and ecological change

This chapter will outline some of the projects undertaken at the
Centre for Sustainable Fashion (CSF) which highlight how fashion
can be used to honour and empower those who produce, consume
and use it, and which also recognise the need for stewardship and
nurture of the Earth. The chapter starts with a short outline of
CSF's vision for understanding fashion. It then highlights some of
CSF's key projects, which aim to show how fashion can bring about
social and ecological change. It concludes with some final thoughts
about the importance of fashion as a form of action in bringing
about social and ecological change.

The Centre for Sustainable Fashion (CSF) is a University of
the Arts London research centre based at the London College of
Fashion. It was established in 2008 by Professor Dilys Williams,
who has 'created a place for exploration [...] an academic research
centre with sustainability as its starting point and fashion as its
means of application'.[1] In using fashion in this way, there is an
explicit recognition of the potential of fashion to challenge current
power structures and discourses around resilience, community,
care and resource use to create a more just and equitable society
for all. CSF's aim is to bring sustainability approaches to fashion
through academic research and education (for both undergraduate
and postgraduate students), and to share these approaches through
a two-way knowledge exchange with key players in the fashion

industry. CSF offers new perspectives on fashion's relationships and processes, which balance ecology, society and culture within both the artistic and the business context of fashion.

Since CSF's approach to fashion is multidimensional, it recognises that those involved have sometimes conflicting goals and ideals. Fashion as an industry is located within current mainstream business practices, which are dictated by neoliberal market forces and demand a particular pattern of production and consumption. It also requires workers with a particular set of skills, who exist in a particular set of relationships to all those others involved in fashion in the broadest sense. Fashion is also about items of clothing. The physical garments embody a choice about the use of resources from a design perspective and also represent an opportunity cost in terms of land and resource use. 'Fashion' is also a social practice of communication, expression and identity formation, which, for some people at least, is in contradiction with the mainstream business practices in which garments are produced. Indeed, not dismissed by all, Marx recognised the importance of fashion in signifying social relations, terming them 'social hieroglyphics',[2] recognising both the items and their meanings.

Similarly, CSF's engagement with sustainability is equally multifaceted, recognising the need for deeper change rather than tweaks in efficiency that ultimately do nothing to challenge the current model of economics, production and the values inherent within this. The contradictory and paradoxical nature of sustainability as applied to fashion certainly requires looking beyond market solutions. We need to challenge many of our preconceived ideas regarding fashion as apolitical and our general failure to realise the agential possibilities of change within both the industry and wider social practice.

Why fashion?

Despite the importance of the fashion industry both culturally and economically (fashion contributes £26 billion annually to the UK economy[3] and is part of the much celebrated and exported 'creative industries'), it has not always been given the consideration or recognition that architecture or food, for example, have received, given the indisputable human dependence on such industries. Bruzzi and Church Gibson highlight the difficultly in theorising fashion, as all too often it is seen as being 'too trivial to theorise, too serious to ignore'.[4] This leaves fashion in a difficult space where its cultural strength and power to engage, express and communicate are ignored while it is also dismissed as wasteful, narcissistic, feminine and superficial. Lipovetsky also recognises this neglect: 'it [fashion] turns up everywhere on the street, in industry, and in the media, but it has virtually no place in the theoretical inquiries of our thinkers [… It is] seen as a superficial issue.'[5] The challenge then is twofold: to recognise the importance of fashion culturally and as an industry, but also to develop an approach within fashion which will challenge dominant discourses and systems of power, and give a more central position to values such as care, compassion and the cultivation of relationships.

Challenging values such as competition, individualism and material success, which are currently given prominence within the fashion industry perhaps at the expense of care and compassion, allows more space to recognise the gendered nature of fashion in production, consumption and the creation of social meaning. To discuss fashion and its potential to bring about positive change in the lives of all involved in its production, consumption and use means acknowledging the value contributed by all involved, recognising, as Yuniya Kawamura does, that 'fashion is not created by a single individual but by everyone involved in the production of fashion, and thus fashion is a collective activity'.[6] And those involved are, for the most part, women. It is an industry in which the majority of makers are women who in turn are making things for other women. However, it is also worth remembering that when it comes to the balance of power within the fashion industry, men – as conglomerate owners, factory owners and in factories – hold the senior roles in many fashion businesses: therefore, there is a gender power imbalance throughout the industry which needs to be addressed. In this respect it is no different from many other industries.

Asking questions

Fashion's complicated relationship with the media and the proximity of these gendered industrial relations add further layers to the analysis of fashion's relevance to questions of social and ecological change as well as women's empowerment. Whose voice is being heard? Who makes the decisions and on what values are they based? These are questions that constantly need asking and answering. Femininities and feminisms are central to the equation, and, within current fashion and sustainability discourse, it is as consumers that women are largely discussed – which is not surprising given that much of the discourse is dominated by commercial thinking. As Mirjam Southwell asks, within the paradigm of sustainable fashion as consumption, is it women's responsibility to demand sustainable fashion?[7]

Around the world, millions of women buy fashion items as a move towards distinction and independence, sometimes conforming and at other times subverting and challenging the disciplining discourses around women's bodies. At the same time, millions of women are engaged in its making and production. In some cases, this too is a means to independence; in others, quite the opposite. The production of fashion garments illustrates only too well the gendered and racial exploitation contained within the structures of global capitalism. Again, the question is what will we do to change this reflection we see in the mirror? In Bangladesh, for example, 80 per cent of the workforce are women, making garments largely for export, and we (as consumers) are then linked directly through the clothes on our bodies to the hands of those making the garments and of those whose lives, as *other*, are treated as disposable, as the collapse of the Rana Plaza garment factory in 2013, killing more than 1,100 workers, showed only too well.

Clearly, within fashion considered as a whole, there are complex and interlinking issues that need to be challenged and changed. Within its various facets, from lighter-touch industry initiatives to research and educational projects, various approaches are being utilised, and there is now a greater acknowledgement that change needs to happen, even if this is motivated by the bottom line. The following projects highlight ways in which CSF uses fashion to challenge some of the issues raised above, through giving voice to others, or being used in place making and in promoting alternative economic systems in which equity, cooperation and care all matter. These are values that can challenge the overt and subtler power structures in play within fashion as a business and as a mode of communication.

Habit(AT)

Habit(AT) is a research project led by CSF's Director, Professor Dilys Williams, that seeks to explore our habits of living, through fashion's actions, relationships and locations framed in the context of the city. It also focuses on the role of the fashion designer in mediating conversations in place using a fashion garment, in this case a T-shirt, to explore the concerns of people that arise from living in urban locations.

It is a body of research, which engages participatory design methods to explore ways in which fashion can contribute to social resilience in an increasingly urban-centric world. It was born out of a small ethnographic study in Ahmedabad, India, where conversations and photographic evidence about clothes in relation to place and self were gathered and then displayed through the exhibition 'Unbox Future Cities' entitled 'I Wear My Culture'.[8]

With 66 per cent of the world's population expected to be living in cities by 2050 (up from 54 per cent in 2014),[9] what we can do within the city environment, both as individuals and collectively, matters greatly. Human ingenuity and collaboration between individuals and groups will create a space for positive and active solutions, while education and new approaches to fashion can create empathy and compassion, which are vital to the empowerment of those rendered vulnerable within our current economic and political systems.

There is an opportunity here to engage and develop a fashion design methodology that encourages designers actively to mediate through the public and other collaborators and to facilitate 'fashion making as community and place making'.[10] Through this project, the design and wearing of clothes is explored as a social process and fashion becomes associated with conviviality, active participation and the 'making together' of both the social and material elements.[11] The most recent iteration of the project took place at Chrisp Street Market in Poplar, East London: it offered an opportunity to use fashion design and garments to recognise community in place, to contribute to a more resilient society, and to explore a local community's thoughts and ideas about nature and biodiversity.

'Craft of use'

Professor Kate Fletcher, also of CSF, explores the 'craft of use' through her work. It is an approach to fashion that frees it from the confines of market-based exchange and challenges the very nature of economic growth inherent within the current fashion industry and our economic system more widely.

> In contemporary consumer culture we organize our ideas about fashion around commerce and consumerism and end up becoming dependent on them […] within this distinctive hierarchy of fashion provision and its ideology of continuous market growth, independent and shared expectation of creating fashion have been increasingly forgotten.[12]

Her approach is to look deeply into how we use and engage with our clothes. By moving away from a discourse of consumption and production, fashion can more freely address creativity, resourcefulness, ingenuity and skill. We can learn to recognise and appreciate the value of clothes while at the same time more thoroughly examining the system within which fashion currently operates and where there is room for resistance and change. The focus on use draws upon, and values, the knowledge and skills that are vital in fashion and in life: 'use presents fashion opportunities and experience differently, as grounded in people's actions and approaches, as part of an iterative on-going engagement with garments that thread through and mark our lives'.[13] As well as providing a challenge to the current 'fashion as consumption' mentality, this approach also has implications for fashion design and emphasises fashion as a place and form of action, for action is crucial to empowerment and hope.

Dress for our time

Fashion is a powerful tool of communication and can be harnessed both to amplify important social messages and to involve people actively rather than as passive recipients of a sustainable garment. Professor Helen Storey's most recent work, *Dress for our Time*, uses the allure and cultural power of fashion to address directly issues of climate change and the mass displacement of people. Professor Storey created a dress from a decommissioned UN refugee tent, which once housed a family of displaced people at the Za'atari Refugee Camp in Jordan and which was gifted to her by the Office of the United Nations High Commissioner for Refugees (UNHCR). Through the relationships developed in the making and exhibiting of the dress, Professor Storey has visited the Za'atari Camp in her academic capacity and is co-creating a cross-disciplinary educational, cultural and business programme focused on women and girls in the camp. To date, the project has engaged seventy women, delivering short accredited beauty courses. A high number of participants are now going on, in partnership with CSF, the UNHCR and other partners, to set up female-run enterprises within the Za'atari Camp. Through fashion as both a material and symbolic object, Professor Storey has been able to create a series of practical projects that seek to improve the lives of refugees in the camp.

This brief snapshot of some aspects of CSF's work highlights the importance of a holistic approach to fashion, and indeed one in which fashion is understood and taken seriously beyond the boundaries of the market. It is widely accepted that the current neoliberal economic model is flawed from both a social and an ecological perspective; that the Earth has now entered a new geological age, the Anthropocene, in which human behaviour is now irreversibly impacting on the Earth's ecosystem; that the 'safe operating space for humanity' as laid out by the Stockholm Resilience Centre[14] is already under strain; and that wealth inequality is increasing both within and between nations. In short, there is much to change. And while fashion is not unique in adopting business practices that champion deregulation and engage in the 'race to the bottom' through supply chains which snake across the globe, the detrimental role it plays does not go unseen. Within this context, mainstream fashion practices are part of an exploitative neoliberal model of production and consumption that continues to heap pressure on natural resources and the delicate ecological balance of our Earth, while social injustices and dominant political discourses seem to go unchallenged.

Through the work done at CSF, one call to action is that a socially and environmentally foregrounded approach to guide an examination of the fashion system is in order, and this is something the projects outlined above seek to do. We need to step back and approach the root of social and ecological problems with a wider lens, giving room to the complications, contradictions and nuances inherent in the system. In this way, fashion can value the human. As Professor Dilys Williams states, 'fashion is derived from the bringing together of people through the crafting of form with beauty and value. At the heart of humanity lies the ability to cherish and to be cherished, so processes of creation, enjoyment and caring should imbue the relationships that fashion makes real.'[15] Fashion must be recognised as a viable tool of empowerment on multiple levels.

A second feature that grounds the work done at CSF and is integral to its approach to sustainability is the recognition that fashion is a collective activity, since it is through the lens of fashion that we can all look for ways of making connections with others and empowering them. To echo Kate Fletcher, CSF's Professor of Sustainability, Design and Fashion:

the whole is the problem – the cumulative values, discern-
ments, habits of mind, industrial practices, business models,
economic logic, deep societal forces and aggregated individual practices that make up the fashion and textile sector
[...] and it is the whole we must understand before we
consider the functions and needs of its elements. Sustainability is dependent on how the parts work together, not on
how the parts work in isolation.[16]

As well as embracing this holistic approach, CSF understands
sustainability to be a relational concept, 'a dynamic balance among
three mutually interdependent elements: (1) protection and
enhancement of natural ecosystems and resources; (2) economic
productivity; and (3) provision of social infrastructure such as jobs,
housing, education, medical care and cultural opportunities'.[17]

Like fashion, sustainability is an active and dynamic process,
and therefore the focus of sustainability cannot be focused solely
on the product. A product cannot possess sustainability, but it can
be designed to respond to its makers and users in a sustainable way.
Sustainability is not singularly about minimising negative impact,
but also about maximising positive impact, allowing individuals,
communities and economic systems to flourish. The work outlined
above exemplifies this approach.

Through this chapter, we have seen that fashion is about more
than the clothes we cover our bodies with, and it is important
precisely because it brings together deeply private, personal and
political expressions of ourselves, while opening a space for debate
around the production and consumption practices that shape
this particular historical moment. As an industry, it is a means
to a livelihood and an emotional form of identity expression,
which surpasses and yet includes the individual self. It is a form
of non-verbal and embodied communication, which provides a
mirror in which, if we look closely enough, we can see a reflection of the society we live in. Our gaze, then, must contain both
questions about why things are as they are and a commitment to
actions that will bring about change. Thus, we will understand

that the importance of fashion lies in its embodiment in material objects and in its communicative symbolism, as well as in its capacity to generate a form of praxis.

23

CARINA HIRSCH

The Margaret Pyke Trust, with the Population & Sustainability Network

Family planning: a win-win for women and sustainability

Advancing and improving access to voluntary and rights-based family planning is a win-win for both women and sustainability. Fulfilling and respecting women's and girls' rights to family planning is not only fundamental to ensuring human rights to health, well-being and empowerment (all critical ends in themselves), but also contributes to furthering sustainability goals. In this chapter, we explain the links between family planning, global population and environmental sustainability, and ways in which family planning, when integrated with other development actions, can achieve greater development and sustainability outcomes than single-sector programmes. We also demonstrate how family planning can contribute to improving human and planetary health, including as part of climate change response and resilience.

Meeting the unmet need: unleashing the power of family planning

For those of us fortunate enough to live in developed countries, generally speaking, we have the necessary rights, information and access to a variety of contraceptive options to manage our own fertility, and healthily space and time our pregnancies, should we decide to have children. We are also very likely to be able to choose whether we marry and whom; and we benefit from numerous health services including antenatal care, resulting in, relative to many developing countries, very low levels of maternal and child mortality and morbidity.

In many areas of the world, however, the scenario is very different: an estimated 214 million women and girls in developing countries have an unmet need for modern contraception. The World Health Organization defines the 'unmet need' as those women and girls of reproductive age who either do not want children or want to delay their next child, but are not able to access any method of contraception.

In sub-Saharan Africa, 21 per cent of women and girls have an unmet need for contraception, while Southern Asia is home to the largest absolute number of women and girls who lack access – 70 million.[1] The United Nations Population Fund estimates that 24 per cent of women and girls in Uganda and 14 per cent in Niger have an unmet need for family planning.

The Margaret Pyke Trust, the coordinating body of the Population & Sustainability Network, knows well from its own work undertaken in health facilities in Uganda, South Africa and elsewhere that issues preventing girls and women from freely accessing family planning services are many and various, such as health professionals' negative attitudes towards youth, deeply rooted local myths, patriarchal social structures, insufficient clinical training and supply chain issues, to name just a few.

In many developing countries, girls and women face other related challenges. For instance, one in three girls in developing nations is married before the age of eighteen[2] and women are 300 times more likely to die in childbirth compared with their counterparts in industrialised nations. Their children are fourteen times more likely to die in the first twenty-eight days of life and children in sub-Saharan Africa are more than fourteen times as likely to die before age five than children in developed regions.[3] There is also great variation within countries: these alarming statistics tend to be even worse in rural areas. Fulfilling the unmet need for modern contraception in developing regions, and ensuring that pregnant women and their newborns receive essential care, would result in the following declines from 2017 levels:

» 67 million fewer unintended pregnancies (a 75 per cent decline);
» 23 million fewer unplanned births (a 76 per cent decline);
» 36 million fewer induced abortions (a 74 per cent decline);
» 2.2 million fewer newborn deaths (an 80 per cent decline);
» 224,000 fewer maternal deaths (a 73 per cent decline).[4]

By helping women prevent unintended pregnancies, we can also reduce unsafe abortions.[5] For all these reasons, those of us in the sexual and reproductive health and rights sector understand the critical importance of family planning, but the impacts of family planning are greater than those outside the health sector might realise. Empowering women with contraceptive options and other vital reproductive health services also supports progress towards a number of development priorities and reduces population growth and the overall costs of achieving development goals. Economists estimate that every US$1 invested in universal access to contraception saves countries US$120 in reduced need for infrastructure and social spending.[6] Similarly, up to US$6 can be saved in interventions aimed at achieving other development goals, including those related to gender equality, the elimination of poverty and hunger, education, HIV/AIDS and environmental sustainability.[7] Family planning saves lives, and it does much else besides.

When girls can avoid unintended pregnancies and complete their education, there are positive ripple effects. Of course, maternal mortality drops, as do the mortality rates of their children, but this also leads to a lower incidence of HIV/AIDS and malaria, and educated girls realise higher wages and greater upward mobility, contributing to women's economic empowerment.

Sustainability: what's population got to do with it?

It is clear that family planning directly benefits women, their children and families, and there is increasing understanding that furthering women's rights benefits women *and* the environment; it's a win-win. Women with more years' education have fewer, healthier children and are better able to manage actively their reproductive health. It is precisely in those areas of the world where girls are having the hardest time accessing education that population growth is fastest and environmental degradation is greatest. Addressing these issues together can kick-start a positive chain reaction, improving women and girls' well-being, while also responding to environmental concerns.

For instance, the Margaret Pyke Trust is working closely with two Population & Sustainability Network member organisations, Pathfinder International and the Endangered Wildlife Trust, to implement a project responding to a poor, rural community's inter-related health, environmental and livelihood needs. At a rural site in South Africa, near the border with Botswana, a community is struggling to support their families in the face of degraded agricultural land, erratic rainfall, climate change, population pressures and an unstable ecosystem, upon which they rely for their livelihoods. Environmental actions alone, livelihood actions alone, or family planning actions alone cannot adequately respond to the inter-related challenges faced by this community. Three Population & Sustainability Network members working with the community are combining environmental, livelihood and family planning actions, to lead to long-term sustainable change, benefiting both human and ecosystem health.

There is growing recognition among development experts that when development challenges are interrelated, as they are in the age of the Sustainable Development Goals, then the solutions must be too. While this growing recognition is encouraging, it has yet to lead to the necessary actions being taken on the ground that are critical for sustainable development. But there are some promising developments, such as the formal recognition of family planning as a potential climate adaptation strategy.

Family planning as a recognised climate change adaptation strategy

The Intergovernmental Panel on Climate Change, the global scientific authority informing the United Nations Framework Convention on Climate Change (UNFCCC), affirmed in a 2014 report that family planning can play a role in reducing climate change vulnerability and is a potential adaptation strategy.[8] The reference to family planning in the report should lead to UNFCCC decisions and policies on adaptation planning, encouraging the inclusion of it in national climate change plans and recommending action on these issues moving forward. To date, few countries have included family planning in their national adaptation programmes of action (or similar national climate change plans), though the majority of developing countries cite a direct connection between population and climate change.

The recent publication *Drawdown: The Most Comprehensive Plan Ever Proposed to Reverse Global Warning* details the top hundred solutions that have the greatest potential to reduce emissions or sequester carbon from the atmosphere.[9] The majority of these are 'no-regret' solutions, or initiatives that the world should implement regardless of their ultimate impact on emissions and climate as they are practices that benefit society and the environment in multiple ways.

In *Drawdown*, educating girls ranks sixth and family planning ranks seventh in the top hundred solutions as the authors cite the powerful positive impacts on health, welfare and life expectancy of women and their children, as well as the myriad benefits for social and economic development and the effects on curbing greenhouse gas emissions. The potential is greatest in developed countries such as the United States, which has the highest global levels of consumption *and* high levels of unintended pregnancy (45 per cent of all pregnancies). Improving access to family planning in high-consumption countries will improve women's sexual and reproductive health and contribute to reducing emissions. Enhanced access to family planning will also increase the resilience and adaptation capacity of the world's poorest countries. While those in poor countries bear no responsibility for climate change, many are already feeling its effects.

Empowering women and girls as agents of change

The critical role that women play in advancing environmental sustainability has been recognised for some time. The 1992 Rio Earth Summit noted that: 'Women have a vital role in environmental management and development. Their full participation is therefore essential to achieve sustainable development.'[10] In developing countries, women make up 43 per cent of the agricultural labour force and produce 60 to 80 per cent of food crops.[11] Women are responsible for collecting water in almost two-thirds of households. This experience makes them an invaluable source of ecological knowledge and expertise on environmental management and appropriate conservation actions.[12]

As the primary resource managers for households, women are disproportionately affected by environmental degradation, including water scarcity and deforestation, and they may also have a stronger impetus to ensure that local natural resources are used sustainably.[13] Compared with their male counterparts, women have less access to a range of resources, including land, credit, technology and education. Several studies demonstrate that if women had access to the same resources as men, their outputs would actually surpass parity. This has significant implications in low-income countries; it would lift large numbers of people out of poverty and hunger. The Food and Agriculture Organization of the United Nations estimates that, under the scenario of equal access to resources, 100 million to 150 million people would be lifted out of extreme poverty and hunger. Therefore closing the gender gap would also benefit carbon emissions; with improved agricultural output, the pressure to deforest additional land is less and soil quality is better preserved.

Indeed, there is evidence to suggest that women are more responsive to changing their behaviour towards environmentally friendly practices. Women are more likely to recycle, buy organic food and eco-friendly products, and place a higher value on energy-efficient transport.[14] Women increasingly play roles as stewards and managers of land, food, soil, trees, water and other natural resources. When girls and women are educated they can marshal multiple ways of knowing how to observe, understand and take action to sustain themselves and those who depend on them.[15] A study of 130 countries found that countries with higher female parliamentary representation are more likely to ratify international environmental treaties.[16] Local institutions of forest governance with a higher proportion of women have been shown to be associated with significantly greater improvements in forest conditions and conservation.[17] Likewise, community water and sanitation projects run with the full participation of women are more effective and sustainable than those without.[18] It becomes very clear that what is good for gender equity is also good for the environment.

What has this got to do with sexual and reproductive health and rights?

Worldwide, women and girls bear a higher burden of unpaid domestic work and undertake most of the parenting.[19] As well as negatively impacting their health and options for pursuing educational and employment opportunities, this presents a gendered barrier to women's full participation in governing their community and society, including environmental management and decision-making. Research looking specifically at women's role in forestry management in developing countries has found that frequent pregnancies, and the associated childcare and increased domestic responsibilities of women with larger families, reduced the involvement of women in forest conservation efforts.[20]

In contrast, a woman who is healthy and able to choose the number and timing of her pregnancies is more resilient to natural resource constraints and climate change, and better able to manage resources effectively for her family and community. A woman with access to family planning is also better able to balance her reproductive and productive roles, allowing her to engage more effectively in livelihood and income-generating activities. Additionally, being able to plan her family means that her domestic burden is more manageable, she faces fewer constraints in realising her aspirations, and she has more capacity to engage in environmental activism and stewardship. As shown below, a number of 'Population, Health and Environment' projects in developing countries are achieving just that.

Population, Health and Environment: a revolution for women and the environment?

For too long, conservation and human development agendas have been distinct from one another – and even in competition – and have failed to address the critical relationships between people, their health and well-being, gender equality and the environment. But this may be starting to change, thanks to a growing movement of community-based projects in developing nations combining reproductive health interventions, and primary healthcare more broadly, and education with natural resource management, conservation and other sustainable development initiatives. These 'Population, Health and Environment' (PHE) programmes take a pragmatic and holistic approach to the interconnected issues of poor health, unmet family planning needs, food insecurity, poverty, unsustainable use of natural resources and environmental degradation. Integrating these factors creates synergies and reverses this vicious cycle, improving the health of both communities and the ecosystems on which they depend.[21] Their effectiveness over single-sector approaches is proven. A comprehensive review of ten years of PHE projects funded by USAID revealed that PHE projects often have greater buy-in from communities and more rapid mobilisation of community efforts, leading to quicker short-term results in the first one to two years of the project, and longer-term, sustainable impact.

The success of these projects is by no means limited to addressing the unmet need for contraception and associated fertility reductions. By responding to the priority needs of communities, these projects are able to foster greater local trust and buy-in, helping build local ownership of conservation programmes and grassroots movements with the potential to deliver sustainable change.[22] This has been the finding of an integrated programme in an isolated coastal community in rural Madagascar.[23] The project, implemented by Population & Sustainability Network member Blue Ventures Conservation, started as a marine conservation programme but quickly evolved to include reproductive health actions, including offering family planning services. This evolution was in response to a community-articulated understanding about declining fish stocks, with locals citing that the pressure on fish stocks was partly due to the number of people fishing and the lack of alternative livelihood options. Offering reproductive health information and services has provided opportunities to engage women and foster their involvement in natural resource management, and in turn men have become more supportive and involved in reproductive health issues.[24]

PHE programmes often lead to increased access to and involvement of men in reproductive health. Simultaneously, the integrated messaging and interventions often result in increased access to and involvement of women in conservation and natural resource management activities, when compared with single-sector interventions. The PHE Ethiopia Consortium, another Population & Sustainability Network member, found that, in communities integrating family planning and environmental livelihood interventions, more husbands (30.2 per cent) were supportive of their wives' choices to use family planning than in communities that did not benefit from such integrated programmes (7.3 per cent).[25] Women whose husbands support their use of family planning were seventeen times more likely to use family planning methods. The findings suggest that, overall, the PHE approach has positive outcomes in fertility and family planning behaviours and environmental conservation when compared with a single-sector approach addressing only reproductive health.

An integrated development agenda: a win-win for human and planetary health

Environmentalists sometimes include population-related perspectives in their work and specifically advocate for reproductive rights. An example is provided by the collaboration between the Population & Sustainability Network and Friends of the Earth on a common position on global population, consumption and rights. The paper concludes that 'a rights-based approach to accelerating the positive trend of declining rates of population growth is necessary' and provides a number of shared, wide-ranging recommendations.[26]

Programmatic actions, as well as policy actions, can promote family planning as a win-win for women and sustainability. The joint project of the Margaret Pyke Trust, Pathfinder International and the Endangered Wildlife Trust mentioned above, which is being implemented in Groot Marico, in the North West Province of South Africa, is one example. The community named the project '*A Re Itireleng*' (a local Setswana phrase meaning 'Let's do it ourselves') and it is designed to respond to the community's related needs for sustainable livelihoods, access to family planning information and services, and improved general health. The Endangered Wildlife Trust is providing the community with sustainable livelihood training, Pathfinder International is undertaking family planning clinical training, and the Margaret Pyke Trust is coordinating activities and leading the integration of project actions, including by developing integrated community education materials on the project themes. By integrating conservation and community health actions, PHE projects such as *A Re Itireleng* have led to greater health, gender and environmental outcomes compared with traditional single-sector projects.

Similarly, the International Planned Parenthood Federation, one of the largest global providers of sexual and reproductive health services, working in 172 countries, called on the Margaret Pyke Trust to collaborate with them on a joint advocacy and communications toolkit highlighting the links between family planning and climate change, to help family planning advocates in those

172 countries engage in climate policy discussions and to promote family planning as an adaptation strategy. Clearly, some conservation organisations and some sexual and reproductive health and rights organisations are seeing the connections.

The advancement of gender equality and meeting the unmet need both offer rights-based ways to address population-related environmental concerns, delivering benefits for women and the environment. By pursuing these strategies, environmental activists can help empower women and girls to make decisions that are a win-win for themselves, their families, their communities and the planet. One cannot rationally argue with a development approach placing women's rights at its core that also responds to environmental issues from a human rights perspective.

Two common population questions

1. Isn't the problem consumption, not population?

Both need to be addressed in a rights-based manner. It is true that the vast majority of future population growth is projected to take place in the poorest countries of the world,[27] where per capita consumption rates are much lower than in the developed world. Developing regions have contributed least to environmental degradation and climate change but it is precisely these areas that are already bearing the brunt. At the same time, developing countries are experiencing pressures at the local level caused by population growth. For example, the majority of developing countries have identified high population growth and density as undermining their capacity to adapt to climate change by exacerbating environmental problems and undermining other development efforts.[28] Furthermore, to lift growing numbers of people out of poverty, the world's poorest will need to consume more[29] – in line with their right to development. However, given the pressing nature of the global environmental challenges we face, especially in developing countries, we should be drawing on all potentially beneficial strategies at our disposal. Only human rights-based strategies should ever be implemented, and voluntary family planning is one such strategy.

2. With global fertility on the decline, hasn't the problem been 'solved'?

It's not quite that simple: global fertility levels may be declining but fertility is not declining in all areas of the world. Forty-six per cent of the world's population live in countries with below-replacement fertility (where women have on average fewer than 2.1 children over their lifetimes).[30] But the population in some developing countries is still growing rapidly, and even when fertility does drop to replacement level, the population will continue to grow for several decades, as the youngest generations reach reproductive age. Between now and 2050, the world population is projected to increase from today's 7.3 billion to 9.7 billion.[31] More than half of this growth is projected to take place in Africa, where the population will double between today and 2050, and quadruple by the end of the century, reaching over 4 billion.[32] These levels of growth in the world's poorest countries will inevitably exacerbate the challenges already faced in alleviating poverty, ensuring food and water security, and providing access to health and education services for all. In Niger, for example, one of the world's poorest countries, women have, on average, 7.6 children, and only 8 per cent of sexually active women of reproductive age use a modern method of contraception. The population is growing by 4 per cent each year.[33]

This chapter is an updated and revised version of the chapter originally written by Sarah Fisher.

24

KATE METCALF
and colleagues

UK Women's Environmental Network

The power of grassroots action for women's empowerment and the environment

Women's Environmental Network (WEN) is the only organisation in the UK that has worked consistently to make the links between women, health and the environment. WEN was established in 1988 by a group of women involved in the green movement who felt that women's perspectives were overlooked by mainstream environmental organisations. WEN's vision is of an environmentally sustainable world in which we have achieved gender equality; we attach equal importance to both and believe they can and should be achieved simultaneously. Achieving one without the other is not possible or desirable.

In real terms, this means WEN aims to inspire women to make environmentally informed choices and to empower women to become agents of change in their families, networks and society. We focus on five key programme areas of health, waste, food, climate change and women's empowerment; but all of our work highlights the intersectionalities of gender, inequality and environmental issues, especially in the urban setting in which we work, in Tower Hamlets, London.

Past projects and successes

Since forming in 1988, the Women's Environmental Network has campaigned, published high-quality information and run practical sessions on issues which lie at the nexus between women and the environment. We have brought a gendered analysis to environmental debates such as climate change, where a gender-blind focus has been the norm, but also have broadened the scope of what is considered an 'environmental issue'. This focus has seen us tackling a range of subjects such as sanitary products, menstruation, harmful chemicals in cosmetics, breast cancer as an environmental disease, stress incontinence, cloth nappies, food growing and seed saving.

Enviromenstrual issues

Many of WEN's campaigns have centred on products which cause both health risks and waste. In 1989, WEN campaigned for dioxin-free and unbleached products and achieved the widespread agreement of manufacturers to use chlorine-free pulp in papers. In 1992, WEN persuaded tampon manufacturers to provide clear health warnings about toxic shock syndrome on the outside of all tampon packs, also pushing for new research on this condition. WEN continues to provide regularly updated information on alternatives to sanitary towels and tampons which are both environmentally friendly and avoid the numerous associated health problems. This work has helped to break down the taboos surrounding menstruation.

In 1992, WEN persuaded tampon manufacturers to provide clear health warnings about toxic shock syndrome on the outside of all tampon packs, also pushing for new research on this condition. WEN's briefing 'No laughing matter' provided free information on preventing and managing stress incontinence, another taboo issue which affects nearly 17 per cent of women over eighteen and has extensive environmental and social impacts.[1] An awareness-raising campaign examining the environmental causes of breast cancer in 1995 continued to explore the links between women's health and the environment and pushed for precautionary chemical regulation.

Waste and real nappies

At the beginning of the 1990s WEN launched its first packaging waste campaign, Wrapping is a Rip Off, which involved the promotion of reusable products such as cloth handkerchiefs. We initiated the Waste Prevention Bill, which was first presented to Parliament in 1995 and evolved into the 1998 Waste Minimization Act, which gave local authorities power to introduce waste reduction measures.

WEN has consistently campaigned to raise awareness of the environmental impacts of disposable nappies, and in 2003 pressure from WEN resulted in the government prioritising nappy waste in its Waste Implementation Programme. WEN launched Real Nappy Week, which takes place at the end of April and has become a mainstream event supported by numerous UK local authorities, and developed Real Nappies for London and the Real Nappy Exchange to provide parents with information and access to local real nappy sellers.

Harmful chemicals

WEN's work around chemical hazards has included a 1993 campaign around the pesticides, lindane in particular, used on cocoa which then end up in chocolate. A year of campaigning led to the regular testing of chocolate by the Ministry of Agriculture, Fisheries and Food. Lindane also had an adverse effect on the women cocoa harvesters as it was alleged to cause miscarriage. Towards the end of the 1990s, WEN also published a set of briefings on genetic engineering and was one of the founding members of the Five Year Freeze. In 2005 this became the GM Freeze campaign, which continues to push for a precautionary approach with regard to the propagation of genetically modified food and the patenting of genetic resources.

WEN's work on harmful chemicals in cosmetics began with our 2002 report, *Pretty Nasty*, which exposed the use of phthalates in European cosmetic products.[2] This was followed by *Getting Lippy: Cosmetics, toiletries and the environment*, a briefing addressing both the social pressure on women to use cosmetic products and the specific health risks accompanying them.[3] Alongside this, WEN began providing resources and workshops on making your own natural beauty products, known as Fruity Beauty, and also Toxic

Tour workshops inviting women to undertake a toxic tour of their bathroom cabinets to find out about the potential harmful effects of the chemicals in their toiletries.[4]

Gender and climate change

WEN has consistently pushed for the promotion of gender aware-ness in climate change action and policy. In 2007, we launched a Women's Manifesto on Climate Change in partnership with the National Federation of Women's Institutes, calling on the UK government to involve women in decision-making on climate change and provide economic incentives and carbon labelling to enable them to reduce their environmental impact.[5] During the 2009 Copenhagen Summit, this was developed into a comprehen-sive report (*Gender and the Climate Change Agenda*), which found that climate change is exacerbating existing gender inequality and demanded efforts to address this inequality, as well as gender-sen-sitive climate change mitigation and adaptation strategies.[6] We condensed this report into a four-page briefing, 'Why women and climate change', in order to make it more accessible to a wider audience.[7] The briefing outlined how women are more affected by climate change owing to gender inequality, have contributed less to it and are not equally involved in decisions about solutions to address it, despite often being best placed to report on and tackle the problems. For example: women are more likely to suffer from an increased workload as a result of climate-change-related disas-ters such as an increased burden of water and fuel collection, and they are more likely to suffer violence, including sexual violence, in resource conflicts exacerbated by climate change.

Current grassroots work: the Local Food project

For the past fifteen years, WEN has been working on food-growing projects with low-income and unemployed women from black, Asian and minority ethnic (BAME) backgrounds in the London Boroughs of Tower Hamlets and Hackney, both of which have some of the highest levels of deprivation in England.[8]

It is estimated that 40 per cent of Asian and black women live in poverty in the UK, and Pakistani and Bangladeshi women are the most disadvantaged, earning the lowest salaries of any ethnic group and experiencing poverty at greater rates.[9] Thirty per cent of Tower Hamlets' residents are Bangladeshi.[10] Therefore, WEN's food-growing project aims to address the problems of poor health, social exclusion and barriers to education associated with this deprivation, particularly for women, as well as contributing towards a more sustainable food system.[11]

The WEN Local Food project encompasses a number of smaller projects, which complement and enchance one another. As the local lead for Capital Growth in the borough, WEN coordinates the Tower Hamlets Food Growing Network: a network of food growers supported by four seasonal gatherings a year, a community seed library, email updates and a resource directory. The Network is comprised of individuals, community groups, community gardens, mental health groups, housing associations, council representatives and Tower Hamlets Public Health, and was set up in 2010. The Network is an easily replicable model which serves to enhance and promote the community food-growing activity already taking place in the borough, as well as to raise the profile of food growing and access to healthy, fresh food for people on low-incomes, and enabling environmental issues to be addressed in an accessible way. Bringing people together from all different cultural backgrounds around a common issue has proved to be very beneficial. WEN also offers Spice it Up! organic food growing training, which empowers disadvantaged women to grow their own organic food and to share their knowledge and expertise with others. The project addresses the social isolation of marginalised groups such as Somali and Bangladeshi women, while also promoting biodiversity and green spaces in a densely populated urban area. It aims to help the many women in East London who lack access to formal horticultural and other training owing to gender, language, cultural and financial barriers. Spice it Up! provides a space for women to develop new skills and confidence and places value on their cultural food-growing knowledge.[12]

WEN has a unique role in the area, providing women-only activities for disadvantaged BAME women, who are often reluctant to attend mixed-sex groups and who face particular cultural, practical, psychological and institutional barriers to learning.[13] The social and health benefits of community food growing are becoming widely known and locally valued. In an evaluation of the Tower Hamlets Healthy Borough Programme, coordinated by NHS East London and the City, community food growing was found to be particularly positive, generating a wide range of health and social benefits, strong community enthusiasm and buy-in from social housing landlords. Given the wide recognition of the importance of community food growing, the London Borough of Tower Hamlets recently commissioned a community gardening service which WEN successfully bid for in partnership with a number of local Registered Social Landlords (RSLs), including Eastend Homes, Poplar HARCA and Tower Hamlets Community Housing, and Capital Growth/ Sustain. WEN coordinated this project, 'Gardens for Life: Tower Hamlets Community Gardens', creating fifteen new community gardens with residents on housing estates, at community centres and in sheltered accommodation centres. Beneficiaries of this project received training and ongoing support and were linked into the Tower Hamlets Food Growing Network to ensure sustainability. The Network has been a great way to integrate people of different cultural, social and economic backgrounds, but above all a safe space for women and men to share.

Food growing for domestic use can provide its own economic benefits, such as improved access to healthy affordable food. Organic food is often regarded as a luxury, but growing food without the use of chemical pesticides and fertilisers is a straightforward cost-saving measure for the majority of small-scale and low-income growers. From our experience, Bangladeshi women in particular are expert organic gardeners, using agricultural skills and a culture of gardening that have been passed down through the generations in Bangladesh. Valuing traditional knowledge of this kind is important in empowering women, fostering community and making the most of community diversity.

Developing skills

Volunteering at community food-growing and urban agriculture projects has also been found to increase employability of individuals and aid the transition to work through the development of transferable skills, increased confidence and social support, the development of technical skills and formal qualifications, and linking participants to networks that increase their chances of finding employment opportunities.[14] This has particular significance for BAME women, who are more likely to face cultural and psychological barriers to formal employment, but for whom food growing can offer an enjoyable and culturally appropriate form of engagement, with the potential to lead on to further opportunities.

Women's role in the alternative food economy: successes and constraints

One goal of WEN is to facilitate the self-empowerment of women as social, economic and environmental actors in accordance with feminist principles. WEN also seeks to build communities both among women as well as among larger communities of interest where women and the environment are prioritised. These efforts have been and continue to be successful in many respects, but challenges and constraints are ever present. Constraints include working with women who don't speak English, making empowerment efforts challenging. Time constraints mean that many women have very little spare time and often have to be back at noon to cook lunch. Successes include training hundreds of local women in organic food growing as well as building relationships through Spice it Up! and helping to set up numerous community gardens. Working with partner organisations, WEN is building a borough-wide network of community gardens, as well as a network of women who support each other in their food-growing efforts. WEN is also very proud of their community seed library, which is continuously developing. There are, however, ongoing challenges to our goals, primarily in relation to sustainability. Women's organisations and services across the board are facing huge funding crises. It is not an easy sell when people and funders think that gender equality issues have been solved and mainstreamed, so therefore do not see the need for a separate women's organisation or a specific gender focus on environmental issues.

Gardening allows ethnic minorities to express their cultural identities in the crops (e.g. okra, chilli, coriander, sweet potato, callaloo) they choose to grow and how they organise their gardens.[15] Programmes such as Spice it Up! celebrate cultural diversity and women's knowledge and allow Asian women, in particular, the opportunity to share their gardening and culinary culture with their neighbours. Gardening in a community of women can also give women the confidence to become involved in larger community greening efforts.

Through these same avenues of renegotiation, acts of growing and other forms of self-sufficiency by women can also be seen as a feminist act.[16] By taking the power of production back from some of the large-scale exploitative economic processes, women can gain a greater say in their own economies. This is not without its tensions, as women have historically and still largely remain responsible for food provision,[17], making tough choices concerning nutritional value when providing food on a tight budget.[18] Valuing these women's existing food-growing skills is vital as these skills are routinely devalued in the mainstream economy.

It is easy to see how food growing positively impacts women in terms of their familial food budget. It can, however, be a challenge to translate those skills into direct economic power for women outside of the home. Possible economic benefits might involve selling produce locally, or perhaps finding paid employment using agricultural skills. One possible means of making community gardens financially sustainable is to sell produce to local restaurants or markets, as mentioned above, and we are beginning to see relationships develop between community gardens and local business, yet more work needs to be done in this area to help ensure success. WEN would also like to see food provision and other domestic tasks shared equally with men to reduce women's burden.

Spice it Up! revalues food-growing skills that are going to become increasingly important in the face of peak oil and climate change – challenges which our current economic system cannot resolve. Small-scale food growing projects are one way of reinvigorating local communities to take more control of their food security and put sustainability at the forefront. Crucially these projects develop vital skills such as cooperation, working with nature and fostering community resilience in the face of the above challenges. Local small-scale action is often devalued in the global economy, along with women's skills and knowledge. We believe that projects such as Spice it Up! are valuable not just economically, but above all socially, culturally and environmentally, and play a small part in creating an alternative food economy with women at the forefront.

Planning sustainable cities: ensuring participation of marginalised voices

There are many authors with greater knowledge and experience of the planning system and its limitations or possibilities for creating positive change in light of the environmental crisis than WEN. We can only share our experiences of working with marginalised communities on community gardening projects, but we feel there are useful lessons to be learned from this for how we can create truly participatory processes for consultation in planning for sustainable cities.

In our Gardens for Life project, we were aware that how we went about setting up new gardens would affect how well the project delivered for people who needed it the most. If we had advertised an open call for submissions on ideas of vacant plots of land or even people who were interested in helping to set up a new garden, we would not have reached the most marginalised people in the borough who might not have been able to read the advert, respond to it or have had the confidence to do so. We decided to do this by working with providers of social housing who identified possible plots of land, then knocking on people's doors in the area and asking them if they wanted to grow their own vegetables. Our experience was that a small number of people were interested initially, but once the project got physically started many more people would come forward and want to get involved. In one particular place just three people were interested at first, but this quickly grew to over 20 households in a block of 60 flats. Most of our participants on housing estates were from the Bangladeshi community, and most were women. Many did not speak English or read and write. It is highly unlikely that these participants would have come forward as a result of seeing an advert either in the mainstream or social media, or even after seeing a poster in their building. However, these participants were the most engaged and the most invested in the project as it grew.

Our experience demonstrates that what could be perceived as a less 'open' and transparent system for community engagement is actually what is needed to directly target the most marginalised and oppressed groups in our society.

We are planning to work on a project that promotes the integration of a gendered approach to climate change policies at a city level in London. We will be using participatory approaches to work with women – particularly low-income BAME women – as we are committed to an intersectional approach which looks at how multiple inequalities can compound the effects of climate change. The aim is to work with these communities to co-produce gender sensitive climate policies for London.

Conclusion

At the grass roots is where Women's Environmental Network currently works, educating and enabling women and men (through the Tower Hamlets Food Growing Network) in disadvantaged areas of London to take back control over their food, positively impacting their health and the environment by growing their own food in community gardens.

We would advocate that similar approaches be used more extensively in environmental and gender equality struggles. WEN is creating and facilitating spaces where women can share and value their knowledge and skills, which are routinely devalued by the mainstream economy and patriarchal society. Food growing and gardening are non-threatening, non-controversial ways to engage with many women who are isolated and not participating in wider societal structures. It is a useful strategy to address their practical gender needs, although we also aim ultimately to address their strategic gender needs. It provides not only a platform to talk about wider environmental issues such as climate change in an accessible way with very concrete examples rooted in people's lives, but also works as a tool for language learning and social inclusion.

We have also found that while many women we work with would be uncomfortable attending any social activism events such as an anti-GM protest, they do feel strongly about the topics and are keen to engage in a practical way. We take them on a journey, because for many women just getting out of the house is a big hurdle to overcome. We have seen that the Tower Hamlets Community Seed Library empowers women by providing a way for them to take action by saving and sharing seeds with one another; engaging with the environmental issues in a way that they are comfortable with. WEN would like to see similar inclusive approaches bringing people together to build networks for sustainability and gender equality. In this context, using a covert feminist approach is more effective than an overt one, although we do endeavour to engage the women we work with in wider political and environmental issues such as biofuels, seed sovereignty, climate change and gender equality. Our vision is an environmentally sustainable world in which we have achieved gender equality. Not an easy task, but one where we are going to need multifaceted approaches to foster an awareness of the importance and benefits of working towards this vision. This entails working with both women and men to promote this agenda.

WEN is calling for recognition of the fact that the future of the planet, and everyone on it, relies on policy-makers and governments including women in decision-making, and empowering them, through achieving greater gender equality, to make the changes that need to be made for all our sakes. This means we need

25

MARYLYN HAINES EVANS

National Federation of Women's Institutes

One hundred years of collective action for environmental change

> We are yet bound together in one great, unbreakable sisterhood.
>
> Grace Hadow

In writing these words, NFWI's first vice-chair, Grace Hadow, recognised the strength of women coming together – and captured the imagination of a generation of women united in the WI's vision of a movement that could unlock the potential of all women and so create a strong, informed and active civil society. Since the 1920s, this has included taking responsibility for our impact on the planet and empowering women as agents of environmental change.

The ethos of the WI has always been to inspire, to educate, and to improve the lives of women and those around them. More than one hundred years on, the organisation has changed in many ways yet this ethos, and the ideals of community and friendship under-pinning it, still holds true.

Grace's recognition of the value of collective action for bringing about change still permeates every level of the WI. A look back through the WI's history books offers a case study on how the empowerment of women can be harnessed to bring about environmental change.

The WI set out to empower women to get to grips with issues of concern to members and their communities. The founding members recognised: 'if one person alone cannot make her wants heard it becomes much easier when there are numbers wanting the same kind of things. That is why large numbers of women organised in bodies such as the National Federation of Women's Institutes can become a real power.' At a time when few women participated in public life and the vote for women had not yet been won, the organisation took a democratic and coordinated approach to mobilising women in the belief that if women learnt how to conduct meetings and run committees, and gained confidence in speaking in public, these skills would equip them for a changing world and stand them in good stead for participating in other areas of public life. This approach offered British women training in democracy and the exercise of the vote, enabling members, who perhaps had little prior experience of exerting power, to exercise influence and through the WI come together with other women in the numbers needed to become a force to be reckoned with; gradually forging the organisation a reputation as an effective force for change.

> This meeting, realising the significant changes which are rapidly taking place in agriculture and rural life, calls on the NFWI Executive Committee and the County Federations to encourage WI members to study these changes and to help to adapt new conditions to old.
>
> 1938 AGM

The WI's initial focus centred on the war effort. In 1917, with word out that only three weeks' food supply remained in the country, the newly formed National Federation of Women's Institutes began urging WIs to get behind food production efforts. WIs began growing more for villages and communities and, at a time when fruit conservation was something of a novel concept, members began bottling and preserving excess fruit in tremendous volumes; during the Second World War efforts were again stepped up with members preserving nearly twelve million pounds of fruit for the nation between 1940 and 1945. The jam-making label stuck.

While it is now something of a stereotype, it's one which the WI is rightly proud of – demonstrating the organisation's commitment to encouraging members to give help where needed, tackling some of society's major challenges along the way.

Since then, the WI has campaigned on a wide range of issues that matter to women and their communities. With its roots in the countryside, the WI has been at the forefront of protecting and promoting the countryside, and understanding the symbiotic relationship between humans and nature. As early as 1927, the WI was speaking out on the threats our seas and coastal shores faced (at the time being polluted by waste oil from ships) and the impact on sea-life. Concerned by the need for greater planning regulation to protect the countryside from urban expansions and the effect this had on the health of people and wildlife, in 1938 WI members called for the preservation of 'wide areas of special beauty'. A decade later, Areas of Outstanding Beauty were established as part of the National Parks and Access to the Countryside Act 1949.

Often these campaigns have not only triggered important national conversations, but have responded to local need and, in many cases, left a rich legacy. One of the most memorable and long-standing WI initiatives stems from a resolution calling for a campaign to 'preserve the countryside against desecration by litter'. This resolution, passed in 1954 under the then chair, Elizabeth Brunner, led to the formation of the Keep Britain Tidy campaign, now an independent charity that celebrated its Diamond Jubilee in 2014.

In more recent years, WI campaigns have ranged from tackling the plight of the honey bee to reducing waste and conserving the countryside. A 2005 resolution on protecting natural resources inspired a nationwide action day that saw WIs up and down the country return excess packaging to supermarkets, as part of efforts to encourage retailers to reduce waste. The WI Carbon Challenge, launched in 2008, saw 10,000 members signed up, pledging to reduce their carbon footprint by 20 per cent. The savings achieved were equivalent to filling the Royal Albert Hall 108 times with CO_2. Each campaign, and the resolutions that inspire them, is underpinned by the founding members' vision of the potential of an empowered group of women; agents of change with the ambition to build a well-informed and active society that takes responsibility for our impact on the planet.

> Members must learn to realise their responsibility toward the community in which they live and, from an interest in their own village and their own county, come to see the connection between their affairs and those of the nation at large.
>
> Grace Hadow

Worldwide, women are both an influential and positive force for change and some of the most vulnerable individuals in the face of our changing climate. Globally, women remain influential consumers of domestic products and utilities, responsible for the tremendous spending power that accompanies their holding the purse strings on the vast majority of consumer spending. Management professor Gloria Moss suggests women buy 93 per cent of all groceries and 92 per cent of holidays, along with, perhaps more surprisingly, 60 per cent of new cars and 55 per cent of home computers. With UK women so critical to household spending, and so influential on others' purchases, women's economic and social capital means they hold the potential for powering tremendous environmental change through individual lifestyle and consumer choices.

The social roles women play as primary caregivers for children and older people in most societies throughout the world also offer women a unique perspective on sustainability, and the power to positively influence the way in which today's children consider their coexistence with our planet. NFWI research, undertaken ahead of the People's Climate Marches and the UN Climate Summit in New York City in September 2014, revealed that 74 per cent of British women believe that responsibility for tackling climate change cannot be left to future generations. And when asked what worried women the most when thinking about the effects of climate change, 35 per cent were concerned about the challenges that will face the future generations set to inherit a warmer planet, with all the difficulties around both resource and human security that will accompany this.

This awareness of the legacy that we leave with the choices we make has been a constant theme within the WI movement over the past 100 years. While we may feel that individually we are unable to have an impact or change the course of events, by working together it's easier to see how every person making seemingly small changes can contribute towards a huge collective effect.

Looking again at the NFWI's women and climate polling, it starts to become apparent why the formula to which the WI works is effective. The study found that women were more likely than men to believe that they as individuals could make a difference in tackling climate change (16 per cent of men felt that individuals cannot do much about climate change, compared to 9 per cent of women). It also found that women believed that the government had an important role to play in supporting the public to make more sustainable choices in their day-to-day lives, such as through improved recycling schemes or making it easier for people to use public transport.

> Women's Institutes have awakened the members' responsibility towards the community. It has led them to realise their power and to exert it for the improvement of conditions of rural life.
>
> WI Handbook, 1953/54

The WI campaigns model frequently sees members take a twofold approach: pressing for change from decision-makers; while examining the role of individuals as change agents, leading the way in their own communities by driving environmental changes by taking their own lives as a start point for practical action.

Take the WI's SOS for Honey Bees campaign, for example. Members across England and Wales, concerned at the accelerating decline in the UK honey bee population, backed an AGM resolution that launched a campaign calling on the government to increase funding for research into bee health in 2008. By 2013, with the research funding in place but the situation for bees and other pollinators remaining bleak, members got behind national campaigning for more comprehensive action for bees, through the development of a government-led national pollinator strategy. This important national campaigning was underpinned by awareness-raising among the public to build understanding about the declining honey bee population and the vital role that pollinators play in the country's ecosystem and food production.

Thousands of WI members have embraced the campaign by taking action in their own homes and communities. Nottingham City WI offers one such example, taking SOS for Honey Bees to the centre of the community with their vision to create a bee-friendly village. They won funding through the national pocket park scheme to revitalise Barker Gate Rest Garden in Nottingham's Creative Quarter. The park will be planted with bee-friendly plants to give year-round support to urban bees, and to support the city's Bee Action Plan.

Many more WIs took up the challenge, turning unused land into community bee paradises, securing hives or donated plants, and mobilising the whole community to transform once neglected space into areas to be proud of. Others encouraged local authorities to plant bee-friendly flowers, giving out seed packs and planting guides at community fetes and fairs. Members from Liverpool WI took the campaign one step further by training as beekeepers to care for honeybees kept on the roof of Blackburne House in the city. Campaigns such as these are rooted in the recognition that we all have a role to play in protecting our environment, and that collective action brings about wider change in society and government policy.

> Although for 55 years we've worked to improve the conditions of the countryside, now we must hurry. We can't afford to be slow [...] Let's make thousands know what we're doing, positively, to conserve the countryside.
>
> Mrs Jacob, 1972 (at the launch of the
> 'This Green and Pleasant Land' competition)

The concept of women as agents of change is one that resonates strongly with members. Right from the start, the WI was about giving women a voice and ensuring that women used that voice. And that this voice be an informed voice. But just as importantly, the NFWI worked hard to make sure that this informed voice was heard. This was not always easy, however, even with the strong leadership of resourceful and connected women such as Lady Denman, Dame Frances Farrer and Lady Brunner – and a look through the NFWI archives highlights moments when the NFWI rebuked ministers for their lack of female representation on influential committees or international delegations. In one such letter, addressed to The Rt Hon. Anthony Wedgwood Benn, MP (then Secretary of State for Energy), NFWI chairman Mrs Patricia Batty Shaw urged action to address the poor representation of women on the Energy Commission, noting 'that the representation of the non-industrial consumer might well be strengthened, possibly by the inclusion of another woman, as we have noted that there is only one on the Commission at present'.

In 2015, the Women's Institute celebrated 100 years of action. Despite its many successes, further action is needed, in particular to give women a proper place and a voice at decision-making tables, whether in government, in business or elsewhere. Only then can women's potential to create a fairer, more sustainable world be fully realised.

26

JULIET DAVENPORT
CEO of Good Energy

The impact of gender balance in the renewable energy sector

Broadly, what's your vision for energy, for our energy system?
My vision broadly has always been renewable. I do believe we could
have a 100 per cent renewable Britain and I think that's good on
many levels. Firstly, from the climate point of view, secondly from
an energy security and global security point of view, and thirdly it's
about ownership. It's about the fact that renewable energy doesn't
have to be owned by one person; it can be developed by people in
their own homes, and it can be developed by communities. It gives
access at all different levels of society. My vision is one of lots of
people generating their own power, becoming much more responsible for the power they use and using renewables to achieve this.

**Among the problems that we face in getting to that vision,
how important is the issue of gender inequality, do you think?**
It's a really interesting question. I can't say directly that these issues
are just driven by men, because this is about a wider part of society
taking responsibility – both men and women. So it's not just about
women being in positions of power. It's also about women understanding that they hold as much responsibility as the people who
have traditionally worked in this area. By bringing women into the
workforce, particularly in energy, you bring first of all different views
and ideas, but also you bring a wider sense of responsibility about
issues like energy use, where it's produced and how it impacts on
other people's lives.

How important is gender equality within the context of Good Energy itself? Do you actively promote gender equality? What do you do about it?

As part of the energy industry, I got very used to being a lone female voice in a fairly male-dominated area, but there are now more women employed across the sector. From Good Energy's perspective, we're now doing pretty well on gender balance. I remember back in our early days sitting down at a meeting, and realising that I was pretty much the only female face there. We did some analysis of gender equality in the company, and started to measure it, which is the first stage for any organisation. Where are we losing women? When are they coming in? What we found is that we had gender equality at the start stage, among students and graduates and, as time went on, we slowly lost our women, so a lot of our staff in senior positions were male. So I wanted to look at how we could support women through coming back to work, making sure that they got career progression and ensuring they were interested in what they were doing. We now have a Board with four women out of seven, and currently over two-thirds of our senior leadership team are women.

We've not deliberately set out to promote women but I put it on the agendas of our headhunters and our HR team and told them I wanted to see a balance. You always want to choose the best person, but also to make sure that you're seeing enough people. Then within the company, we've also tried to give people a lot of support in coming back to work: mentoring about how to manage childcare, because that is the key issue for women coming back to work. How do you make sure that, firstly, their job is interesting enough for them to want to come back to work, because otherwise they will want to stay at home. Secondly, can we support them to come back – through offering flexible working wherever possible (to mothers and fathers), and fostering a culture which supports peoples' need for a good work-life balance.

Can you see an impact from an improved gender balance in a company? Has that had an impact on the business?

We've definitely seen more senior women come in who've had a very can-do attitude, which has been great, and it's broken down some of the barriers in terms of getting things moving. It also means people have got to think slightly more holistically, seeing it all from slightly different angles, so you get a much better debate on areas of risk. If you get too much of a male environment, it can sometimes be the case that people are worried about asking the 'stupid questions which can quite often be the most important ones'. They're worried about looking silly and that becomes a major issue, because then you don't discover what's really going on. I don't know if it's the same if you get too much of a female environment, that's probably got its negatives as well.

And you'd attribute that to a difference in gender, that in a way we're wired differently?

I think so, I do see that. When you put one gender in place, you get all the assets reinforced and all the negatives reinforced. Where you get a balance between men and women working together, they balance each other out really well and bring different aspects to the table. If you only have one gender, you tend to start to see biases. To say it's a gender bias isn't quite correct, because there are different types of biases, but you do run the risk of everybody beginning to say the same thing, rather than challenge anyone.

Is it true that the energy business is very male-dominated?

Although more women work in the sector than ever before, it's still very much dominated by men. Energy is still seen as an engineering discipline, and with the large proportion of girls dropping STEM subjects, energy is not seen as a natural career choice for them. But the energy sector is multi-faceted with a score of opportunities in a range of different areas, so an engineering or a science degree is definitely not a pre-requisite – there are other routes in too. We are seeing a growing number of female leaders in the energy sector, but the numbers are still comparatively low. The sector is gradually waking up to the issue, and lots of organisations are putting programs in place to help address it.

If so, what made you personally want to get involved in it? Was that a challenge that you welcomed, or was there a barrier in it, deterrent to you?
My working life and my career started when I studied science at university and there was probably a worse gender balance then than there is currently in the energy industry. I studied physics, and 10 per cent of us were women – maybe even less. But I really enjoyed physics. I then studied climate change and, if you want to do something about climate change, you end up in the energy sector. It wasn't because I was wanted to be a female in a male-dominated area but because it was the area that I was interested in. In terms of gender equality, it is quite dull being in the minority all the time and it's quite hard work. When there are more women around, you feel slightly more confident that you may be heard. If you sit in a room with twelve people and you're the only woman, you stick your hand up to say something, you stand out. You do. You can't help it. So having more women in the room, you feel more normalised.

You started off as a scientist. What kind of action would you say is needed to get more women into science, technology, business, politics?
It's a wider societal issue. I see girls being given the idea that science is boring, or 'male', at the age of ten. I think we need to look at primary schools and how we teach science. I think science is absolutely fundamental. Our lives are so based around science. Everything we do in our lives – whether it's using a tablet or phone, or, the electricity we supply our houses with – everything is underpinned by science. Yet the majority of the people who use it don't understand it and I think that makes us very vulnerable to people who do understand it and people who can blind us with science.

In my view, if society's going to shift its perception, we need to celebrate scientists as much as we celebrate the arts – writers, actors, personalities. We need to see science as a really positive thing. Brian Cox and Helen Czerski are good examples, where you see a focus on somebody who is a career scientist, working hard to communicate science in an engaging way to the public. We need to make programmes about science that are really interesting and help women and men see that it is part of their lives, not just something that someone else does. It's vital that this starts at a really early age, because by the time girls are eleven, most of them have made their decision about whether they're going to be a writer or not. Well, not quite, but they've already got that scientific or non-scientific bent.

I've worked with South East Physics Network, SEPnet, which is about getting more people into science – and about getting more women into science. If you look at a lot of companies and businesses worldwide, a lot of people who run them, or are involved in them, have got some type of scientific background, because you need to be hugely numerate, you need to be able to understand how things work. The more we can see women coming through to science, the more we'll see women at high levels in business, especially in energy.

The political world, which obviously shapes energy policy, is also obviously male-dominated. Has this made your job and your vision more difficult to achieve, do you think?
I look at politics and think, 'I don't want to be a politician. It's bad enough being a business leader!' You get your life put in the spotlight and that can be hard. I guess that's true no matter what gender you are.

I think politics has got to look at itself very hard if it wants to encourage more women into it – starting with confronting sexist behaviour in Parliament. Whether it's made my job more difficult? I don't know. You have to try harder to relate to a man than a woman, and a lot of talking to politicians is about relatedness, an understanding of where they're coming from. So it does make it a little harder, yes.

Switching tack slightly, are you aware of any gender bias in your customer base, particularly among those involved ... you spoke about community ownership earlier. Is there a gender bias in the customer base, do you know of, among those involved in micro-generation?

There used to be. When we first set up, we definitely had a gender bias with more men as customers. That has shifted over the years, as we've seen more women get involved in energy. I'm not seeing a bias at the moment. From our recent analysis of our customer base, we're seeing fewer families, more singles, more couples without families and young couples. If you look at that mix, the family side may be where we're missing out, which is interesting because our core purpose is to help to prevent climate change: to preserve the planet for the next generation. We're now looking at innovative ways of connecting with families to make sure that message gets across.

And that's with regard to micro-generation specifically?

Yes, but also energy customers, as well. There's real opportunity to engage with people through how they use energy, what appliances they have in their home, how much energy they use – and of course the opportunities of generating their own electricity. One of the least talked about benefits we have seen from the huge increases in solar deployment in recent years is how it has allowed people to become more engaged with the energy they use. The role of electricity generator has passed from the hands of a few large companies into the hands of millions of households in just a few years – and that is a revolutionary thing. The more we can engage everyone in where their energy comes from, the greater our chances of avoiding catastrophic climate change.

So can you say, broadly speaking, for example, the decision for a family to install solar panels or to sign up to a green tariff would be led by the male partner or the female partner?

It's really difficult, actually. I used to be able to, but I can't any more. It's a very interesting question. It's quite tricky to figure out, because quite often, you'll have two people on the bill, male and female. So it's much more difficult to see who the decision-makers are. We're seeing it as much more of a joint decision now, which is great.

More broadly than energy, do you think women have a particular role to play in creating a green economy?
Yes. There have been a lot of women leaders in fashion, in the arts, in companies like People Tree, Body Shop, in terms of beauty products – we've seen quite a lot of female leaders break through in those areas, maybe partly because those are traditionally more female-dominated areas. You could say that, in some senses, we've seen green ideas coming through earlier, where there's a greater balance of women in those sectors. It would be good to unpick how that comes about. Is it the case that if you've got more of a balance of women involved in an industry, they actually start looking at the environment as something that should be looked after as much as the economy? What drives this different approach and how can we encourage more organisations to expand their gender balance so that they can benefit from the green economy?

If you could do one thing to improve the number of women in positions of power, or gender equality more generally, what would that be?
To be honest, I would take a fiscal measure. I would make childcare – particularly for those on middle and low incomes – tax deductible. I know that we've already got various childcare support mechanisms, but this is one of the biggest issues women face when returning to work. When you're working your way through to becoming more senior – which might be late twenties, early thirties – if you decided to have a child, coming back to work becomes a huge decision on a personal basis, on a financial basis, and on the basis that you like your job, as well, because I think that's really important. If we can make at least one of those an easier decision and start to encourage people, to make it easier for them to go back to work if they want to then I think that would be brilliant. I read somewhere that if you have a chauffeur, that's tax deductible! If you have childcare, that

should be tax deductible, as well. That would deliver a much more balanced society.

And conversely, would you like to see it incentivised for men to be at home, or do more of the childcare?

You have to think how you would incentivise that. I think you have to make it acceptable. I think that has to become a more societal norm. So how do you teach that? That's about education. Trying to make it tax-appealing? Maybe there could be a tax break for people staying at home. But I think a lot of it is getting over the stigma men feel if they decide to stay at home. If we can get over that, as a society, then why not? To a certain extent, it's a bit like having a sabbatical, but with children on the side. We can take time out. We can see it as enriching our lives to spend it with our children, and then make sure that going back to work is straightforward and not seen as a negative thing.

So to come back to the overarching question we're looking at in this book, is it possible for you to say, we think we'll get better environmental outcomes if there were greater gender balance? If there were more women in positions of power, in energy particularly, in business, politics, more generally?

I think the answer is yes, because we bring in a wider balance of society. We bring in different views, we bring in different challenges and the idea of 'group think' begins to diminish. That's the danger in organisations where you have a gender bias. You begin to move to 'group think', where you just reinforce what you think already, and you don't question it. For me, gender balance is all about questioning and challenging things, asking if this is the best way to do something and checking what impact an action or idea might have somewhere else. Having more women across the board – whether that's in energy companies, in all companies, in government – is a really good thing. Having a proper gender balance throughout your organisation, from top to bottom, makes a real difference. We need women on the board, as managers and as senior leaders if we really want to get the right business and environmental outcomes.

27

EMMA HOWARD BOYD

Chair, Environment Agency and 30% Club for
women in business leadership

More women in business for a
sustainable economy

'We cannot return to the old macho ways'

In February 2009, the then business editor of the *Observer*, Ruth
Sunderland, invited me to join a round-table discussion with seven
women from the world of business and finance to discuss 'City
culture, machismo's role in the financial crisis and how women can
help bring about a resolution'.[1]

For a while, Ruth had been observing that women's voices had
been conspicuously absent from the debate on what went wrong
with the banking system. If men were the architects of a risky
and fragile financial system whose flaws have now been laid bare,
should we be looking to women to help create a more balanced and
sustainable economy?

Our discussion was wide-ranging, covering several pages of the
newspaper, but with a core theme: that the financial crisis highlighted the dangers of homogeneous boards and the need for
diversity of thinking. The *zeitgeist* was right for change.

One of the comments I made during the discussion focused on
the contribution gender diversity can make to diversity of perspective, bringing a greater understanding of a broad range of issues,
including those relating to environmental sustainability:

> I would hope that we get a mind-set that comes into this
> debate that allows a different type of thinking about other

areas, about the environment, about green issues. We are going through a financial crunch but there are a whole range of other crunches coming up around carbon, around water and a lot of those will impact first on developing countries. We need to think about some of the risks that have built up in the financial system and also to understand the other risks that are building up.[2]

While I plan to explore whether greater representation of women at senior levels of business can help in the transition to a sustainable economy, later in this chapter, before I do, I want to describe the important work of the 30% Club.

Since the spring of 2011, I have been a member of the steering committee of the 30% Club, founded by Helena Morrissey, CBE, CEO of Newton Investment Management. The 30% Club launched in the UK in 2010 with an initial goal of FTSE-100 boards having female representation of 30 per cent or more by the end of 2015.

Over this period, the under-representation of women at senior levels in almost every area of society – business, politics, the public sector, professional services, sports bodies, academia and the arts – has attracted a huge amount of attention, not just here in the UK, but globally.

But after decades of snail-like progress, accelerated results over this relatively short time indicate that finally we are taking the right actions to address the issue – in a sustainable and meaningful way.

So first, let's look at what has been achieved in the FTSE-100 and FTSE-250, the UK's largest and next tier of public companies:[3]

» 46 FTSE-100 companies have at least 25 per cent women on their board
» 25 have reached 30 per cent
» By May 2015 we had reached 24.7 per cent of the FTSE-100 total (up from 12.5 per cent at the 30% Club's launch in 2010
» And, since May 2014, no all-male FTSE-100 boards, as the last bastion fell

» And in the FTSE-250 strong momentum, with only 20 all-male boards left, down from 131 (yes, over half)
» Rather encouragingly, since 1 March 2013, 33 per cent of all board appointments to the FTSE-100 have been women
» And of great importance, all delivered without resorting to quotas – a real achievement.

There is no doubt that a key breakthrough has been the acceptance that better gender balance at senior levels is a business issue, not just a women's issue – taking the issue beyond a specialist diversity effort and into mainstream talent management.

There is increasing agreement that diversity at board and top executive level in terms of skills, gender and nationality is a key factor in the quality and performance of boards. Improved board-room dynamics, greater diversity of perspective, varying attitudes to risk and a better ability to connect with consumers are all acknowledged as powerful benefits of a mixed-gender board.

As a result, we have seen a radical shift in the way business leaders are approaching the issue of what makes a more effective corporate board – including by institutional shareholders, who simply want the opportunity to invest in more successful companies.

So what has been the catalyst behind this breakthrough? How have we improved outcomes and moved away from a period where efforts exceeded results?

While there has been no 'silver bullet', there has been a combination of factors coming together to powerful effect – a formula for change that might prove useful elsewhere.

» The most important driver was undoubtedly senior business leaders' involvement – those who could make a real difference in terms of female appointments. There are now over one hundred members of the 30% Club – chairs of listed companies, professional services firms and public sector bodies. The impact of their visible commitment – most of them are, of course, men – cannot be overstated. Their public support has made a big impact, for example on the board recruitment process, especially that of the executive search firms.

» The focus of a specific and measurable goal – an aspirational target, not a mandatory quota – has provided real impetus for change. The original emphasis on boards has widened to include developing the executive pipeline of female talent; the aim is now 30 per cent women at all senior levels.

There were a number of other key ingredients:

» One has been timing. The financial crisis highlighted the dangers of homogeneous boards – 'groupthink' – and the status quo. In 'The moral DNA of performance',[4] a report published by the Chartered Management Institute in October 2014, one of the top ten steps to an ethical organisation was to 'harness diversity to challenge "groupthink"'.

» Similarly, the European Commission threatening to introduce quotas, which the 30% Club does not support, has brought a sense of urgency to the debate, and helped highlight voluntary action as the preferred way.

» This increased political attention was a key driver behind Lord Davies publishing his excellent report into the (then) scarcity of 'women on boards'. The Davies Report[5] set out ten clear recommendations in 2011 – a useful and replicable blueprint for change.

» Where no initiative existed around a Davies recommendation, we set out to address this. For example, establishing an investor group, which I chair, representing over £5 trillion in assets, to engage with companies.

» Importantly, the UK's Financial Reporting Council (FRC) made changes to the UK Corporate Governance Code which reflect the view that gender diversity strengthens board effectiveness by reducing the risk of 'groupthink', making fuller use of the talent pool and keeping companies in touch with their customers.

» The 30% Club investor group's approach is one of constructive engagement with listed companies as part of a broader analysis of a company's governance and development of future top talent. We have been encouraging improved disclosure beneath the board and executive committee levels. Where insufficient action is taken, individual members of the investor group are prepared to use their voting rights to encourage greater response. This approach is set out in our paper 'Diversity and stewardship – the next steps'.[6]

Growing the female talent pipeline needs to be high on the agenda for every board and executive committee

While progress has been made in increasing female representation on boards over the last three years, this has, on the whole, been achieved through an increase in the appointment of female non-executive directors.

The FTSE-100 has moved from 12.5 per cent female directors in 2010 to 24.7 per cent as of May 2015, while only 8.6 per cent of executive directors in the FTSE-100 are women. Attention now needs to be focused on achieving real, measurable progress – not by 'fixing the women' or 'beating up the men', but through men and women working together to improve business culture and achieve more diversity of thought at all company levels.

For a real step change to occur, more women must progress from senior management to executive board roles. Having the focus of a specific and measurable goal – an aspirational target, not a mandatory quota – can provide real impetus for change.

As the CBI noted in its position paper 'Building on progress: boosting diversity in our workplace',[7] published in June 2014: 'More firms should take on the example set by some leading firms of extending diversity targets, on a comply-or-explain basis, down through their middle and senior management cohorts.'

Notable examples include Sky, which in 2015 set a target of 50:50 gender split in its top 500 senior management roles, increasing from the current level of a third.

The CBI is leading by example and has committed to becoming a more diverse organisation. Currently eight of its thirteen senior managers are women, it has recently appointed its first female director general and the CBI board has approved a target of 30 per cent female representation at its events and in its policy-making processes.

This chimes with our own ambition. Our original emphasis on boards (with an initial goal of FTSE-100 boards having female representation of 30 per cent or more by the end of 2015) has widened to include developing the executive pipeline of female talent.

Investors are in a unique position to encourage companies to improve their gender diversity – but not just at board level

In July 2014, the 30% Club held its fourth annual London seminar in which we set out the next steps for accelerating change towards better gender balance from 'schoolroom to boardroom', demonstrating that the momentum behind our campaign has spread to a number of initiatives based on a collaborative approach.

In his introductory remarks to our seminar one of our founding chairmen, Sir Roger Carr, reminded the audience of the moment when the critical role of investors was underlined:

'Now, whilst chairmen can influence board behaviour, the Club recognised that it is ultimately the owners who really call the shots – and reinforcement of the message was powerfully nailed when Martin Gilbert of Aberdeen Asset Management stood up at an earlier meeting of this type [our first annual seminar] and encouraged investors to challenge boards and demand action.'

Investors are in a unique position to encourage companies to improve their gender diversity – but not just at board level. The 30% Club's investor group has the clout to make a big impact – now with more than twenty members, including PIMCO and Blackrock, and combined assets under management of around £5 trillion.

So what is it that investors, in particular, can focus on?

» Investors are increasingly aware that talent management is a mainstream issue and are in a unique position to encourage companies to improve their gender diversity – but not just at board level. Whilst many companies say that their people are their most valuable asset, in which they invest significantly, there is no established framework for reporting on human capital. This makes it difficult in turn for investors to assess this vital aspect of a company's future prospects. The Investment Association has been leading a project to consider ways of addressing this shortcoming, working with a small group of investors and representatives from other groups. Growing the female talent pipeline needs to be high on the agenda for every board and executive committee, and seen as a crucial part of business strategy and a key determinant of future performance.

» With the focus moving from boardroom to senior management teams it was agreed that this issue needs to be considered by mainstream fund managers, not just by specialist governance teams, and raised in meetings with CEOs, as well as chairmen, as part of the assessment of companies' longer-term prospects.

» There is a need for greater transparency surrounding talent management in companies. This will be helped by the new requirements for companies to report on the number of male and female directors, senior managers and employees that they have, as set out in the guidance on the strategic report, published by the UK Financial Reporting Council in June 2014.[8]

» A focus on board refreshment could accelerate the pace of change. Data published by BoardEx in January 2015 shows that out of 839 non-executive FTSE-100 directorships, 83 non-executive directors (NEDs) – 10 per cent – have served on the board for more than nine years, the maximum recommended term under the UK Corporate Governance Code. Of these, seventy-four are men.

More women in business makes for better business overall

A whole raft of research has been published linking women leaders with business success.[9]

Most recently, a study of companies in the UK, US and India found that companies perform better when they have at least one female executive on the board. Only one in ten of the companies surveyed had female board executives, and the report concluded that those publicly traded companies with male-only executive directors missed out on £430 billion of investment returns last year.[10]

McKinsey also published a report making the economic case for advancing women's equality. In a 'full potential' scenario in which women participate in the economy identically to men, as much as 26 per cent would be added to global gross domestic product by 2025 compared with a business-as-usual scenario.

This is equivalent to adding the combined value of the US and Chinese economies. Taking a more realistic 'best in region' scenario in which all countries simply match the rate of improvement in gender equality of the best-performing countries in their region, McKinsey finds that $12 trillion of additional GDP growth would be achieved by 2025.[11]

Other studies have looked at whether women leaders create positive return beyond financial performance, i.e. whether women are making companies 'better' or 'better companies' have stronger female representation on the board.

One 2012 study, 'Women create a sustainable future',[12] investigated the correlation between having at least one woman on a board and improved environmental, social and governance (ESG) performance among 1,200 Fortune companies.

Environmental performance proved most statistically significant – the research concluded that businesses with more women on their board of directors are more likely to: manage and improve their energy efficiency; measure and reduce their carbon emissions; reduce their packaging impacts; invest in renewable power.

Social performance came in second: businesses with more women on their board of directors are more likely to improve access to healthcare in developing countries; have strong partnerships with local communities; offer products with nutritional or health benefits; proactively manage human capital development.

Finally, on governance issues, women on boards correlate to: less fraud, corruption and misreporting of numbers. In short, fewer CEOs charged with misconduct.

The 'MSCI 2014 survey of women on boards'[13] explored this area further and found some interesting correlations between women on boards and broader ESG metrics.

» Boards with gender diversity above and beyond regulatory mandates or market norms had fewer instances of governance-related scandals such as bribery, corruption, fraud, and shareholder battles.
» There was preliminary evidence that companies with more women on their boards tend to display overall stronger management of ESG-related risks.
» Companies with a higher percentage of women on their boards tend to have higher ESG ratings than their peers.
» Interestingly, subsequent to appointing a female CEO, companies exhibit a greater rate of female director appointments compared to male-led companies.

Catalyst's latest research published in January 2015 ('Companies behaving responsibly: gender diversity on boards'[14]) also suggests that gender-diverse boards are good for business *and* society. The research highlights that what is good for women is good for men, business, communities and, indeed, good for the world. Companies with both women and men in the boardroom are better equipped to oversee corporate actions and ensure corporate citizenship standards are not only met, but exceeded – building stronger, more sustainable companies.

A company that holds its supply chain accountable, values customer loyalty, and improves both the community and the environment creates a positive cycle of influence. This approach not only makes the world a better place, but also increases the likelihood of sustainable big wins for the company and its stakeholders. Research published in Australia in July 2015, based on a sample of 128 Australian publicly listed companies, confirmed that having larger representations of women on corporate boards is associated with lower occurrences of fraud.[15]

Gender-diverse boards can help companies and stakeholders alike

Are companies that empower women more likely to be companies that act sustainably? As explored earlier, empirical evidence suggests that companies with at least one woman on their boards achieve superior financial results than those with all-male boards. While causality cannot be proved at this stage – that this is due to the women – it is noticeable that those companies which 'get' this particular issue also tend to be more forward-looking on other aspects of good governance, including sustainability. And that, in itself, is a big prize, well worth having.

NOTES

INTRODUCTION

1 See www.un.org/en/development/desa/population/publications/urbanization/urban-rural.shtml

2 CoP 21 President Ségolène Royal, High-Level Climate Champions Laurence Tubiana and Moroccan Minister of Environment Hakima El Haite, SEforALL Chief Executive Officer Rachel Kyte, former Green Climate Fund Executive Director Héla Cheikhrouhou, GEF Chief Executive Officer and Chair Naoko Ishii ...

3 See https://cmsdata.iucn.org/downloads/disaster_and_gender_statistics.pdf

4 See www.metoffice.gov.uk/learning/learn-about-the-weather/weather-phenomena/case-studies/heatwave

3 SUSAN BUCKINGHAM

1 J. Jacobs, *The Death and Life of Great American Cities*, Harmondsworth, Pelican, 1961.

2 Reported in R. Solnit, *Storming the Gates of Paradise: Landscapes for Politics*, University of California Press, Berkeley, 2007.

3 D. Hayden, 'What would a non-sexist city look like? Speculations on housing, urban design and human work', *Signs*, 5(3), 1980, pp. 170–87.

4 E. Beyazit, 'Gendered mobilities: commuting experiences of female domestic workers in Istanbul', Engendering Habitat III International Conference, Madrid, 5–7 October 2016.

5 P. Jiron, 'Mobility on the move: examining urban daily mobility practices in Santiago de Chile', PhD thesis, London School of Economics and Political Science, 2008.

6 I. Sanchez de Madariaga, 'Mobility of care: introducing new concepts in urban transport', in I. Sanchez de Madariaga and M. Roberts (eds), *Fair Shared Cities: The Impact of Gender Planning in Europe*, Ashgate, Farnham, 2013, pp. 33–48.

7 J. Laghaei, A. Faghri and M. Li, 'Impacts of home shopping on vehicle operations and greenhouse gas emissions: multi-year regional study', *International Journal of Sustainable Development and World Ecology*, 23(5), 2015, pp. 381–91.

8   See www.1millionwomen.com.au/blog/whats-environmental-impact-your-online-shopping-habits/, accessed 20 July 2017.

9   Jacobs, *The Death and Life of Great American Cities*.

10 S. Buckingham and R. Kulcur, 'It's not just the numbers: challenging masculinist working practices in climate change decision-making in UK government and non-governmental organizations', in M. Griffin Cohen (ed.), *Climate Change and Gender in Rich Countries: Work, Public Policy and Action*, Routledge, London, 2017.

11 'Making it happen: Roisin Willmott reflects on International Women's Day', Royal Town Planning Institute, 19 March 2015, www.rtpi.org.uk/briefing-room/rtpi-blog/making-it-happen-celebrating-international-day/, accessed 20 July 2017.

12 R. Waite, 'Number of women architects in AJ100 practices rises again', *Architects' Journal*, 3 June 2016, www.architectsjournal.co.uk/news/number-of-women-architects-in-aj100-practices-rises-again/10007191.article, accessed 6 July 2017.

13 Architects' Council of Europe, *The Architectural Profession in Europe 2014: A Sector Study*, Architects' Council of Europe, Brussels, 2015, www.ace-cae.eu/fileadmin/New_Upload/7._Publications/Sector_Study/2014/EN/2014_EN_FULL.pdf, accessed 6 July 2017.

14 L. C. Chang, 'Where are the women? Measuring progress on gender in architecture', Association of Collegiate Schools of Architecture, Washington, DC, 2014, www.acsa-arch.org/resources/data-resources/women, accessed 6 July 2017.

15 B. Tether, 'How architecture cheats women: results of the 2017 Women in Architecture survey revealed', *Architectural Review*, 27 February 2017, www.architectural-review.com/rethink/how-architecture-cheats-women-results-of-the-2017-women-in-architecture-survey-revealed/10017497.article?blocktitle=Women-in-architecture-survey&contentID=16263&v=1, accessed 18 July 2017.

16 E. Irschick and E. Kail, 'Vienna: progress towards a fair shared city', in I. Sanchez de Madariaga and M. Roberts (eds), *Fair Shared Cities: The Impact of Gender Planning in Europe*, Ashgate, Farnham, 2013, pp. 193–230.

17 Senatsverwaltung für Stadtentwicklung, *Gender Mainstreaming in Urban Development*, Berlin, Senatsverwaltung für Stadtentwicklung, 2011, p. 10.

18 See www.cohousing-berlin.de/en/about, accessed 20 July 2017.

19 L. Tummers, 'Co-housing: a double shift in roles?', in S. Buckingham and V. Le Masson (eds), *Understanding Climate Change through Gender Relations*, Routledge, London, 2017, pp. 239–56.

20 S. Buckingham, 'Gendered nature and ecofeminism', in T. Cannon (ed.), *Sage Handbook on Nature*, Sage, London, 2018.

21 See www.punt6.org/en/, accessed 17 July 2017.

22 See https://urbanistasuk.wordpress.com/urbanistas-london-3/, accessed 20 July 2017.

23 L. Hartley, 'Space for women to "do urban"', *Town and Country Planning*, November 2015, pp. 514–15.

5 DIANE ELSON

1 UNCED (United Nations Conference on Environment and Development), *Rio Declaration on Environment and Development*, A/CONF.151/26, 1992, www.un-documents.net/rio-dec.htm

2 IUCN (International Union for Conservation of Nature), *The Environment and Gender Index (EGI) 2013 Pilot*, IUCN, Washington, DC, 2013.

3 United Nations Conference on Sustainable Development, *Outcome Document: The Future We Want*, Resolution adopted by the General Assembly, A/RES/66/288, 2012, sustainabledevelopment.un.org/futurewewant.html, paras 31, 45.

4 UNDP (United Nations Development Programme), *Powerful Synergies: Gender Equality, Economic Development and Environmental Sustainability*, ed. B. Cela, I. Dankelman and J. Stern, New York, 2012, p. 40.

5 L. Schalatek, *The Post-2015 Framework: Merging care and green economy approaches to finance gender-equitable sustainable development*, Heinrich Böll Stiftung, Washington, DC, 2013; World Bank, *Gender and climate change: 3 things you should know*, World Bank, Washington, DC, 2011.

6 IUCN, *The Environment and Gender Index (EGI) 2013 Pilot*.

7 B. Agarwal, *Gender and Green Governance: The political economy of women's presence within and beyond community forestry*, Oxford University Press, New Delhi, 2010.

8 UN Women, *World Survey on the Role of Women in Development*, UN Women, New York, 2014, p. 40.

9 Committee on the Elimination of Discrimination Against Women (2004) *General Recommendation 25* on Article 4, paragraph 1, of the Convention on the Elimination of All Forms of Discrimination against Women, on temporary special measures, para. 8, www.un.org/womenwatch/daw/cedaw/recommendations/General%20recommendation%2025%20%28English%29.pdf, para. 8.

10 Ibid., para. 10.

11 M. Sepulveda Carmona, *Report of UN Special Rapporteur on Extreme Poverty and Human Rights to UN General Assembly*, A/68/293, 2013.

12 J. W. Rockström et al., 'Planetary boundaries: exploring the safe operating space for humanity', *Ecology and Society*, 14(2), 2009, p. 32.

13 K. Raworth, 'A safe and just space for humanity: can we live within the doughnut?', Oxfam Discussion Paper, Oxfam, Oxford, 2012.

14 WCED (World Commission on Environment and Development), *Our Common Future: Report of the WCED* (Brundtland Report), Oxford University Press, Oxford, 1987, ch. 2, para. 1.

15 S. Fukuda-Parr, J. Heintz and S. Seguino, 'Critical perspectives on finan-cial and economic crises: heterodox macroeconomics meets feminist economics', *Feminist Economics*, 19(3), 2013, pp. 4–31.

16 UN Women, 'Gender equality and the global economic crisis', Research paper, UN Women, New York, 2014.

17 See, for example, ILO, *Working towards Sustainable Development: Opportu-nities for decent work and social inclusion in a green economy*, International Labour Organization, Geneva, 2012.

18 World Bank, *World Development Report 2012: Gender equality and develop-ment*, World Bank, Washington, DC, 2012.

19 UNEP (United Nations Environment Programme), 'Global green new deal', Policy brief, Nairobi, 2009.

20 Ibid.

21 Ibid., p. 6.

22 O. Strietska-Ilina et al., 'Skills for green jobs: a global view', Synthesis report based on twenty-one country studies, ILO, Geneva, 2011, p. 126.

23 ILO, *Working towards Sustainable Development*.

24 Ibid.

25 UN Women, *World Survey on the Role of Women in Development*, pp. 74–5.

26 D. Elson, 'Economics for a post-crisis world: putting social justice first', in D. Jain and D. Elson (eds), *Harvesting Feminist Knowledge for Public Policy*, Sage, New Delhi, 2011.

8 NATHALIE HOLVOET and LIESBETH INBERG

1   This contribution is based on our paper in *Climate and Development*, 6(3), 2014, pp. 266–76.

2   UNDP, *Human Development Report*, New York, UNDP, 2011; World Bank, 'Local institutions and climate change adaptation', *Social Dimensions of Climate Change*, 113, World Bank, Washington, DC, 2008.

3   The UNFCC was agreed upon during the 1992 United Nations Confer-ence on Environment and Development (UNCED), yet it neglected the UNCED Rio principle that 'women have a vital role in environmental management and development', and that 'their full participation is therefore essential to achieve sustainable development'. UNCED, *Rio Declaration on Environment and Development*, UNCED, Rio de Janeiro, 1992, p. 4.

4   IUCN, *Draft Guidelines to Mainstreaming Gender in the Development of National Adaptation Plans (NAPs)*, UNFCCC, Bonn, 2011.

5   UNFCCC, *Report of the Conference of the Parties on its sixteenth session, held in Cancún from 29 November to 10 December 2010. Addendum. Part Two: Action taken by the Conference of the Parties at its sixteenth session*, UNFCCC, Cancún, 2010, pp. 3–4.

6   UNFCCC, *Draft decision –CP.18. Promoting gender balance and improving the participation of women in UNFCCC negotiations and in the representa-*

tion of Parties in bodies established pursuant to the Convention or the Kyoto Protocol, UNFCCC, Qatar, 2012.

7   UNFPA and WEDO, *Climate Change Connections*, UNFPA and WEDO, New York, 2009.

8   The guidelines prescribe the following structure: 1) Introduction and setting; 2) Framework for adaptation programme; 3) Identification of key adaptation needs; 4) Criteria for selecting priority activities; 5) List of priority activities; and 6) NAPA preparation process. Least Developed Countries Expert Group, *Annotated guideless for the preparation of national adaptation programmes of action*, UNFCCC, Bonn, 2002.

9   Ibid.

10 Skinner, E., *Gender and Climate Change Overview Report*, Institute of Development Studies, Brighton, 2011.

11 IUCN, *Draft Guidelines to Mainstreaming Gender in the Development of National Adaptation Plans (NAPs)*.

12 UNFPA and WEDO, *Climate Change Connections*, p. 28.

13 The sub-Saharan African countries that have elaborated a NAPA in the period 2004–11 are (in alphabetical order): Angola, Benin, Burkina Faso, Burundi, Cape Verde, Central African Republic, Chad, Comoros, Democratic Republic of Congo, Djibouti, Eritrea, Ethiopia, Gambia, Guinea, Guinea-Bissau, Lesotho, Liberia, Madagascar, Malawi, Mali, Mauritania, Mozambique, Niger, Rwanda, Senegal, Sierre Leone, Sudan, Tanzania, Togo, Uganda, Zambia.

14 The IUCN is the partner of the three Rio conventions and the Global Environment Facility (GEF) in mainstreaming gender into the implementation of the three conventions. IUCN Gender Office, *Harmonizing Gender in the Three Rio Conventions and the GEF*, IUCN, n.d.

15 National Adaptation Plans were agreed upon in the context of the 2010 Cancún Adaptation Framework and, in contrast to NAPAs, they are focused on the middle and long term (S. Kreft, A. O. Kaloga and S. Harmeling, 'National Adaptation Plans towards effective guidelines and modalities', Discussion paper, Germanwatch and WWF International, 2011). In 2011, the Gender Office of the International Union for Conservation of Nature (IUCN) elaborated draft gender guidelines for these National Adaptation Plans (IUCN, *Draft Guidelines to Mainstreaming Gender in the Development of National Adaptation Plans (NAPs)*).

16 As discussed in detail in S. Arora-Jonsson, 'Virtue and vulnerability: discourse on women, gender and climate change', *Global Environmental Change*, 21, 2011, pp. 744–51.

17 See J. Demetriades and E. Esplen, 'The gender dimension of poverty and climate change adaptation', *IDS Bulletin*, 39(4), 2008, pp. 24–31.

18 See H. Djoudi and M. Brockhaus, 'Is adaptation to climate change gender neutral? Lessons from communities dependent on livestock and forests in northern Mali', *International Forestry Review*, 13(2), 2011, pp. 123–35.

19 See, e.g., D. Elson, 'Male bias in macroeconomics: the case of structural adjustment', in D. Elson (ed.), *Male Bias in the Development Process*, Manchester University Press, Manchester, 1991.

20 See M. Hemmati and U. Röhr, 'Engendering the climate-change negotiations: experiences, challenges, and steps forward', *Gender and Development*, 17(1), 2009, pp. 19–32; G. Terry, *Climate Change and Gender Justice*, Practical Action Publishing in association with Oxfam GB, Warwickshire, 2009; UNFPA and WEDO, *Climate Change Connections*; UNDP, *Powerful Synergies. Gender Equality, Economic Development and Environmental Sustainability*, UNDP, New York, 2012.

21 See C. D. North, *Institutions, Institutional Change and Economic Performance*, Cambridge University Press, Cambridge, 1990.

22 See, e.g., B. Agarwal, *A Field of One's Own: Gender and Land Rights in South Asia*, Cambridge University Press, Cambridge, 1994.

23 L. Lessa and C. Rocha, 'Food security and gender mainstreaming: possibilities for social transformation in Brazil', *International Social Work*, 55(3), 2012, pp. 337–52.

24 See also A. Cornwall, E. Harrison and A. Whitehead, 'Gender myths and feminist fables. The struggle for interpretive power in gender and development', *Development and Change*, 38(1), 2007, pp. 1–20.

25 UNFPA and WEDO, *Climate Change Connections*.

26 Terry, *Climate Change and Gender Justice*.

27 B. Rodenberg, *Climate Change Adaptation from a Gender Perspective. A cross-cutting analysis of development-policy instruments*, German Development Institute, Bonn, 2009.

28 *NAPA-RIM*, Islamic Republic of Mauritania, Ministry of Rural Development and of Environment, Department of the Environment Project Coordination Unit, Nouackchott, 2004, p. 7.

29 See S. Theobald, R. Tolhurst, H. Elsey and H. Standing, 'Engendering the bureaucracy? Challenges and opportunities for mainstreaming gender in Ministries of Health under sector-wide approaches', *Health Policy and Planning*, 20(3), May 2005, pp. 141–9.

30 Cornwall et al., 'Gender myths and feminist fables'.

31 Ibid., p. 16.

9 ATTI WORKU

1 See www.unicef.org/education/; the Universal Declaration of Human Rights, proclaimed by the United Nations General Assembly in Paris on 10 December 1948, www.un.org/en/universal-declaration-human-rights/

2 'Chapter 3: Education', in United Nations Department of Economic and Social Affairs, *The World's Women 2015: Trends and Statistics*, United Nations, New York, 2015, https://unstats.un.org/unsd/gender/downloads/WorldsWomen2015_chapter3_t.pdf, accessed 22 October 2017.

3   L. Moodley, T. Holt, A. Leke and G. Desvaux, *Women Matter Africa*, McKinsey & Company, 2016.
4   'Chapter 3: Education', in United Nations Department of Economic and Social Affairs, *The World's Women 2015*.
5   Ibid., p. 63.
6   Ibid., p. 69.
7   Ibid., p. 74.

10 SHUKRI HAJI ISMAIL BANDARE and FATIMA JIBRELL

1   As a consequence of the civil war, in 1991 north-western Somalia broke off its union with the rest of Somalia and declared independence. Its secession remains internationally unrecognized. Instead it is defined as an autonomous region of Somalia.
2   See F. Musse and J, Gardner, *A Gender Profile for Somalia*, EC Somalia Unit, 2014.

12 GOTELIND ALBER

1   G. Alber, *Gender, Cities and Climate Change: Thematic Report Prepared for Cities and Climate Change Global Report on Human Settlements 2011*, UN-Habitat, Nairobi, 2010, https://unhabitat.org/wp-content/uploads/2012/06/GRHS2011ThematicStudyGender.pdf; G. Alber, *Gender and Urban Climate Policy: Gender-sensitive Policies Make a Difference*, GIZ, UN-Habitat and GenderCC, Bonn, 2015, http://gendercc.net/fileadmin/inhalte/dokumente/8_Resources/Publications/Guide book_Gender_and_Urban_Climate_Policy_June_2015.pdf; G. Alber and K. Cahoon, 'Urbanisation and global environmental change from a gender and equity perspective', in K. Ching-Yee Seto, W. Solecki and C. Griffith (eds), *The Routledge Handbook of Urbanization and Global Environmental Change*, Routledge, New York, 2015, pp. 310–24.
2   See http://gendercc.net/our-work/current-projects/gender-into-urban-climate-change-initiative.html
3   These are often called co-benefits. However, this is based on the assumption that climate policy has some kind of primacy over all other concerns, while we believe that social issues have to be treated on an equal footing.
4   *Manual: Gender Mainstreaming in Urban Planning and Urban Development*, Urban Development Vienna, Vienna, 2013, www.wien.gv.at/stadtentwicklung/studien/pdf/b008358.pdf
5   *Gender Issue Guide: Housing and Slum Upgrading*, UN-Habitat, Nairobi,2012,https://unhabitat.org/books/housing-and-slum-upgrading-gender-issue-guide/

13 LYLA MEHTA and MELISSA LEACH

1   This chapter draws on M. Leach et al., 'Gender equality and sustainable development: a pathways approach', Background working paper for UN Women World Survey on the Role of Women in Development, 2014.

2   B. Unmüßig, W. Sachs and T. Fatheuer, *Critique of the Green Ecology –
    Toward Social and Environmental Equity*, Ecology Series no. 22, Heinrich
    Böll Stiftung, Berlin, 2012.

3   Ibid.

4   See ibid.; W. Harcourt (ed.), *Feminist Perspectives on Sustainable Develop-
    ment*, Zed Books, London.

5   See C. Wichterich, *The Future We Want. A feminist perspective*, Ecology
    Series no. 21, Heinrich Böll Stiftung, Berlin, 2012.

6   See ibid.; UN Women, *World Survey on the Role of Women in Development
    2014: Gender Equality and Sustainable Development*, New York, 2014.

7   J. Rockström et al., 'A safe operating space for humanity', *Nature*, 461, 209.

8   C. Folke et al., 'Reconnecting to the biosphere', *Ambio*, 40, 2011.

9   K. Raworth, 'A safe and just space for humanity: can we live within the
    doughnut?', Oxfam Discussion Paper, Oxfam, Oxford, 2012.

10 Unmüßig et al., *Critique of the Green Ecology*.

11 UNEP, *What is the Green Economy Initiative?*, www.unep.org/greene-
    conomy/AboutGEI/WhatisGEI/tabid/29784/Default.aspx, 2013.

12 J. Clancy, *Economy or Environment? It's a false choice*, National Union of
    Public and General Employees, Canada, 2009 nupge.ca/content/815/
    economy-or-environment-its-false-choice .

13 T. Jackson, *Prosperity without Growth: Economics for a Finite Planet*, Earth-
    scan/Routledge, London, 2009.

14 Wichterich, *The Future We Want*; Unmüßig et al., *Critique of the Green
    Ecology*.

15 For example Natural Capital Committee, *The State of Natural Capital:
    Towards a framework for measurement and valuation*, Defra, London,
    2013, www.defra.gov.uk/naturalcapitalcommittee

16 See J. Fairhead and M. Leach, *Misreading the African Landscape: Society
    and ecology in a forest-savanna mosaic*, Cambridge University Press,
    Cambridge, 1996; L. Mehta, G. J. Veldwisch and J. Franco, 'Introduction
    to the Special Issue: Water grabbing? Focus on the (re)appropriation of
    finite water resources', *Water Alternatives*, 5(2), 2012; S. M. Borras, Jr,
    R. Hall, I. Scoones, B. White and W. Wolford, 'Towards a better under-
    standing of global land grabbing: an editorial introduction', *Journal of
    Peasant Studies*, 38(2), 2011.

17 See M. Naret Guerrero and A. Stock, 'Green economy from a gender
    perspective', www.academia.edu/1604568/Green_economy_from_a_
    Gender_perspective, 2012, accessed February 2015.

18 See L. Schalatek, *The Post-2015 Framework: Merging Care and Green
    Economy Approaches to Finance Gender-Equitable Sustainable Development*,
    Heinrich Böll Foundation, 2013.

19 See Unmüßig et al., *Critique of the Green Ecology*.

20 For example G. Vaughan (ed.), *Women and the Gift Economy: A Radically
    Difference Worldview Is Possible*, Inanna Publications & Education Incor-

porated, 2007; M. Mellor, 'Ecofeminist political economy and the politics of money', in A. Salleh (ed.), *Eco-Sufficiency and Global Justice: Women write political ecology*, Pluto Press, London, 2009.

21 See L. Mehta, *The Limits to Scarcity. Contesting the Politics of Allocation*, Earthscan, London, 2010; A. Salleh (ed.), Eco-Sufficiency and Global Justice: Women write political ecology, Pluto Press, London, 2009.

22 See Wichterich, *The Future We Want*.

23 See B. Agarwal, 'Gender inequality, cooperation and environmental sustainability', Workshop on 'Inequality, collective action and environmental sustainability', Working Paper 02-10-058, Santa Fe Institute, New Mexico, November 2002; S. Buckingham-Hatfield, 'Gender equality: a prerequisite for sustainable development', *Geography*, 2002, pp. 227–33; UNDP, 'Powerful synergies: gender equality, economic development and environmental sustainability', New York, 2012, www.undp.org/content/dam/undp/library/gender/Gender%20and%20Environment/Powerful-Synergies.pdf; G. Johnsson-Latham, 'A study on gender equality as a prerequisite for sustainable development: Report to the Environment Advisory Council, Sweden 2007:2', Ministry of the Environment, Sweden.

24 M. Leach, I. Scoones and A. Stirling, *Dynamic Sustainabilities: Technology, environment, social justice*, Earthscan, London, 2010.

25 M. Leach, L. Mehta and P. Prabhakaran, 'Gender equality and sustainable development: a pathways approach', Background working paper for UN Women World Survey on the Role of Women in Development, 2014; UN Women, *World Survey on the Role of Women in Development 2014*.

16 JULIE A. NELSON

1 Earlier research underlying this chapter was funded by a grant from the Institute for New Thinking in Economics (INET).

2 G. Lakoff, *Women, Fire, and Dangerous Things: What Categories Reveal About the Mind*, University of Chicago Press, Chicago, IL, 1987; K. M. Knutson, L. Mah et al., 'Neural correlates of automatic beliefs about gender and race', *Human Brain Mapping*, 28, 2007, pp. 915–30; J. E. B. Wilkie and G. V. Bodenhausen, 'Are numbers gendered?', *Journal of Experimental Psychology: General*, 2011, advance online publication.

3 Heterodox approaches – including Marxist, feminist and ecological approaches to economics – exist, but are much marginalized within the profession.

4 W. D. Nordhaus, *A Question of Balance: Weighing the Options on Global Warming Policies*, Yale University Press, New Haven, CT, 2008; US Department of Energy, 'Final Rule Technical Support Document (TSD): Energy Efficiency Program for Commercial and Industrial Equipment: Small Electric Motors', Appendix 15A (by the Interagency Working Group on Social Cost of Carbon): 'Social Cost of Carbon for Regulatory Impact Analysis Under Executive Order 12866', 2010.

5   IPCC, 'Final Draft Report of the Working Group III contribution to the IPCC 5th Assessment Report, "Climate Change 2014: Mitigation of Climate Change"', Intergovernmental Panel on Climate Change, 12 April 2014.

6   E. Stanton, 'Negishi welfare weights in integrated assessment models: the mathematics of global inequality', *Climatic Change*, 2010, online.

7   Some economists with strong mainstream credentials have recently publicly split from some or all of these views. But they are not yet carrying the day, nor do they tend to re-evaluate the mainstream assumptions as a whole. See, for example, Nicolas Stern, 'The structure of economic modeling of the potential impacts of climate change: grafting gross underestimation of risk onto already narrow science models', Journal of Economic Literature, 51(3), 2013, pp. 838–59.

8   J. A. Nelson, 'Economists, value judgments, and climate change: a view from feminist economics', *Ecological Economics*, 65(3), 2008, pp. 441–7.

9   E. F. Keller, *Reflections on Gender and Science*, Yale University Press, New Haven, CT, 1985.

10 S. Harding, *The Science Question in Feminism*, Cornell University Press, Ithaca, NY, 1986.

11 J. A. Nelson, 'Gender, metaphor, and the definition of economics', *Economics and Philosophy*, 8, 1982, pp. 103–25; A. L. Jennings, 'Public or private? Institutional economics and feminism', in M. A. Ferber and J. A. Nelson (eds), *Beyond Economic Man*, University of Chicago Press, Chicago, IL, 1993, pp. 111–29.

12 J. A. Nelson, 'Does profit-seeking rule out love? Evidence (or not) from economics and law', *Washington University Journal of Law and Policy*, 35(69), 2011, pp. 69–107.

13 J. A. Nelson, *Economics for Humans*, University of Chicago Press, Chicago, IL, 2006; H.-J. Chang, *23 Things They Don't Tell You about Capitalism*, Bloomsbury Press, New York, 2010; V. A. R. Zelizer, *Economic Lives: How Culture Shapes the Economy*, Princeton University Press, Princeton, NJ, 2011.

14 R. E. Freeman, *Strategic Management: A Stakeholder Approach*, Pitman, Boston, MA, 1984; L. Stout, *The Shareholder Value Myth: How Putting Shareholders First Harms Investors, Corporations, and the Public*, Berrett-Koehler, San Francisco, 2012.

15 Y. Smith, *Econned: How Unenlightened Self Interest Undermined Democracy and Corrupted Capitalism*, Palgrave Macmillan, New York, 2010.

16 E.g. J. Gillespie and D. Zweig, *Money for Nothing: How CEOs and Boards Are Bankrupting America*, Free Press, New York, 2011.

17 S. Sivaraksa, 'Alternatives to consumerism', in A. H. Badiner (ed.), *Mindfulness in the Marketplace: Compassionate Responses to Consumerism*, Parallax Press, Berkeley, CA, 2002, pp. 135–41; M. Bookchin, 'What is social ecology?', in M. E. Zimmerman, J. B. Callicot, K. J. Warren, I. J.

Klaver and J. Clark (eds), *Environmental Philosophy: From Animal Rights to Radical Ecology*, Pearson Prentice Hall, Upper Saddle River, NJ, 2005, pp. 462–78; 463, 474.

18 J. A. Nelson, 'Ethics and the economist: what climate change demands of us', *Ecological Economics*, 85, January 2013, pp. 145–54.

18 CELIA ALLDRIDGE

1 WMW international actions take place every five years, starting in 2000, and international meetings take place every two to three years.

2 The WMW Action Area documents were published in 2009 and are available on the WMW international website at www.marchemondiale.org/index_html/fr

3 WMW, 'Women in the fight against the commodification of nature and life!', WMW Report from Rio+20, 2012.

4 An activist drumming group using recycled materials as drums and percussion.

5 A. Salleh, 'Rio+20 and the Green Economy: Technocrats, Meta-industrials, WSF and Occupy', ZNet, 31 March 2012, zcomm.org/znetarticle/rio-20-and-the-green-economy-technocrats-meta-industrials-wsf-and-occupy-by-ariel-salleh/

6 A. Bosch, C. Carrasco and E. Grau, 'Verde te quiero violeta: encuentros y desencuentros entre feminismo y ecologismo', in E. Tello, *La Historia Cuenta: Del crecimiento económico al desarrollo humano sostenible*, El Viejo Topo, Barcelona, 2005.

7 7th National Congress Declaration, CONAMURI (a member organisation of the Paraguayan WMW National Coordinating Body).

8 D. Harvey, *The New Imperialism*, Oxford University Press, Oxford, 2003.

9 WMW, Preparatory document for the 4th International Action, 2013, www.marchemondiale.org/structure/9rencontre/context/en

10 MAB (Movimento dos Atingidos por Barragens – Movement of People Affected by Dams), in SOF (Sempreviva Organização Feminista), Nosso Corpo Nos Pertence, video, 20 February 2014, www.youtube.com/watch?v=UvS4hwSa8So

11 S. Federici, *Caliban and the Witch: Women, the Body and Primitive Accumulation*, Autonomedia, New York, 2004; S. Federici, 'Feminism and the politics of the commons', *The Commoner*, 24 January 2011, www.commoner.org.uk/?p=113

12 Federici, *Caliban and the Witch*, p. 97, emphasis in original.

13 Ibid.

14 Federici, 'Feminism and the politics of the commons'.

15 Ibid., p. 5.

16 See Declaration of the 10th International Meeting 'Women in resistance, building alternatives for a better world', www.marchemondiale.org/news/mmfnewsitem.2016-10-28.0582816348/en

17 At the time of revision, WMW activists in Kurdistan, Turkey and Palestine were being held illegally by the Turkish and Israeli governments. The WMW demands the immediate release of Ayse Gokkan, Ilknur Ustun, Khitma Saafin and all other political prisoners in Turkey, Palestine and across the world.

18 CONAMURI (Coordinadora Nacional de Organizaciones de Mujeres Trabajadoras Rurales e Indígenas), 7th National Congress Political Declaration, 2014.

19 See www.facebook.com/events/1800364480290805

20 See the Global Campaign to Reclaim Peoples Sovereignty, Dismantle Corporate Power and Stop Impunity, www.stopcorporateimpunity.org/

21 NIDHI TANDON

1 The industrial nature and mode of agricultural investment often go beyond the visible immediacy of land grab to the destruction of land itself. The use of inorganic fertilizers, synthetic pesticides and herbicides, increased landscape homogeneity, reduced fallow periods, the wholesale drainage of water systems and decimation of ecological diversity, all contribute to damaging soils and ecosystems, the effects lasting long after the industrial investors have left. The intensification of agriculture and subsequent degradation of ecosystem services further erode local food systems.

2 UNEP's *Towards a Green Economy* (2011) defines natural capital as natural assets such as forests, lakes, wetlands and river basins, essential components of natural capital at an ecosystem level. These underlying ecosystems provide services and values in the diversity and abundance of species and variability in genes that can be used for different services and products.

3 R. Knight et al., *Protecting Community Lands and Resources*, Namati and International Development Law Organization, 2013.

4 Studies such as S. Kpanan'Ayoung Siakor, *Uncertain Futures: The impacts of Sime Darby on communities in Liberia*, World Rainforest Movement and Sustainable Development Institute, 2012, and L. Balachandran, E. Herb, S. Timirzi and E. O'Reilly, *Everyone must eat? Liberia, Food Security and Palm Oil*, Columbia/Sipa, 2012.

5 The long-term implications of losing land and dignity and the particular impacts for rural women are being acknowledged by the international community. See Oxfam, *Promises, Power, and Poverty: Corporate land deals and rural women in Africa*, 2013, and Action Aid, *From under their feet: A think piece on the gender dimensions of land grabs in Africa*, 2012.

6 Rights and Resources Initiative, *Investments into the Agribusiness, Extractive and Infrastructure Sectors of Liberia: An Overview*, February 2013, www.rightsandresources.org/publication/investments-into-the-agribusiness-extractive-and-infrastructure-sectors-of-liberia/

7 Ministry of Agriculture stats, Ghana (2010), puts total nucleus (hectares) of land under oil palm plantations at 21,574 hectares.

8   The global palm oil industry has recently witnessed unprecedented growth, with a cumulative annual growth rate (CAGR) of 8 per cent, although West Africa's CAGR is 1.5 per cent. The competitive landscape is dominated by South-East Asian producers who have better production efficiency (higher productivity at comparable costs of production, hence able to capture larger shares of the world market) and ideal climatic conditions. K. Ofosu-Budu and D. Sarpong, 'Oil palm industry growth in Africa: a value chain and smallholders study for Ghana', in A. Elbehri (ed.), *Rebuilding West Africa's Food Potential*, FAO/IFAD, 2013.

9   See www.youtube.com/watch?v=ocDWFcbGts8 and, e.g., Oxfam, *Promises, Power, and Poverty*, and Action Aid, *From under their feet*.

10 www.uneca.org/sites/default/files/uploaded-documents/fg_on_land_policy_eng.pdf. This would be consistent with commitments made by African states in the AU's 2003 Maputo protocol to the ACHPR on the Rights of Women in Africa and the 2004 Solemn Declaration on Gender Equality in Africa, which call for action to address gender inequalities, including women's unequal access to land.

11 The UN's International Assessment of Agricultural Knowledge, Science and Technology for Development (IAASTD) concludes that 'small-scale farmers and organic, agro-ecological methods are the way forward to solve the current food crisis and meet the needs of local communities'. Greening agriculture in developing countries and concentrating on smallholders can reduce poverty while investing in the natural capital on which the poor depend. Greening the small farm sector through promotion and dissemination of sustainable practices could be the most effective way to make more food available to the poor and hungry, reduce poverty, increase carbon sequestration and access growing international markets for green products. See www.unep.org/greeneconomy/Portals/88/documents/ger/GER_synthesis_en.pdf

12 The '*poro*' association for men has declined in significance in large part because the political situation in the past made such associations illegal. However, there may be a role for other sacred institutions, including the '*sande*' for women, and in Garpu Town, a sacred institution called '*nigi*' is organized around a river in the forest – it is forbidden to fish or hunt in the vicinity of the grove. (See IUCN, 'Understanding diversity: a study of livelihoods and forest landscapes in Liberia', 2009, p. 39, cmsdata.iucn.org/downloads/liberia_lls_report_sept_2009.pdf.) The '*sande*' societies, for instance, retain knowledge of plant species for medicinal purposes and valuable traditional folklore.

13 IUCN, 'Understanding diversity', p. 20.

14 Ibid., p. 30.

15 E. Ostrom, *Governing the Commons: The Evolution of Institutions for Collective Action*, Cambridge University Press, Cambridge, 1990.

16 OECD, 'Empowerment of poor rural people through initiatives in agriculture and natural resource management', 2012, p. 2.

22 ANNA FITZPATRICK

1   D. Williams, 'Fashion design', in K. Fletcher and M. Tham (eds), *Routledge Handbook of Sustainability and Fashion*, Routledge, London, 2015, p. 234.
2   Marx quoted in M. Barnard, *Fashion as Communication*, Psychology Press, Abingdon and New York, 2002, p. 9.
3   www.londonfashionweek.co.uk/news/623/Facts--Figures-AW14
4   S. Bruzzi and P. Church Gibson, *Fashion Cultures Revisited: Theories, Explorations and Analysis*, Routledge, Abingdon and New York, 2013.
5   G. Lipovetsky, *The Empire of Fashion: Dressing Modern Democracy*, Princeton University Press, Princeton, NJ, 1994.
6   Y. Kawamura, *Fashion-ology: An Introduction to Fashion Studies*, Berg, Oxford, 2005.
7   M. Southwell, 'Fashion and sustainability in the context of gender', in *Routledge Handbook of Sustainability and Fashion*, p. 104.
8   D. Williams, 'Fashion as a means to recognise and build communities in place', *She Ji: The Journal of Design, Economics and Innovation*, 2017.
9   United Nations, *World Urbanization Prospects: The 2014 Revision Highlights*, United Nations, Department of Economic and Social Affairs, Population Division, New York, 2014, https://esa.un.org/unpd/wup/publications/files/wup2014-highlights.Pdf
10 Personal communication, April 2015.
11 D. Williams, 'Fashion as a means to recognise and build communities in place'.
12 K. Fletcher, *Craft of Use: Post-growth Fashion*, Routledge, London, 2016, pp. 60–1.
13 K. Fletcher and K. Toth-Fejel (eds), *The Craft of Use Event*, London, London College of Fashion, 2014, http://ualresearchonline.arts.ac.uk/7545/1/Craft_of_Use_Event_%281%29.pdf, accessed July 2017.
14 See www.stockholmresilience.org
15 Personal communication, April 2015.
16 K. Fletcher, *Sustainable Fashion and Textiles: Design Journeys*, Routledge, London, 2013.
17 Domenski et al. (1992) quoted in S. Bell and S. Morse, *Sustainability Indicators: Measuring the Immeasurable?*, Routledge, London, 2012, p. 79.

23 CARINA HIRSCH

1   'Adding it up: investing in contraception and maternal and newborn health, 2017', Guttmacher Institute factsheet, July 2017, www.guttmacher.org/fact-sheet/adding-it-up-contraception-mnh-2017
2   UNFPA, *Marrying Too Young: Ending Child Marriage*, United Nations Population Fund (UNFPA), New York, 2012, www.unfpa.org/sites/default/files/pub-pdf/MarryingTooYoung.pdf

3   'Children: reducing mortality', World Health Organization (WHO) fact-sheet, updated September 2016, www.who.int/mediacentre/factsheets/fs178/en/

4   'Greater investments needed to meet women's sexual and reproductive health needs in developing regions', Guttmacher Institute news release, 29 June 2017, www.guttmacher.org/news-release/2017/greater-investments-needed-meet-womens-sexual-and-reproductive-health-needs

5   G. Sedgh, L. S. Ashford and R. Hussain, *Unmet Need for Contraception in Developing Countries: Examining Women's Reasons for Not Using a Method*, Guttmacher Institute, New York, 2016, www.guttmacher.org/report/unmet-need-for-contraception-in-developing-countries#1

6   W. Harris, 'Meeting global demand for contraception is possible: new report shows first ever decrease in unmet need', Marie Stopes International press release, 29 June 2017, www.mariestopes.org/news/2017/6/new-report-shows-first-ever-decrease-in-unmet-need-for-contraception/

7   S. Moreland and S. Talbird, 'Achieving the Millennium Development Goals: the contribution to fulfilling the unmet need for family planning', USAID, Washington, DC, 2006.

8   'New IPCC report recognizes family planning among social dimensions of climate change adaptation', Population Action International press release, 2014, http://pai.org/wp-content/uploads/2014/03/IPCCMediaKit1.pdf

9   Paul Hawken (ed.), *Drawdown: The Most Comprehensive Plan Ever Proposed to Reverse Global Warming*, Penguin Books, New York. 2017.

10 'Report of the United Nations Conference on Environment and Development', Rio de Janeiro, 3–14 June 1992, www.un.org/documents/ga/conf151/aconf15126-1annex1.htm

11 'The role of women in agriculture', ESA Working Paper No. 11-02, Food and Agriculture Organization of the United Nations (FAO), March 2011, www.fao.org/docrep/013/am307e/am307e00.pdf

12 UNEP, *Women and the Environment*, United Nations Environment Programme (UNEP), New York, 2004.

13 M. Wan, C. J. P. Colfer and B. Powell, 'Forests, women and health: opportunities and challenges for conservation', *International Forestry Review*, 13(3), 2011, pp. 369–87.

14 OECD, *Environmental Policy and Household Behaviour: Review of Evidence in the Areas of Energy, Food, Transport, Waste and Water*, Organisation for Economic Co-operation and Development (OECD), Paris, 2008.

15 Paul Hawken (ed.) *Drawdown*.

16 K. Noorgard and R. York, 'Gender equality and state environmentalism', *Gender and Society*, 19(4), 2005, pp. 506–22.

17 B. Agarwal, *Gender and Green Governance: The Political Economy and Women's Presence within and beyond Community Forestry*, Oxford University Press, Oxford, 2010.

18 World Bank, *Linking Sustainability with Demand, Gender, and Poverty*, World Bank, Washington, DC, 2001.

19 World Bank, *World Development Report 2012: Gender Equality and Development*, World Bank, Washington, DC, 2011.

20 M. Wan, C. J. P. Colfer and B. Powell, 'Forests, women and health: opportunities and challenges for conservation'.

21 V. Mohan, J. Castro, D. Pullanikkatil et al., 'Population health environment programmes: an integrated approach to development post-2015', Paper presented at the 2nd International Conference on Sustainable Development Practice, New York, 17–18 September 2014, psda.org.uk/wp-content/uploads/2014/09/PSDA-SDSN-paper-FINAL.pdf, accessed 26 September 2014.

22 R. De Souza, 'Resilience, integrated development and family planning: building long-term solutions', *Reproductive Health Matters*, 22(43), 2014, pp. 75–83.

23 See blueventures.org

24 V. Mohan and T. Shellard, 'Providing family planning services to remote communities in areas of high biodiversity through a Population-Health-Environment programme in Madagascar', *Reproductive Health Matters*, 22(43), 2014, pp. 93–103.

25 'Effectiveness of the PHE approach for achieving family planning and fertility outcomes in Ethiopia', Population, Health and Environment Ethiopia Consortium policy brief, http://phe-ethiopia.org/pdf/GPSDO_policy_brief.pdf, accessed 20 July 2017.

26 'Global population, consumption and rights', Friends of the Earth briefing, August 2013, www.foe.co.uk/sites/default/files/downloads/population_friends_of_the.pdf, accessed 6 September 2014.

27 UN, 'World population prospects: the 2015 revision, key findings and advance tables', Working Paper No. ESA/P/WP.241, United Nations, Department of Economic and Social Affairs, Population Division, New York, 2015.

28 L. Bryant, L. Carver, C. D. Butler and A. Anage, 'Climate change and family planning: least-developed countries define the agenda', *Bulletin of the World Health Organization*, 87, 2009, pp. 852–7.

29 Royal Society, *People and the Planet*, Royal Society, London, 2012.

30 UN, 'World population prospects: the 2015 revision, key findings and advance tables'.

31 Ibid.

32 Ibid.

33 Ibid.; UN, *World Contraceptive Use 2015*, POP/DB/CP/Rev2015, United Nations, Department of Economic and Social Affairs, Population Division, New York, 2015.

24 KATE METCALF and colleagues

All Women's Environmental Network resources are available at wen.org.uk/all-resources

1 Women's Environmental Network, *No Laughing Matter. Stress incontinence and the environment*, 2004.

2 Women's Environmental Network, *Pretty Nasty – questions & answers about phthalates*, 2003.

3 Women's Environmental Network, *Getting Lippy. Cosmetics, toiletries and the environment*, 2003.

4 Women's Environmental Network, *Toxic Tour: What's in my cosmetics?*, 2003.

5 Women's Institute and Women's Environmental Network, *Women's Manifesto on Climate Change*, 2007.

6 Women's Environmental Network, *Gender and the Climate Change Agenda. The impacts of climate change on women and public policy*, 2010.

7 Women's Environmental Network, *Why Women and Climate Change?*, 2010.

8 Greater London Authority, *English Indices of Deprivation. A London perspective*, June 2011.

9 Fawcett Society, *A Fawcett Society Briefing on Ethnic Minority Women, Poverty and Inequality*, 2008.

10 ONS, *Population Estimates for UK, England, Wales, Scotland and Northern Ireland, mid 2006*, Office for National Statistics, London, 2006.

11 K. Metcalf et al., 'Community food growing and the role of women in the alternative economy in Tower Hamlets', *Journal of the Local Economy Policy Unit*, Special Issue: 'Women and the local economy', 27(8), 2012.

12 Ibid.

13 J. Ward and R. Spacey, *Dare to Dream: Learning journeys of Bangladeshi, Pakistani and Somali women*, NIACE, Leicester, 2008.

14 O. Varley-Winter, 'Roots to work: developing employability through community food-growing and urban agriculture projects', Summary Report, City & Guilds Centre for Skills and Development, London, 2011.

15 L. E. Baker, 'Tending cultural gardens and food landscapes in downtown Toronto', *Geographical Review*, 94(3), 2004, pp. 305–25.

16 S. Hayes, *Radical Homemakers: Reclaiming Domesticity from a Consumer Culture*, Left to Write Press, Richmondville, NY, 2010.

17 N. Charles and M. Kerr, *Women, Food, and Families*, Manchester University Press, Manchester, 1988.

18 M. L. DeVault, *Feeding the Family: The Social Organization of Caring as Gendered Work*, University of Chicago Press, Chicago, IL, 1994; K. Wiig and C. Smith, 'The art of grocery shopping on a food stamp budget: factors influencing the food choices of low-income women as they try to make ends meet', *Public Health Nutrition*, 12(10), 2009, pp. 1726–34; V. Inglis, 'Does modifying the household food budget predict changes

in the healthfulness of purchasing choices among low- and high-income women?', *Appetite*, 52(2), 2009, pp. 273–9.

27 EMMA HOWARD BOYD

1   Ruth Sunderland, 'We cannot return to the old macho ways', *Observer*, 15 February 2009, www.theguardian com/business/2009/feb/15/gender-recession-credit-crunch

2   Ibid.

3   www.boardsforum.co.uk/boardwatch.html

4   www.moraldna.org/wp-content/uploads/2014/10/The-MoralD-NA-of-Performance-Infographic-October-2014.pdf

5   www.gov.uk/government/uploads/system/uploads/attachment_data/file/31480/11-745-women-on-boards.pdf

6   30% Club, 'Diversity and stewardship – next steps', November 2012.

7   www.cbi.org.uk/media-centre/press-releases/2014/06/we-need-a-uk-target-on-reducing-gender-pay-gap-cbi/

8   www.frc.org.uk/Our-Work/Publications/Accounting-and-Reporting-Policy/Guidance-on-the-Strategic-Report.pdf

9   For example, www.mckinsey.com/client_service/organization/latest_thinking/unlocking_the_full_potential

10 Grant Thornton, 'Women in business: the value of diversity', September 2015, www.grantthornton.global/en/insights/articles/diverse-boards-in-india-uk-and-us-outperform-male-only-peers-by-us$655bn

11 McKinsey Global Institute, 'The power of parity: How advancing women's equality can add $12 trillion to global growth', September 2015, www.mckinsey.com/insights/growth/how_advancing_womens_equality_can_add_12_trillion_to_global_growth?cid=mckwomen-eml-alt-mgi-mck-oth-1509

12 responsiblebusiness.haas.berkeley.edu/Women_Create_Sustainable_Value_FINAL_10_2012.pdf. By K. A. McElhaney and S. Mobasseri, UC Berkeley Haas School of Business. Research sponsored by KPMG with Women Corporate Directors (WCD).

13 30percentclub.org/wp-content/uploads/2014/11/2014-Survey-of-Women-on-Boards-1.pdf

14 www.catalyst.org/system/files/companies_behaving_responsibly_gender_diversity_on_boards.pdf

15 A. Capezio and A. Mavisakalyan, 'Women in the boardroom and fraud: Evidence from Australia', *Australian Journal of Management* 07/2015, July 2015.

ABOUT THE CONTRIBUTORS

Gotelind Alber

Gotelind Alber is based in Berlin and is an independent researcher and consultant. She is a physicist and has thirty years' experience in research, policy and management, including as a past managing director of the Climate Alliance of European Cities. Since 2006 Gotelind has worked as an independent consultant on energy and climate policy, energy efficiency and renewable energy, multi-level governance, gender and climate justice. She was also one of the co-founders of GenderCC – Women for Climate Justice. She has been following the UNFCCC process from the beginning in order to connect international climate policy with local approaches in industrialised and developing countries. Her recent projects include papers and a policy guidebook on 'gender, cities and climate change' for UN-Habitat and the GIZ, research and pilot projects on gender and climate change, as well as various national and EU evaluation panels, including for the EU Horizon 2020 programme. http://gendercc.net; www.goalber.eu

Celia Alldridge

Celia Alldridge has contributed a piece on behalf of the World March of Women (WMW), an international feminist, anti-capitalist movement bringing together organised grassroots women in the struggle against all forms of inequality and discrimination against women. WMW recognises the deep relationship between feminist activism and territorial self-determination, with parallels between the exploitation and commodification of women and the environment. Celia was International Liaison Officer at the WMW International Secretariat from 2007 to 2013. She is currently International Membership Development Officer at the International Secretariat of Friends of the Earth International.

www.worldmarchofwomen.org

Nicola Baird

Interviews: Christiana Figueres, Jude Kelly, Karin Nansen, Lola Young.

Nicola Baird is a journalist, editor and blogger and also teaches at the University of the Arts London. She worked at Friends of the Earth's publications department from 1999 to 2008 and was co-author of their popular book *Save Cash & Save the Planet* (2005). Nicola has a Politics BA and an MSc in Environmental Management. She was a trustee of FSC UK for some years. Her focus on climate change mitigation and environmental justice was sparked by two years volunteering with VSO as a journalist trainer for the Solomon Islands Development Trust in Honiara, in the South Pacific. Nicola has written ten books, mostly on environmental subjects, including *Homemade Kids: Thrifty, Creative and Eco-friendly Ways to Raise Your Child* (2010).

Shukri Haji Ismail Bandare

Shukri Haji Ismail Bandare has served as the Minister for the Environment of Somaliland since 2013. Before her political appointment, she was an active campaigner on environmental issues and founded a local NGO, Candlelight for Environment, Education and Health. The charity continues to deliver training, education and healthcare programmes with communities across Somaliland.

www.candlelightsomal.org

Susan Buckingham

Susan Buckingham is a feminist geographer whose main focus is on gender and environmental issues. Her research and activist work is interlinked through a commitment to environmental and social justice. Susan is the editor of a new book, *Understanding Climate*

Change Through Gender Relations (with Virginie Le Masson), and is currently writing a second edition of *Gender and Environment.* Until 2015 she was a professor in the Centre for Human Geography at Brunel University London; she now works independently with universities, government institutions and NGOs in Europe and internationally.

www.susanbuckingham.org

Juliet Davenport

Juliet Davenport is the founder and CEO of Good Energy, one of the UK's first entirely renewable electricity supplier and generator companies. A true renewable industry entrepreneur, Juliet built Good Energy from scratch in 1999. Her mission then, as it is now, was to tackle climate change, help deliver energy security for the UK, and give consumers the opportunity to buy and invest in 100 per cent renewable electricity. Today, the company supplies electricity and gas, administrates feed-in-tariff payments, generates its own renewable electricity and plays an important role on the renewable energy stage. In 2013 Juliet was awarded an OBE for services to renewables and in June 2015 was appointed to the board of the Natural Environment Research Council. Since 1999, Good Energy has received a number of awards, including being named Company of the Year at the 2016 Renewable Energy Association awards and 2015 BusinessGreen Leaders Awards.

www.goodenergy.co.uk/about-us/our-story/juliet-davenport

Diane Elson

Diane Elson is Emeritus Professor of Sociology at the University of Essex and former Chair of the UK Women's Budget Group (a network of researchers and activists producing critical analysis of UK government budgets). She is the author of many publications on gender and development, and was the lead author of the first edition in 2000 of the UNIFEM *Progress of the World's Women* report. She currently serves as an adviser to UN Women and is a member of the United Nations Committee for Development Policy. In 2006, she was named as one of fifty key thinkers on development.

Patricia Espinosa

Patricia Espinosa has served as the Mexican Ambassador to Germany since 2013 and as Executive Secretary of the United Nations Framework for Convention on Climate Change (UNFCCC) since 2016. Previously, Patricia served as Mexican Ambassador to Austria, Slovenia and Slovakia and as Secretary of Foreign Affairs in the cabinet of President Felipe Calderón. Embarking on what would become an ongoing tenure of more than thirty years of experience in high-level international relations, Patricia began serving at the Mexican delegation to the United Nations in Geneva when she was just twenty-three years old; she was ultimately promoted to Ambassador within the Foreign Service in 2000. She graduated from El Colegio de México with a Bachelor's degree in International Relations and earned a degree in International Law at the Graduate Institute of International and Development Studies in Switzerland.

Christiana Figueres

Christiana Figueres assumed responsibility for the international climate change negotiations after the failed Copenhagen conference of 2009, serving as Executive Secretary of the United Nations Framework Convention on Climate Change (UNFCCC) from 2010 to 2016. She was determined to lead the process to a universally agreed regulatory framework. Building towards that goal, she directed the successful Conferences of the Parties in Cancun (2010), Durban (2011), Doha (2012), Warsaw (2013) and Lima (2014), and her efforts culminated in the historic Paris Agreement of 2015, forging a new brand of collaborative diplomacy.

Christiana is currently the convener of Mission 2020, a global initiative that seeks to ensure that the world bends the curve on greenhouse gas emissions by 2020 in order to protect the most vulnerable from the worst impacts of climate change and to usher in an era of stability and prosperity. Her responsibilities include being Vice Chair of the Global Covenant of Mayors for Climate and Energy, Climate Leader for the World Bank, Distinguished Fellow of Conservation International, a board member of ClimateWorks and the World Resources Institute, a member of the Rockefeller Foundation Economic Council on Planetary Health, and a member of the Leadership Council of the Global Alliance for Clean Cookstoves.

http://christianafigueres.com; @cfigueres

Anna Fitzpatrick

Anna Fitzpatrick has worked at the Centre for Sustainable Fashion (CSF) at the University of the Arts London for the past four years. CSF's work explores new perspectives, relationships and processes that balance ecology, society and culture within the artistic and business context of fashion. At CSF, Anna has developed her interests in the intersection of fashion and politics, thinking through engagement and apathy in a fashion context. Prior to the 2015 General Election, she organised an event at the Houses of Parliament for young people to express their voice through fashion. Anna was particularly affected by the Rana Plaza disaster, which shaped her focus on workers' rights and the ultimate cost of fashion to women. Previously, Anna lived in São Paulo for four years, where she supported the work of a women's textile cooperative and worked as a journalist for the *Rio Times* and *Time Out*.

www.sustainable-fashion.com

Zandile Gumede

Zandile Gumede began her tenure as mayor of the eThekwini Municipality – Durban's first female mayor – in 2016 and will serve until 2020. Her political career has unfolded over three decades – Zandile has been a constant advocate for women in high-level political positions and worked to empower people as a councillor from 2000 onwards. Zandile also served as treasurer to the eThekwini Municipality from 2007 to 2015, focusing her work on health, disaster management, and parks and recreation. Zandile has worked to establish the link between climate action and women's rights, recognising that women are more vulnerable to climate change. Zandile has also worked to mitigate the impacts of extended periods of drought and pollution in Durban and has established the effects of climate change as an urban emergency.

She has been a constant advocate for women in climate leadership and has worked to encourage more women to earn degrees in the sciences.

Marylyn Haines Evans

Marylyn Haines Evans was Public Affairs Chair of the National Federation of Women's Institutes between 2009 and 2017. The Women's Institute (WI) was formed in the UK in 1915 to revitalise rural communities and encourage women to become more involved in producing food during the First World War. Since then, the WI's aims have broadened and it is now the largest voluntary women's organisation in the UK. The WI currently has 220,000 members in around 6,300 WIs. It celebrated its centenary in 2015. www.thewi.org.uk

Jenny Hawley

Interviews: Juliet Davenport, Vandana Shiva, Shukri Haji Ismail Bandare and Fatima Jibrell.
Jenny Hawley has worked for human rights, environmental sustainability and wildlife conservation in British and international charities for more than twenty years. She worked freelance for Friends of Earth as editor for the first edition of *Why Women Will Save the Planet*.

Anne Hidalgo

The first woman to be elected Mayor of Paris, Anne Hidalgo took office in April 2014. Her agenda is focused on social inclusion, sustainable development, solidarity, citizen participation and innovation, essential topics in building the Paris of tomorrow. After co-hosting the Climate Summit for Local Leaders in December 2015 with Michael Bloomberg, the UN Secretary-General's Special Envoy for Cities and Climate Change, she was elected as the new Chair of C40 Cities. Born in Spain, she is the mother of three children and married to Jean-Marc Germain, a Member of Parliament. A former labour inspector, she occupied several positions in national and international organisations before becoming First Deputy Mayor of Paris

(2001–14), in charge of gender equality and later in charge of urban planning and architecture. She holds a Master's degree in Labour Law from the Labour and Social Security Institute of Paris.

Carina Hirsch

Carina Hirsch is Advocacy and Projects Manager at the Margaret Pyke Trust, with the Population & Sustainability Network. She leads the organisation's engagement in policy discussions such as CoP and manages integrated projects in South Africa aimed to improve family planning information, knowledge and services and environmental objectives. Previously, Carina worked for the Food and Agriculture Organization of the United Nations on women's empowerment and food security programmes in India and West Africa, and advocated for the role of women farmers as Advocacy Officer at the World Farmers' Organisation. She holds postgraduate degrees in Economics and Public Management.
www.margaretpyke.org

Nathalie Holvoet and Liesbeth Inberg

Nathalie Holvoet and Liesbeth Inberg wrote this while working as academics at the Institute of Development Policy and Management (IOB) at the University of Antwerp in Belgium. Their piece for this book, based on their paper in the journal *Climate and Development*, investigates to what extent and in what way thirty-one sub-Saharan African national adaptation programmes of action (NAPAs) integrate a gender dimension in the different sectors that are especially related to climate change. Nathalie is still based at IOB. Liesbeth has moved to the Netherlands.
www.uantwerpen.be/en/staff/nathalie-holvoet

Emma Howard Boyd

Emma Howard Boyd has spent her twenty-five-year career working in financial services, initially in corporate finance and then in fund management, specialising in sustainable investment and corporate governance. As Director of Stewardship at Jupiter Asset Management until July 2014, Emma was integral to the development of their reputation in the corporate governance and sustainability fields. Emma is currently Chair of the Environment Agency and serves on various boards and advisory committees, including Share-Action (Chair of Trustees), Future Cities Catapult (Vice Chair), Menhaden Capital plc, the Aldersgate Group, the 30% Club Steering Committee, the Executive Board of the Prince's Accounting for Sustainability Project and the Carbon Trust Advisory Panel.

Her past board and advisory roles have included being a director of Triodos Renewables plc, Vice Chair and Chair of UKSIF (the UK Sustainable Investment and Finance Association), and a member of the Commission on Environmental Markets and Economic Performance, set up by the UK Government to make detailed proposals specifically on enhancing the UK's environmental industries, technologies and markets.

Naoko Ishii

Naoko Ishii is the CEO and Chairperson of the Global Environment Facility (GEF). She has held these positions since 2012, was appointed for a second term in 2015, and will serve until 2020. Before beginning at GEF, Naoko managed Japan's global policies on environmental issues and international development as the Deputy Vice Minister of Finance of Japan. During her tenure in this role, Naoko led a committee responsible for designing Japan's Green Climate Fund. Over the course of her prolific career, Naoko has also served as the World Bank's Country Director for Sri Lanka and the Maldives, the World Bank's Country Program Coordinator for Vietnam, a project manager at the Harvard Institute for International Development, an economist at the International Monetary Fund, and a Professor of Sustainable Development and Environment at Keio University. She is also an author, the inaugural recipient of the 2006 Enjoji Jiro Memorial Prize, and a graduate of the University of Tokyo.

Fatima Jibrell

Fatima Jibrell is the founder of the international NGO Adeso: African Development Solutions (previously known as Horn Relief), whose mission is to work with communities to create environments in which Africans can thrive. In 2014 Fatima received the Champions of Earth award from the United Nations Environment Programme as a Laureate for Inspiration and Action for 'building environmental and social resilience amidst war and devastation'. adesoafrica.org

Jude Kelly

Jude Kelly has been Artistic Director of Southbank Centre since 2006. A director of more than 100 theatre and opera productions, Jude has also founded several major arts organisations, including Solent People's Theatre (1976), Battersea Arts Centre (1980), West Yorkshire Playhouse (1990) and Metal (2002). In 2011 Jude founded WOW – Women of the World festival – which has become a global platform for celebrating the potential of girls and women on every continent. A well-known speaker on the power of creativity at all levels of society to trigger positive change, Jude advises a range of communities and organisations on how to build and realise their ambitions. Jude developed the Cultural Strategy for London's 2012 Olympic and Paralympic Games. She is the recipient of fourteen honorary doctorates and in 2017 won the inaugural Veuve Clicquot Social Purpose Award.

Melissa Leach

Melissa Leach is Director of the Institute of Development Studies (IDS) at the University of Sussex in the UK. She founded and directed the STEPS Centre from 2006 to 2014 and co-chaired the Science Committee of Future Earth from 2012 to 2016. As a social anthropologist and geographer, her research in Africa and beyond has addressed a variety of environmental, agricultural, health and technology issues, integrating gender and feminist political ecology perspectives. Her recent books include *Green Grabbing: A New Appropriation of Nature* (2013), *The Politics of Green Transformations* (2015) and *Gender Equality and Sustainable Development* (2015). www.ids.ac.uk/person/melissa-leach

264 » Why Women Will Save the Planet

Caroline Lucas

Caroline Lucas is the first Green Party MP in the UK, re-elected for a third term in 2017. She joined the Green Party in 1986 and served as a county councillor on Oxfordshire County Council until 1997; she became one of the UK Green Party's first MEPs in June 1999. She is an active campaigner on a range of issues including climate change, international trade and peace issues. Caroline sits on the Environmental Audit Committee and is also a UNICEF parliamentary champion.

www.carolinelucas.com

Lyla Mehta

Lyla Mehta is a Professorial Research Fellow at the Institute for Development Studies at the University of Sussex in the UK, and a Visiting Professor at Noragric, Norwegian University of Life Sciences. She trained as a sociologist (University of Vienna) and has a PhD in Development Studies (University of Sussex). Her work focuses on water and sanitation, forced displacement and resistance, scarcity, rights and access, resource grabbing and the politics of environment/development and sustainability.

www.ids.ac.uk/idsperson/lyla-mehta

Kate Metcalf and colleagues from the Women's Environmental Network

The Women's Environmental Network (WEN) is the only organisation in the UK that has worked consistently to make the links between women, health and the environment. WEN's vision is of an environmentally sustainable world in which we have achieved gender equality. WEN aims to inspire women to make environmentally informed choices and to empower women to become agents of change in their families, networks and society. It focuses on the five key programme areas of health, waste, food, climate change and women's empowerment, but all of its work highlights the intersectionalities of gender, inequality and environmental issues, especially in the urban setting in which WEN works in Tower Hamlets, London. WEN's piece for this book

was prepared by Kate Metcalf, Connie Hunter, Julia Minnear and Georgie Johnson.
www.wen.org.uk

Maria Mies

Maria Mies, now eighty-six, was Professor of Sociology at the Cologne University of Applied Sciences. She worked for many years at the Goethe-Institut in India and is the founder of the programme 'Women and Development' at the Institute of Social Studies (ISS) in The Hague. She is the author of a number of books on women's issues worldwide, on ecology, and on the question of why our present political economy is based on capitalism and patriarchy. Her main books are *Patriarchy and Accumulation on a World Scale* and *Ecofeminism*, which she co-authored with Vandana Shiva. Her works have been translated into many languages. She stresses that a new perspective or a new vision of our world is necessary, but this vision can no longer be based on permanent economic growth; instead, it must be based on *subsistence*. She co-founded a number of international feminist and other social movements. Having retired from teaching in 1993, she continues to be active in feminist and ecological movements.

Karin Nansen

Karin Nansen is an environmental justice campaigner and co-founder of REDES, based in Uruguay. In December 2016, she became Chair of Friends of the Earth International. Karin has been a member of the national coordination panel of the Native and Local Seeds Network, an initiative that involves more than thirty local groups from all over the country engaged in the recuperation, reproduction and exchange of local seed varieties and agroecological small-scale farming. Karin has many years' experience working with the Network of Rural Women's Groups to assert the role of women as political actors in building food sovereignty. As a member of REDES, she was active in the National Campaign for the Human Right to Water, which led to a constitutional reform to stop water privatisation.
www.redes.org.uy; www.foei.org

Julie A. Nelson

Julie Nelson is Professor of Economics at the University of Massachusetts, Boston. A leading writer on feminist economic thought, she currently conducts research on feminism and economics with special interests in ethics, methodology and implications for social and environmental policies. She was a founding board member of the International Association for Feminist Economics.
www.umb.edu/academics/cla/faculty/julie_a._nelson; sites.google.com/site/julieanelsoneconomist/home

Alexandra Palt

Alexandra Palt is the Chief Corporate Responsibility Officer at L'Oréal, where she has worked since 2012. She is in charge of the L'Oréal Foundation in addition to L'Oréal's sustainability department. During her second year as Chief Sustainability Officer, Alexandra launched L'Oréal's sustainability commitment, 'Sharing Beauty With All', which outlines L'Oréal's goals for 2020. The commitment rests on four principles: innovating, producing, living and developing sustainably. Before L'Oréal, Alexandra founded Fabric of Society, a consulting agency for innovation. A lawyer by training, Alexandra also served as Director of the Promotion of Equality team at the High Commission Against Discrimination and for Equal Opportunities (HALDE). Earlier in her career, Alexandra worked at a law firm and at Amnesty International in Germany, utilising her specialisation in human rights. Alexandra became certified in Sustainability Leadership by the University of Cambridge and holds a Master's degree in Law from the University of Vienna.

Vandana Shiva

Vandana Shiva is a world-renowned Indian philosopher, environmental activist and author. She is one of the leaders and board members of the International Forum on Globalization. She has authored more than twenty books, including the landmark *Ecofeminism* with Maria Mies. She is a member of the International Organization for a Participatory Society. She has received

widespread recognition for her work, including the Right Liveli-hood Award.
http://vandanashiva.com

Nidhi Tandon

Nidhi Tandon, Executive Director at Networked Intelligence for Development, specialises in working with rural and urban commu-nities to support their livelihoods – within the limits of a sustainable and circular economy. With a background in agrarian economics, economics reporting (Zimbabwe International News Agency) and radio broadcasting (BBC Africa Service), much of her work revolves around rights and self-determination, and the relation-ships between humans and water, energy, natural resources and the policy decisions that affect their lives.
networkedintelligence.com/wp/home

Atti Worku

Atti Worku is the Founder and Executive Director of Seeds of Africa, an organisation working to create holistic systems of educa-tion and establish community development centres within urban communities in Africa. Through her work at Seeds of Africa, Atti hopes to build a self-sustaining model for education and commu-nity growth which is adaptable, scalable and replicable. Seeds of Africa does not operate with the traditional aid model, instead working to provide tangible tools to families and communities who need support. Atti graduated with a Bachelor of Arts in Sustain-able Development from Columbia University and is a member of the Aspen Institute's Society of Fellows. Before embarking on her career in the non-profit sector, Atti worked as a model for six years and earned the title of Miss Ethiopia in 2005.

Lola Young

Lola, Baroness Young of Hornsey, is an independent, cross-bench peer who founded and co-chairs the All-Party Parliamentary Group on Ethics and Sustainability in Fashion. After an academic career, and having participated in campaigns for equality and diversity in the cultural and creative sector, she received an OBE in 2001. She has sat on the boards of several national arts, cultural and heritage organisations. Since becoming a Member of the House of Lords in 2004, she has continued to campaign on issues of social, criminal and environmental justice, recently receiving three honorary degrees in recognition of her work in these areas. Baroness Young is currently involved campaigning to improve and strengthen the Modern Slavery Act (2015) through her private members' bill. She was Chair of the Man Booker Prize 2017.

@lolahornsey